CW00833095

JOSEPH L. MANKIEWICZ

INTERVIEWS

CONVERSATIONS WITH FILMMAKERS SERIES
PETER BRUNETTE, GENERAL EDITOR

Photo courtesy Photofest

JOSEPH L. MANKIEWICZ

INTERVIEWS

EDITED BY BRIAN DAUTH

UNIVERSITY PRESS OF MISSISSIPPI / JACKSON

www.upress.state.ms.us

The University Press of Mississippi is a member of the Association of American University Presses.

Manufactured in the United States of America

First edition 2008

∞

Library of Congress Cataloging-in-Publication Data

Mankiewicz, Joseph L.
    Joseph L. Mankiewicz : interviews / edited by Brian Dauth.
    p. cm. — (Conversations with filmmakers series)
    Includes index.
    Filmography: p.
    ISBN-13: 978-1-934110-23-2 (cloth: alk. paper)
    ISBN-10: 1-934110-23-X (cloth: alk. paper)
    ISBN-13: 978-1-934110-24-9 (pbk.: alk. paper)
    ISBN-10: 1-934110-24-8 (pbk.: alk. paper) 1. Mankiewicz, Joseph L.—
Interviews. 2. Motion picture producers and directors—United States—
Interviews. I. Dauth, Brian. II. Title.
    PN1998.3.M35A3 2008
    791.4302'33092—dc22   2007029095

British Library Cataloging-in-Publication Data available

CONTENTS

INTRODUCTION

JOSEPH L. MANKIEWICZ came of age with Hollywood—both the place and the industry. In 1929 at the age of nineteen, he went out to Hollywood to join his successful older brother Herman J. Mankiewicz and got a job at Paramount Studios writing titles for silent movies. With the coming of sound, he went from titling to writing dialogue and then on to screenplays. Moving to Metro-Goldwyn-Mayer in 1936, he became a producer, and finally in 1943 landed at Twentieth Century-Fox where his ambition to direct was realized three years later with *Dragonwyck* (1946).

This none-too-sentimental education allowed Mankiewicz to be both participant in and observer of what he describes in an interview with Paul Attanasio (included here) as "the beginning, rise, peak, collapse, and end of the talking picture." As that piece and the others in this volume demonstrate, Mankiewicz kept his eyes and ears open the entire time. If his movies chronicle American society and culture during the middle decades of the twentieth century, his infrequent, but compelling interviews tell the story of Hollywood and its filmmaking practices during the same period. These interviews also reveal a brilliant and honest man—clear-eyed about himself and the world around him.

The first interview in this volume was published in *Life Magazine* on March 12, 1951, and finds Mankiewicz at the peak of his career in Hollywood. The previous year he had won Academy Awards for Best Direction and Best Screenplay for *A Letter to Three Wives*, and two weeks after the interview appeared, he would repeat those wins for his work on *All About Eve* (this back-to-back accomplishment remains unduplicated to this day and, like Joe DiMaggio's fifty-six-game hitting streak in baseball, may be the only untouchable record in Oscar history).

This interview introduces Mankiewicz's ambivalent feelings toward Hollywood which he dubs an Ivory Ghetto. The director had a passionate, lifelong love/hate relationship with movies and the people who made them: over the course of these interviews, warm and insightful reminiscences about the actors and actresses with whom he worked (especially the actresses) will alternate with icy assessments of the ruling powers who interfered with and cheapened the product they claimed to love so much.

Among Hollywood's villains, Mankiewicz harbors a special scorn for exhibitors. Two years earlier in another article in *Life Magazine* he commented that the movie exhibitor was "a real estate operator whose chief concern should be taking gum off carpets and checking adolescent love-making in the balcony."[1] The remark resulted in an exhibitor backlash which included a boycott of the film he had in release at the time, *House of Strangers* (1949). Never a man to back down from what he believed to be true, Mankiewicz amplifies his assault here and asserts that exhibitor control of the source of production guarantees that bad pictures will be made. This deconstruction of the customs, rituals, and taboos of Hollywood filmmaking will turn up in all of the interviews included here. (Following the tradition established by previous volumes in this series, all interviews are presented uncut and unedited. While this approach results in occasional repetitions, it offers the reader a detailed portrait of the director, revealing his loves, his obsessions, and his bêtes noires).

A third refrain heard here for the first time is Mankiewicz's belief that the writing and directing of a film are two aspects of the same job. He first made this assertion in "Film Author! Film Author!" which he wrote for the Screenwriters Guild house organ *Screen Writer*: "Writing and directing moving pictures, then are—and should be—the two components of a hyphenated entity. Put it as you will—that the direction of a screen play is the second half of the director's work, or the writing of a screen play is the first half of the director's work. The fact remains that a properly written screen play *has already been directed*—in his script, by the trained screen writer who has conceived his film in visual symbols and translated them into descriptive movement and the spoken word" (emphasis in original).[2] The centrality of this idea to Mankiewicz's understanding of himself as a film artist cannot be overemphasized: he will return to it again and again in these interviews.

The next interview included here was published in *Films and Filming* in 1960. During the intervening nine years Mankiewicz had ended his association with Twentieth Century-Fox, moved from Hollywood to New York, and made six films, including *Julius Caesar* (1953), *The Barefoot Contessa* (1954), *Guys and Dolls* (1955), and *The Quiet American* (1958). The occasion of this article was Mankiewicz's shooting of *Suddenly, Last Summer* (1959) at Shepperton Studios in London. Forthright and prescient as always, Mankiewicz says that he is beginning to feel that "my kind of film might have had it . . . I write essentially for audiences who come to listen to a film as well as to look at it." Mankiewicz sees the handwriting on the wall, understands its meaning, and is unafraid to talk about where he believes the motion picture industry is heading.

Another jump, this time of ten years, brings us to Andrew Sarris's interview for *Show* in March 1970. The 1960s had not been kind to Mankiewicz. The decade saw the biggest disaster of his career—the filming and subsequent mangling of *Cleopatra* (1963)—followed by his greatest disappointment—not being able to bring to the screen his adaptation of Lawrence Durrell's *The Alexandria Quartet*. By the time Sarris interviews him, Mankiewicz has given up on doing his own screenplays and is directing those of others instead (in this instance David Newman and Robert Benton's script for *There Was a Crooked Man . . .*). While Mankiewicz plays his accustomed role of witty raconteur, his belief that movie making is changing in ways not for the better is more pronounced than it had been in previous interviews. But even with his misgivings rising, Mankiewicz still exhibits hope. In another 1970 article related to *There Was a Crooked Man . . .*, he asserts to Gordon Gow that while "audiences are conditioned to having their eyeballs jabbed," "the pendulum will swing" and audiences will "begin to demand . . . something other than these easy optical trappings."

If the 1960s were the worst of times for Mankiewicz, the 1970s (or at least the beginning of them) signaled a renaissance. *Sleuth* (1972) was nominated for four Academy Awards including one for Best Direction, Mankiewicz's first nomination in two decades. Suddenly the director who had described himself to Andrew Sarris as "just about the oldest whore on the beat" was hot again. That same year also saw the publication of *More About All About Eve* which contained both Mankiewicz's original screenplay for the film and an in-depth colloquy with Gary Cary—the most sustained interview Mankiewicz ever gave and reprinted here in full for the first time in thirty-five years.

In the interview, Mankiewicz not only details the making of his most famous film, but also reflects on (among many topics) his deep love and respect for actresses, the compromises a director was forced to make under the studio system, and how flights of cinematic ingenuity were often the result of attempting to avoid the censure of the Breen Office. Mankiewicz also offers an extended analysis of his concept of the writer-director.

A sense of having begun a new chapter in his career (and the confidence this upturn inspired) pervades Mankiewicz's interview with Michel Ciment for *Positif*, published in September 1973 and appearing here in English for the first time. An obvious fan, Ciment skillfully draws Mankiewicz out on the way he makes movies, and their conversation is a rare instance where Mankiewicz speaks directly about his visual technique.

The most persistent (and wrong-headed in my estimation) idea about Mankiewicz and his work is that he was inexpert when it came to using the camera. In his article in this volume, Andrew Sarris notes that he is among those critics who "deplore the limitations of [Mankiewicz's] visual style." An exchange between Ciment and Mankiewicz deftly captures Mankiewicz's approach to the visual:

CIMENT: *Your absence-presence, your apparent effacement on the set, approximates your attitude about the* mise en scène *of cinema.*
MANKIEWICZ: For me, it's an essential aspect of direction.

Mankiewicz goes on to say that he is opposed to movies where the director inserts himself between "the public and the screen," believing that the "look at me, I'm a filmmaker" approach destroys a film.

Unfortunately, Mankiewicz's return to the top turned out to be brief. The forces he identified at the end of the *Positif* interview as now being ascendant in Hollywood—accountants—were his undoing and scuttled plans for his next film, an adaptation of Dee Wells's novel *Jane*. But if Mankiewicz would not make another film, he would give more interviews. One of the first of these late interviews, not included in this volume, occurred at the Deauville Film Festival where he was being honored with a retrospective.[3] Mankiewicz is in a "set-the-record-straight" mode and revisits a favorite theme: How Hollywood Really Worked. He regards as "emperor's tailors" those critics and scholars "who look for transcendental meanings in the work of men who couldn't spell the word transcendental . . . They're busy making this invisible clothing."

The following year Mankiewicz appeared on stage at the National Film Theatre in London and the transcript of his remarks was published in *Films and Filming*. Anecdotes about Hollywood and its personalities dominate now as he remembers filmmaking as it once was. These reminiscences, in addition to being great stories, demonstrate Mankiewicz's eternal interest in the "how" of films. As Ciment notes in his introduction to the *Positif* interview, Mankiewicz's tales always help to illuminate the mechanisms of Hollywood filmmaking. Also, the notion that the kind of movies he is interested in making are falling out of favor is now acknowledged by Mankiewicz to be a hard, cold fact: "I've painted myself into an arrogant or an honourable corner, I don't know which . . . if I go back to work, it will be to make movies about human beings. With rare exceptions, today's Hollywood movies are cartoons, rich, yes, and beautifully illustrated, but with no particular depth."

The penultimate interview of this volume appeared in *Interview* in 1989. Peter Stone, himself an accomplished scenarist (*Charade, Sweet Charity*), spoke with Mankiewicz on the afternoon of that year's Academy Awards ceremony and found the director in a reflective mood tinged with anger. Interspersed with memories of his early days, Mankiewicz comments on how he has gone without recognition from either his industry or his country. Rather than a petulant display of pique, Mankiewicz's complaint derives from careful observation, in this case of the quick-to-forget nature of both Hollywood and America. But if Hollywood has forgotten Mankiewicz, he has not forgotten it. Responding to Stone's query about whether or not he will watch the Oscar broadcast that evening, Mankiewicz tells him that not only will he watch, but will be hoping for "something untoward to happen." As always, the director is on the lookout for those crucial moments when "life louses up the script."

The last interview included here was published in *Films in Review* in 1991 and spanned two issues of that journal. Mankiewicz is in a mellow mood and tells stories both old and new. He is even forthcoming about *Cleopatra*, a film he refused to speak about for decades. He corrects misperceptions about the actual cost of the film and lays to rest the falsehood that the movie lost money: it actually turned a profit.

The following year Film Forum in New York City mounted a retrospective of his films. In an interview with Mel Gussow for the *New York Times* (not included here), Mankiewicz provided a summation of his remarkable life and career: "I've lived without caring what anybody thought of me. I followed very few of the rules. I think I've written some good screenplays, gotten some good performances, and made some good movies."[4] As always, Mankiewicz is sharp and succinct in his assessment (though I think he can justly be accused of false and unnecessary modesty). The interviews that follow will augment this self-evaluation and provide a rich portrait of the fascinating and consummate writer-director known as Joseph L. Mankiewicz.

BD

Notes

1. Eric Hodgins, "A Roundtable on the Movies," *Life*, 27 June 1949, 90–110.
2. Joseph L. Mankiewicz, "Film Author! Film Author!" *Screen Writer*, May 1947, 23–28.
3. "Joseph Mankiewicz," *Interview*, November 1981.
4. Mel Gussow, "The Sometimes Bumpy Ride of Being Joseph Mankiewicz," *New York Times*, 24 November 1992, C13.

CHRONOLOGY

1909	Joseph Leo Mankiewicz is born on February 11, 1909, in Wilkes-Barre, Pennsylvania, third child and youngest of Franz and Johanna Mankiewicz.
1913	Mankiewicz family moves to New York City.
1928	Graduates from Columbia University and moves to Berlin, ostensibly to continue his studies, but instead takes a job with UFA translating titles from German into English.
1929	Joins older brother Herman J. Mankiewicz in Hollywood and is hired by Paramount Studios to write titles for silent films.
1931	Academy Award nomination for Writing, Adaptation for *Skippy* (Norman Taurog).
1933	Moves to Metro-Goldwyn-Mayer.
1934	Marries Elisabeth Young.
1936	Begins producing career. Son Eric is born.
1937	Divorces Elisabeth Young.
1939	Marries Austrian actress Rosa Stradner.
1941	Academy Award nomination for Best Picture for *The Philadelphia Story* (George Cukor). Son Christopher is born.
1942	Son Thomas is born.
1943	Joins Twentieth Century-Fox.
1946	*Dragonwyck* (director and screenplay) and *Somewhere in the Night* (director and co-screenplay).
1947	*The Late George Apley* (director) and *The Ghost and Mrs. Muir* (director).
1948	*Escape* (director).
1949	*A Letter to Three Wives* (director and screenplay) and *House of Strangers* (director and uncredited screenplay).
1950	*No Way Out* (director and co-screenplay) and *All About Eve* (director and co-screenplay). Wins Academy Awards for Best

Direction and Best Screenplay (*A Letter to Three Wives*). Elected President of the Screen Directors Guild and wins showdown with Cecil B. DeMille over the imposition of a mandatory loyalty oath.

1951   *People Will Talk* (director and screenplay). Repeats Academy Award wins for Direction and Screenplay (*All About Eve*). Additional nomination for Best Writing, Story and Screenplay for *No Way Out* (shared with Lesser Samuels). Ends association with Twentieth Century-Fox. Moves from Hollywood to New York City.

1952   *5 Fingers* (director and uncredited screenplay). Stages *La Boheme* for the Metropolitan Opera.

1953   *Julius Caesar* (director). Brother Herman dies. Nominated for Academy Award for Best Direction (*5 Fingers*).

1954   *The Barefoot Contessa* (director, screenplay, producer).

1955   *Guys and Dolls* (director and screenplay). Academy Award nomination for Best Writing, Story and Screenplay (*The Barefoot Contessa*).

1958   *The Quiet American* (director, screenplay, producer). Wife Rosa commits suicide.

1959   *Suddenly, Last Summer* (director).

1962   Marries Rosemary Matthews.

1963   *Cleopatra* (director, co-screenplay).

1964   *Carol for Another Christmas* (director and producer).

1966   Birth of daughter Alexandra.

1967   *The Honey Pot* (director, screenplay, producer).

1970   *There Was a Crooked Man . . .* (director and producer).

1972   *Sleuth* (director).

1973   Academy Award nomination for Best Direction (*Sleuth*).

1981   Receives Honorary Lifetime Membership from the Directors Guild of America.

1983   Co-President of the International Jury at the Berlin Film Festival.

1986   Presented with Lifetime Achievement Award by the Directors Guild of America (formerly the D. W. Griffith Award).

1987   Awarded Golden Lion Award for Career Achievement at the Venice Film Festival.

1989   Becomes the first American to receive the Akira Kurosawa
        Award for Lifetime Achievement from the San Francisco Film
        Festival.
1991   Receives Lifetime Membership from the Academy of Motion
        Picture Arts and Sciences.
1993   Dies on February 5, in Bedford, New York.

FILMOGRAPHY

1946
DRAGONWYCK
Twentieth Century-Fox
Producer: Darryl F. Zanuck; Ernst Lubitsch (uncredited)
Director: **Joseph L. Mankiewicz**
Screenplay: **Joseph L. Mankiewicz**, from the novel by
Anya Seton
Cinematography: Arthur C. Miller
Editing: Dorothy Spencer
Art Direction: J. Russell Spencer and Lyle R. Wheeler
Music: Alfred Newman
Cast: Gene Tierney (Miranda Wells), Walter Huston (Ephraim Wells),
Vincent Price (Nicholas Van Ryn), Glenn Langan (Dr. Jeff Turner), Anne
Revere (Abigail Wells), Spring Byington (Magda), Connie Marshall
(Katrine Van Ryn), Harry Morgan (Klaus Bleecker), Vivienne Osborne
(Johanna Van Ryn), Jessica Tandy (Peggy O'Malley), Trudy Marshall
(Elisabeth Van Borden)
35 mm, B&W
103 minutes

SOMEWHERE IN THE NIGHT
Twentieth Century-Fox
Producer: Anderson Lawler
Director: **Joseph L. Mankiewicz**
Screenplay: Howard Dimsdale and **Joseph L. Mankiewicz**, from the
story "The Lonely Journey" by Marvin Borowsky
Cinematography: Norbert Brodine
Editing: James B. Clark
Art Direction: James Basevi and Maurice Ransford
Music: David Buttolph

Cast: John Hodiak (George W. Taylor), Nancy Guild (Christy Smith),
Lloyd Nolan (Police Lt. Donald Kendall), Richard Conte (Mel Phillips),
Josephine Hutchinson (Elizabeth Conroy), Fritz Kortner (Anzelmo),
Margo Woode (Phyllis), Sheldon Leonard (Sam), Lou Nova (Hubert).
35 mm, B&W
110 minutes

1947
THE LATE GEORGE APLEY
Twentieth Century-Fox
Producer: Fred Kohlmar
Director: **Joseph L. Mankiewicz**
Screenplay: Philip Dunne, from the play by George S. Kaufman and
John P. Marquand and the novel by John P. Marquand
Cinematography: Joseph LaShelle
Editing: James B. Clark
Art Direction: James Basevi and J. Russell Spencer
Music: Cyril J. Mockridge
Cast: Ronald Colman (George Apley), Peggy Cummins (Eleanor Apley),
Vanessa Brown (Agnes Willing), Richard Haydn (Horatio Willing),
Charles Russell (Howard Boulder), Richard Ney (John Apley), Edna Best
(Catherine Apley), Mildred Natwick (Amelia Newcombe), Percy Waram
(Roger Newcombe), Nydia Westman (Jane Willing), Francis Pierlot
(Wilson, the Butler)
35 mm, B&W
97 minutes

THE GHOST AND MRS. MUIR
Twentieth Century-Fox
Producer: Fred Kohlmar
Director: **Joseph L. Mankiewicz**
Screenplay: Philip Dunne, from the novel by R. A. Dick (pseudonym of
Josephine Leslie)
Cinematography: Charles Lang, Jr.
Editing: Dorothy Spencer
Art Direction: George W. Davis and Richard Day
Music: Bernard Herrmann

Cast: Gene Tierney (Lucy Muir), Rex Harrison (Captain Daniel Gregg), George Sanders (Miles Fairley), Edna Best (Martha Huggins), Vanessa Brown (Anna Muir as an Adult), Anna Lee (Mrs. Miles Fairley), Natalie Wood (Anna Muir as a Child), Isobel Elsom (Angelica, Mother-in-Law), Victoria Horne (Eva, Sister-in-law)
35 mm, B&W
104 minutes

ESCAPE
Twentieth Century-Fox
Producer: Fred Kohlmar
Director: **Joseph L. Mankiewicz**
Screenplay: Philip Dunne, from the play by John Galsworthy
Cinematography: Freddie Young
Editing: Kenneth Heeley-Ray and Alan Jaggs
Art Direction: Alex Vetchinsky
Music: William Alwyn
Cast: Rex Harrison (Matt Denant), Peggy Cummins (Dora Winton), William Hartnell (Inspector Harris), Norman Wooland (Minister), Jill Esmond (Grace Winton), Frederick Piper (Convict), Marjorie Rhodes (Mrs. Pinkem), Betty Ann Davies (Girl), Cyril Cusak (Rodgers), John Slater (Salesman), Frank Pettingell (Village Constable), Michael Golden (Plainclothesman), Frederick Leister (Judge), Walter Hudd (Defense Counsel), Maurice Denham (Crown), Jacqueline Clarke (Phyllis), Frank Tickle (Mr. Pinkem), Peter Croft (Titch), Stuart Lindsell (Sir James)
35 mm, B&W
78 minutes

A LETTER TO THREE WIVES
Twentieth Century-Fox
Producer: Sol C. Siegel
Director: **Joseph L. Mankiewicz**
Screenplay: **Joseph L. Mankiewicz**, from the novel *Letter to Five Wives* by John Klempner
Cinematography: Arthur C. Miller
Editing: J. Watson Webb, Jr.
Art Direction: J. Russell Spencer and Lyle R. Wheeler

Music: Alfred Newman
Cast: Jeanne Crain (Deborah Bishop), Linda Darnell (Lora Mae
Hollingsway), Ann Sothern (Rita Phipps), Kirk Douglas (George Phipps),
Paul Douglas (Porter Hollingsway), Jeffrey Lynn (Brad Bishop), Connie
Gilchrist (Mrs. Ruby Finney), Florence Bates (Mrs. Manleigh), Hobart
Cananaugh (Mr. Manleigh), Thelma Ritter (Sadie Dugan), Celeste Holm
(Addie Ross)
35 mm, B&W
103 minutes

HOUSE OF STRANGERS
Twentieth Century-Fox
Producer: Sol C. Siegel
Director: **Joseph L. Mankiewicz**
Screenplay: Philip Yordan and **Joseph L. Mankiewicz** (uncredited),
from the novel *I'll Never Go There Anymore* by Jerome Weidman
Cinematography: Milton R. Krasner
Editing: Harmon Jones
Art Direction: George W. Davis and Lyle R. Wheeler
Music: Daniel Amfitheatrof
Cast: Edward G. Robinson (Gino Monetti), Susan Hayward (Irene
Bennett), Richard Conte (Max Monetti), Luther Adler (Joe Monetti), Paul
Valentine (Pietro Monetti), Efrem Zimbalist, Jr. (Tony Monetti), Debra
Paget (Maria Domenico), Hope Emerson (Helena Domenico), Esther
Miniciotti (Theresa Monetti), Diana Douglas (Elaine Monetti), Tito
Vuolo (Lucca)
35 mm, B&W
101 minutes

1950
NO WAY OUT
Twentieth Century-Fox
Producer: Darryl F. Zanuck
Director: **Joseph L. Mankiewicz**
Screenplay: **Joseph L. Mankiewicz** and Lesser Samuels
Cinematography: Milton R. Krasner
Editing: Barbara McLean

Art Direction: George W. Davis and Lyle R. Wheeler
Music: Alfred Newman
Cast: Richard Widmark (Ray Biddle), Linda Darnell (Edie Johnson),
Stephen McNally (Dr. Dan Wharton), Sidney Poitier (Dr. Luther
Brooks), Mildred Joanne Smith (Cora Brooks), Harry
Bellaver (George Biddle), Stanley Ridges (Dr. Sam Moreland),
Dots Johnson (Lefty Jones), Rudolph Anders (Hoodlum)
35 mm, B&W
106 minutes

ALL ABOUT EVE
Twentieth Century-Fox
Producer: Darryl F. Zanuck
Director: **Joseph L. Mankiewicz**
Screenplay: **Joseph L. Mankiewicz**, based on the short story
"The Wisdom of Eve" by Mary Orr
Cinematography: Milton R. Krasner
Editing: Barbara McLean
Art Direction: George W. Davis and Lyle R. Wheeler
Music: Alfred Newman
Cast: Bette Davis (Margo Channing), Anne Baxter (Eve Harrington),
George Sanders (Addison DeWitt), Celeste Holm (Karen Richards), Gary
Merrill (Bill Sampson), Hugh Marlowe (Lloyd Richards), Gregory Ratoff
(Max Fabian), Barbara Bates (Phoebe), Marilyn Monroe (Miss Caswell),
Thelma Ritter (Birdie Coonan), Walter Hampden (Aged Actor), Randy
Stuart (Girl), Craig Hill (Leading Man), Leland Harris (Doorman),
Barbara White (Autograph Seeker), Eddie Fisher (Stage Manager),
William Pullen (Clerk), Claude Stroud (Pianist), Eugene Borden
(Frenchman), Steve Geray (Captain of Waiters)
35 mm, B&W
138 minutes

1951
PEOPLE WILL TALK
Twentieth Century-Fox
Producer: Darryl F. Zanuck
Director: **Joseph L. Mankiewicz**

Screenplay: **Joseph L. Mankiewicz**, based on the play *Dr. Praetorius* by Curt Goetz
Cinematography: Milton R. Krasner
Editing: Barbara McLean
Art Direction: George W. Davis and Lyle R. Wheeler
Music: Alfred Newman
Cast: Cary Grant (Dr. Noah Praetorius), Jeanne Crain (Deborah Higgins), Finlay Currie (Shunderson), Hume Cronyn (Professor Rodney Elwell), Walter Slezak (Professor Barker), Sidney Blackmer (Arthur Higgins), Basil Ruysdael (Dean Lyman Brockwell), Katherine Locke (Miss James), Will Wright (John Higgins), Margaret Hamilton (Miss Sarah Pickett), Esther Somers (Mrs. Pegwhistle), Carleton Young (Dr. Beecham), Lawrence Dobkin (Business Manager), Ray Montgomery (Doctor), Jo Gilbert (Nurse), Ann Morrison (Miss Fillmore), Julia Dean (Old Lady), Gail Bonney (Secretary), William Klein (Student Manager), George Offerman, Jr. (Uriah Haskins), Adele Longmire (Mabel), Billy House (Sergeant Coonan), Al Murphy (photographer), Parley Baer (Toy Salesman), Irene Seidner (Anna), Joyce Mackenzie (Gussie), Maude Wallace (Night Matron), Kay Lavelle (Bella), Billy Mauch (Student)
35 mm, B&W
110 minutes

1952
5 FINGERS
Twentieth Century-Fox
Producer: Otto Lang
Director: **Joseph L. Mankiewicz**
Screenplay: Michael Wilson and **Joseph L. Mankiewicz** (uncredited), based on the book *Operation Cicero* by L. C. Moyzisch
Cinematography: Norbert Brodine
Editing: James B. Clark
Art Direction: George W. Davis and Lyle R. Wheeler
Music: Bernard Herrmann
Cast: James Mason (Diello), Danielle Darrieux (Countess Anna Staviska), Herbert Berghof (Colonel von Richter), Walter Hampden (Sir Frederic), Oskar Karlweis (L. C. Moyzisch), Michael Rennie (Colin Travers), John Wengraf (Count von Papen), Ben Astar (Siebert), Roger Plowden (Macfadden)

35 mm, B&W
108 minutes

1953
JULIUS CAESAR
Metro-Goldwyn-Mayer
Producer: John Houseman
Director: **Joseph L. Mankiewicz**
Screenplay: William Shakespeare
Cinematography: Joseph Ruttenberg
Editing: John D. Dunning
Art Direction: Edward C. Carfagno and Cedric Gibbons
Music: Miklós Rózsa
Cast: Marlon Brando (Marc Antony), James Mason (Brutus), John Gielgud (Cassius), Louis Calhern (Julius Caesar), Edmond O'Brien (Casca), Greer Garson (Calpurnia), Deborah Kerr (Portia), George Macready (Marullus), Michael Pate (Flavius), Richard Hale (Soothsayer), Alan Napier (Cicero), John Hoyt (Decius Brutus), Tom Powers (Metellus Cimber), William Cotrell (Cinna), Jack Raine (Trebonius), Ian Wolfe (Caius Ligarius), Morgan Farley (Artemidorus), Bill Phipps (Servant to Anthony), Douglass Watson (Octavius Caesar), Douglass Dumbrille (Lepidus), Rhys Williams (Lucillus), Michael Ansara (Pindarus), Dayton Lummis (Messala), Paul Guilfoyle (Citizen of Rome), Edmund Purdom (Strato), Lawrence Dobkin (Citizen of Rome), Jo Gilbert (Citizen of Rome), John Hardy (Lucius), Chet Stratton (Servant to Caesar), Lumsden Hare (Publius), Preston Hanson (Claudius), Victor Perry (Popilius Lena), Michael Tolan (Officer to Octavius), John Lupton (Varro), Joe Waring (Clitus), John Parrish (Titinius), Stephen Roberts (Dardanius), Thomas Browne Henry (Volumnius), David Bond (Citizen of Rome), Ann Tyrrell (Citizen of Rome), John O'Malley (Citizen of Rome), Donald Elson (Citizen of Rome)
35 mm, B&W
120 minutes

1954
THE BAREFOOT CONTESSA
Figaro Incorporated
Producer: **Joseph L. Mankiewicz**
Director: **Joseph L. Mankiewicz**

Screenplay: **Joseph L. Mankiewicz**
Cinematography: Jack Cardiff
Editing: William Hornbeck
Music: Mario Mascimbene
Cast: Humphrey Bogart (Harry Dawes), Ava Gardner (Maria Vargas), Edmond O'Brien (Oscar Muldoon), Marius Goring (Alberto Bravano), Valentina Cortese (Eleanora Torlato-Favrini), Rossano Brazzi (Count Vincenzo Torlato-Favrini), Elizabeth Sellars (Jerry), Warren Stevens (Kirk Edwards), Franco Interlenghi (Pedro Vargas), Mari Aldon (Myrna), Bessie Love (Mrs. Eubanks), Diana Decker (Drunken Blonde), Bill Fraser (J. Montague Brown), Alberto Rabagliati (Nightclub Proprietor), Enzo Staiola (Busboy), Maria Zanoli (Maria's Mother), Renato Chiantoni (Maria's Father), John Parrish (Max Black), Jim Gerald (Mr. Blue), Riccardo Rioli (Gypsy Dancer), Tonio Selwart (Pretender), Margaret Anderson (Pretender's Wife), Gertrude Flynn (Lulu McGee), John Horne (Hector Eubanks), Bob Christopher (Eddie Blake), Anna Maria Paduan (Chanbermaid), Carlo Dale (Vincenzo's Chauffeur)
35 mm, Technicolor
130 minutes

1955
GUYS AND DOLLS
Samuel Goldwyn Company
Producer: Samuel Goldwyn
Director: **Joseph L. Mankiewicz**
Screenplay: **Joseph L. Mankiewicz**, based on the musical play by Frank Loesser, Abe Burrows and Jo Swerling
Cinematography: Harry Stradling
Editing: Daniel Mandell
Production Design: Oliver Smith
Music: Frank Loesser
Cast: Marlon Brando (Sky Masterson), Jean Simmons (Sergeant Sarah Brown), Frank Sinatra (Nathan Detroit), Vivian Blaine (Miss Adelaide), Robert Keith (Lieutenant Brannigan), Stubby Kaye (Nicely Nicely Johnson), B. S. Pully (Big Jule), Johnny Silver (Benny Southstreet), Sheldon Leonard (Harry the Horse), Dan Dayton (Rusty Charlie), George E. Stone (Society Max), Regis Toomey (Arvide Abernathy), Kathryn

Givney (General Cartwright), Veda Ann Borg (Laverne), Mary Alan
Hokanson (Agatha), Joe McTurk (Angie the Ox), Kay Kuter (Calvin),
Stapledon Kent (Mission Member), Renee Renor (Cuban Singer), The
Goldwyn Girls (Performers)
35 mm, Eastmancolor
152 minutes

1958
THE QUIET AMERICAN
Figaro Films
Producer: **Joseph L. Mankiewicz**
Director: **Joseph L. Mankiewicz**
Screenplay: **Joseph L. Mankiewicz**, based on the novel by Graham
Greene
Cinematography: Robert Krasker
Editing: William Hornbeck
Music: Mario Nascimbene
Cast: Audie Murphy (The American), Michael Redgrave (Thomas
Fowler), Claude Dauphin (Inspector Vigot), Giorgia Moll (Phuong),
Bruce Cabot (Bill Granger), Fred Sadoff (Dominguez), Kerima (Phuong's
Sister), Richard Loo (Mr. Heng), Peter Trent (Eliot Wilkins), Georges
Brehat (French Colonel), Clinton Anderson (Joe Morton), Yoko Tani
(Rendezvous Hostess), Nguyen Long (Boy with Mask), C. Long Cuong
(Boy in Watchtower), Tu An (Boy in Watchtower)
35 mm B&W
120 minutes

1959
SUDDENLY, LAST SUMMER
Columbia Pictures
Producer: Sam Spiegel
Director: **Joseph L. Mankiewicz**
Screenplay: Gore Vidal and Tennessee Williams, based on the play by
Tennessee Williams
Cinematography: Jack Hildyard
Editing: William Hornbeck and Thomas G. Stanford

Production Design: Oliver Messel
Music: Malcolm Arnold and Buxton Orr
Cast: Elizabeth Taylor (Catherine Holly), Katherine Hepburn (Violet
Venable), Montgomery Clift (Dr. Cukrowicz), Albert Dekker
(Dr. Lawrence J. Hockstader), Mercedes McCambridge (Grace Holly),
Gary Raymond (George Holly), Mavis Villiers (Foxhill), Patricia
Marmont (Nurse Benson), Joan Young (Sister Felicity), Maria Britneva
(Lucy), Shelia Robbins (Dr. Hockstader's Secretary), David Cameron
(Young Blonde Intern)
35 mm, B&W
114 minutes

1963
CLEOPATRA
Twentieth Century-Fox
Producer: Walter Wanger
Director: **Joseph L. Mankiewicz**
Screenplay: **Joseph L. Mankiewicz**, Ranald MacDougall, and Sidney
Buchman
Cinematography: Leon Shamroy
Editing: Dorothy Spencer
Production Design: John DeCuir
Music: Alex North
Cast: Elizabeth Taylor (Cleopatra), Richard Burton (Marc Antony), Rex
Harrison (Julius Caesar), Pamela Brown (High Priestess), George Cole
(Flavius), Hume Cronyn (Sosigenes), Cesare Danova (Apollodorus),
Kenneth Haigh (Brutus), Andrew Keir (Agrippa), Martin Landau (Rufio),
Roddy McDowall (Octavian), Robert Stephens (Germanicus), Francesca
Annis (Eiras), Gregoire Aslan (Pothinus), Martin Benson (Ramos),
Herbert Berghof (Theodotos), John Cairney (Phoebus), Jacqui Chan
(Lotos), Isabelle Cooley (Charmian), John Doucette (Achillas), Andrew
Faulds (Canidius), Michael Gwynn (Cimber), Michael Hordern (Cicero),
John Hoyt (Cassius), Marne Maitland (Euphranor), Carroll O'Connor
(Casca), Richard O'Sullivan (Ptolemy XIII), Gwen Watford (Calpurnia),
Douglas Wilmer (Decimus)
70 mm, DeLuxe Color
246 minutes

1964
CAROL FOR ANOTHER CHRISTMAS
ABC-TV/Telsun Foundation, Inc.
Producer: **Joseph L. Mankiewicz**
Director: **Joseph L. Mankiewicz**
Screenplay: Rod Serling, from the novel *A Christmas Carol* by Charles Dickens
Cinematography: Arthur J. Ornitz
Editing: Nathan Greene and Robert Lawrence
Production Design: Gene Callahan
Music: Henry Mancini
Cast: Sterling Hayden (Daniel Grudge), Percy Rodriguez (Charles), Eva Marie Saint (The Wave), Ben Gazzara (Fred), Barbara Ainteer (Ruby), Steve Lawrence (Ghost of Christmas Past), James Shigeta (The Doctor), Pat Hingle (Ghost of Christmas Present), Robert Shaw (Ghost of Christmas Future), Peter Sellers (Imperial Me), Britt Ekland (The Mother)
B&W
84 minutes

1967
THE HONEY POT
Famous Artists Productions
Producer: **Joseph L. Mankiewicz**
Director: **Joseph L. Mankiewicz**
Screenplay: **Joseph L. Mankiewicz**, based on the play *Mr. Fox of Venice* by Frederick Knott, the novel *The Evil of the Day* by Thomas Sterling, and the play *Volpone* by Ben Jonson
Cinematography: Gianni De Venanzo
Editing: David Bretherton
Production Design: John De Cuir
Music: John Addison
Cast: Rex Harrison (Cecil Sheridan Fox), Susan Hayward (Mrs. Sheridan), Cliff Robertson (William McFly), Capucine (Princess Dominique), Edie Adams (Merle McGill), Maggie Smith (Sarah Watkins), Adolfo Celi (Inspector Rizzi), Hugh Manning (Volpone), David Dodimead (Mosca)
35 mm, Technicolor
132 minutes

1970
THERE WAS A CROOKED MAN . . .
Warner Brothers
Producer: **Joseph L. Mankiewicz**
Director: **Joseph L. Mankiewicz**
Screenplay: David Newman and Robert Benton
Cinematography: Harry Stradling, Jr.
Editing: Gene Milford
Production Design: Edward Carrere
Music: Charles Strouse
Cast: Kirk Douglas (Paris Pitman, Jr.), Henry Fonda (Woodward W.
Lopeman), Hume Cronyn (Dudley Whinner), Warren Oates (Floyd
Moon), Burgess Meredith (The Missouri Kid), John Randolph (Cyrus
McNutt), Lee Grant (Mrs. Bullard), Arthur O'Connell (Mr. Lomax),
Martin Gabel (Warden LeGoff), Michael Blodgett (Coy Cavendish),
C. K. Yang (Ah-Ping), Alan Hale (Tobaccy), Victor French (Whiskey),
Claudia McNeil (Madam), Bert Freed (Skinner), Jeanne Cooper
(Prostitute), Barbara Rhoades (Jessie Brundidge), Gene Evans (Colonel
Wolff), Pamela Hensley (Edwina), J. Edward McKinley (The Governor),
Ann Doran (Mrs. Lomax)
35 mm, Technicolor
126 minutes

1972
SLEUTH
Palomar Pictures
Producer: Morton Gottlieb
Director: **Joseph L. Mankiewicz**
Screenplay: Anthony Shaffer, from his play
Cinematography: Oswald Morris
Editing: Richard Marden
Production Design: Ken Adam
Music: John Addison
Cast: Laurence Olivier (Andrew Wyke), Michael Caine
(Milo Tindle)
35 mm, DeLuxe Color
138 minutes

Films Written and Produced by Joseph L. Mankiewicz but Directed by Others

The Keys of the Kingdom (1944), Twentieth Century-Fox, directed by John M. Stahl

Films Produced by Joseph L. Mankiewicz but Directed by Others

Three Godfathers (1936), Metro-Goldwyn-Mayer, directed by Richard Boleslawski

Fury (1936), Metro-Goldwyn-Mayer, directed by Fritz Lang

The Gorgeous Hussy (1936), Metro-Goldwyn-Mayer, directed by Clarence Brown

Love on the Run (1936), Metro-Goldwyn-Mayer, directed by W. S. Van Dyke

The Bride Wore Red (1936), Metro-Goldwyn-Mayer, directed by Dorothy Arzner

Double Wedding (1937), Metro-Goldwyn-Mayer, directed by Richard Thorpe

Mannequin (1938), Metro-Goldwyn-Mayer, directed by Frank Borzage

Three Comrades (1938), Metro-Goldwyn-Mayer, directed by Frank Borzage

Shopworn Angel (1938), Metro-Goldwyn-Mayer, directed by H. C. Potter

The Shining Hour (1938), Metro-Goldwyn-Mayer, directed by Frank Borzage

A Christmas Carol (1938), Metro-Goldwyn-Mayer, directed by Edwin L. Marin

The Adventures of Huckleberry Finn (1939), Metro-Goldwyn-Mayer, directed by Richard Thorpe

Strange Cargo (1940), Metro-Goldwyn-Mayer, directed by Frank Borzage

The Philadelphia Story (1940), Metro-Goldwyn-Mayer, directed by George Cukor

The Wild Man of Borneo (1941), Metro-Goldwyn-Mayer, directed by Robert B. Sinclair

The Feminine Touch (1941), Metro-Goldwyn-Mayer, directed by W. S. Van Dyke

Woman of the Year (1942), Metro-Goldwyn-Mayer, directed by George Stevens

Cairo (1942), Metro-Goldwyn-Mayer, directed by W. S. Van Dyke

Reunion in France (1942), Metro-Goldwyn-Mayer, directed by Jules Dassin

Films Written in Whole or Part by Joseph L. Mankiewicz but Directed by Others

Slightly Scarlet (1930), Paramount, directed by Louis G. Gasnier and Edwin H. Knopf

Paramount on Parade (1930), Paramount, directed by various directors

The Social Lion (1930), Paramount, directed by A. Edward Sutherland

Only Saps Work (1930), Paramount, directed by Cyril Gardner and Edwin H. Knopf

The Gang Buster (1931), Paramount, directed by A. Edward Sutherland

Finn and Hattie (1931), Paramount, directed by Norman Z. McLeod and Norman Taurog

June Moon (1931), Paramount, directed by A. Edward Sutherland

Skippy (1931), Paramount, directed by Norman Taurog

Newly Rich (1931), Paramount, directed by Norman Taurog

Sooky (1931), Paramount, directed by Norman Taurog

This Reckless Age (1932), Paramount, directed by Frank Tuttle

Sky Bride (1932), Paramount, directed by Stephen Roberts

Million Dollar Legs (1932), Paramount, directed by Edward F. Cline

If I Had a Million (1932), Paramount, directed by various directors

Diplomaniacs (1933), Paramount, directed by William A. Seiter

Emergency Call (1933), Paramount, directed by Edward L. Cahn

Too Much Harmony (1933), Paramount, directed by A. Edward Sutherland

Alice in Wonderland (1933), Paramount, directed by Norman Z. McLeod

Manhattan Melodrama (1934), Metro-Goldwyn-Mayer, directed by W. S. Van Dyke

Our Daily Bread (1934), Viking Productions, directed by King Vidor

Forsaking All Others (1934), Metro-Goldwyn-Mayer, directed by W. S. Van Dyke

I Live My Life (1935), Metro-Goldwyn-Mayer, directed by W. S. Van Dyke

Films Titled in Whole or Part by Joseph L. Mankiewicz but Directed by Others

The Dummy (1929), Paramount, directed by Robert Milton

Close Harmony (1929), Paramount, directed by John Cromwell and A. Edward Sutherland

The Man I Love (1929), Paramount, directed by William A. Wellman

The Studio Murder Mystery (1929), Paramount, directed by Frank Tuttle

Thunderbolt (1929), Paramount, directed by Josef von Sternberg

River of Romance (1929), Paramount, directed by Richard Wallace

The Mysterious Dr. Fu Manchu (1929), Paramount, directed by Rowland V. Lee

Fast Company (1929), Paramount, directed by A. Edward Sutherland

The Saturday Night Kid (1929), Paramount, directed by A. Edward Sutherland

The Virginian (1929), Paramount, directed by Victor Fleming

JOSEPH L. MANKIEWICZ

INTERVIEWS

15 Authors in Search of a Character Named Joseph L. Mankiewicz

ROBERT COUGHLAN/1951

NARRATOR: Let us face the fact at once that our subject's name cannot be pronounced except in Polish—the first of several anomalies, since he is not Polish. Joseph Leo Mankiewicz. He answers to *"Mank-uh-wits."* He is a film writer and director—you have seen his name swim past among the screen credits, along with those of the costume designers, special-effects men, producers, composers, cameramen and all the other functionaries who enforce such a wait before Betty Grable opens the show with a Technicolor high kick. There is no reason why he should again detain us except that, in a way important to us of the movie audience, he is an extraordinary man.

Among the many awards given in the motion picture industry . . .

A PRODUCER: Awards! Awards are a nickel a hundred. You get an award for going to the bathroom here, you get an award for riding down as far as Duvernoy Drive.

NARRATOR: . . . some have real meaning. Among these are the awards of the Academy of Motion Picture Arts and Sciences—the Oscars. Mankiewicz has won Oscars. In 1949 he won two of them for writing and directing a movie called *A Letter to Three Wives*; and two weeks from now, at the Academy's annual Bank Nite at Pantages Theater, he may well win one or two more for writing and directing a movie called

From *LIFE Magazine* (March 12, 1951). Reprinted by permission of Time Life, Inc.

All About Eve. For that, he has already been given the director's award of the New York Film Critics—another very good award to have. *Eve* has been called "brilliantly conceived . . . dazzling . . . devastating . . ." by the New York *Times*; "a triumph of motion picture making" by the New York *Herald Tribune*; "a monumentally satisfying achievement" by the New York *World-Telegram & Sun*. All of which certifies the fact that his pictures have Quality.

The other side of the equation is Box Office. Hollywood has always had a convincing answer to the charge that most movies are made for the twelve-year-old mind: "If you don't make them for that level, you flop at the box office. If you flop at the box office, you go out of business." Now and then a movie has come along—*The Lost Weekend*, *The Best Years of Our Lives*—and shown that money can be made on an adult theme treated in an adult way for an adult audience. But no one has discredited the familiar answer quite so thoroughly—certainly not in rapid order, with two such pictures as *Letter* and *Eve*—as Mankiewicz has done.

And so it is important to ask, "Who is Mankiewicz and where has he been? Can he do it again? Is he a freak, a genius, or can we expect more such products as his from Hollywood?"

A FRIEND: He's not a genius.

A CRITIC: The surprising thing is that he's been around forever. He was practically born in Hollywood; professionally, at least, he's had nothing but Hollywood experience. For years he was just another very competent man, well above average but relatively undistinguished. Then—this metamorphosis. Whatever it was that happened to him should happen to more people in Hollywood.

FRIEND: I've known him for twenty years. I can't tell that he's changed much. He's more inward, perhaps. He seems to worry about his immortal soul or something. But then, maybe he always did. I'm not sure that I've ever *really* known him. He's an elusive character. He's aggressive, disputatious, rude—yet he'll go to *any* length to avoid a personal scene. He's glib and humorous—and intensely serious. He's enormously charming and everybody likes him—and I doubt if he has a really close friend in the world. He's even hard to describe physically. Big gestures with his hands; the way his eyes pop when he gets excited. That pipe—he's always got a pipe in his teeth.

LINDA DARNELL: I wish women could smoke pipes. Joe's pipe is a shield—he gets behind it.

FRIEND: Somehow he doesn't make anecdotes.

ADELAIDE, HIS SECRETARY: He's unathletically inclined. He writes in a small light script with very sharp soft pencils on copybook paper. He really gets warmed up at night and often goes on working until 3 A.M. His hardest job is writing letters: he's never learned to dictate, so he writes them in longhand and I copy them on the typewriter. After seventeen years my shorthand is shot. He's sort of naive about some things. He was the last one on the set of *Eve* to know that Bette Davis and Gary Merrill were in love. He doesn't swear and he very seldom takes a drink. He likes steak, lamb chops, broiled chicken, fresh pineapple, cottage cheese and Kadota figs. He's crazy for peanut brittle.

PRODUCER: This is a town built on fear. The assistant director is afraid of the director. The director is afraid of the producer. The producer is afraid of the production head. The production head is afraid of the owners. The owners are afraid of the exhibitors. Joe's chief characteristic, it seems to me, is that he's not afraid of *any*body. He has convictions and he doesn't take counsel easily. He will interrupt. He'll go charging up San Juan Hill with a knife in his teeth when somebody else might figure, "Maybe there's a way *around* that hill." So he's often in trouble. For instance, that famous crack of his at the *Life* Movie Round Table (June 27, 1949) about the exhibitor as "a real estate operator whose chief concern should be taking gum off carpets and checking adolescent lovemaking in the balcony." All over the country exhibitors screamed, wrote letters, wrote articles, abused him and even boycotted his pictures. There were hundreds of canceled bookings of the one he had out then, *House of Strangers.*

MANKIEWICZ: Boycott! It was just my luck to shoot my mouth off at the same time I made a bad picture. If it had been a good picture, something the audience would have put down its fifty cents to see, there wouldn't have been any boycott. Does a rabbit boycott lettuce? Does a chippy boycott the navy?

There are bound to be bad pictures so long as the exhibitor controls the source of supply, the producer, and milks him for most of the profits. The whole industry is based on the idea that twenty thousand movie theaters have to have a change of bill two or three times a week, that somebody has to produce four hundred pictures a year so those places won't go dark. The whole thing is a real estate proposition—it's all wrong-side-to.

Of course, the studio heads come in for their part of the blame. They refuse to admit that within the last twenty years audiences have grown up. You can tell that just by listening to ordinary conversation. Mrs. Jones used to say, "Mabel Smith certainly is a bitch"; now she says, "Mabel Smith certainly must be neurotic to act that way." Nowadays people want to know *why* people behave the way they do. Mere action isn't enough to hold their interest, their intelligence. What the studio heads are saying should be reversed: it's usually a case now where twelve-year-old minds are making pictures for grownup audiences.

Even if they wanted to, it would be hard for most of them to make anything but formula pictures. How can they know anything about life and people? They live in an Ivory Ghetto out here. The only people they talk to are other picture people. The only conversation is about the movies. When they travel they take the Ivory Ghetto along. They eat the same food, have the same companions, impulses, responses, comforts and concerns—whether it's between trains in Chicago, in New York, London, Paris or Palm Springs. They get back—they've never left home.

CRITIC: Joe is what I call a man of the Third Alternative. There are some people who "go Hollywood"—sell out completely and sink happily into the mire. There are the others who hate it, and protest against it by going "pure" and "arty" and work here only in order to "rob the robbers." Joe has found the happy golden mean. He knows all the faults, but he can also see all the potentialities. He neither victimizes nor is the victim—he's the master of his milieu.

MANKIEWICZ: Don't get me wrong. I love the movies as a medium. It's perfectly possible to do good work here. And I've observed that the criticism of Hollywood you hear from Hollywood people usually is in inverse ratio to their own success. They're really only putting up a smokescreen to cover their own mediocrity. The movies are full of mediocrity. What isn't? How good is the average book, or magazine, or play? They talk about Hollywood's commercialism. Well, thousands of books are published each year and most of them are put out to make a buck. Half of them are trash. Do you think that when the great firm of Macmillan published *Forever Amber* they were motivated by the desire to contribute to Restoration history? And did anybody say, "Isn't that just like the publishing industry?" But it was "just like Hollywood" to make the movie.

They talk about acting—you're not an actor unless you learned it on the stage. The movies actually are the toughest school of acting in the world. The proof of that is when kids like June Lockhart—their only training has been in pictures—go east and do a play, they knock the critics cold. I'll say something really dramatic. The upper strata of writing here is better than the average of Broadway's.

The point is that Hollywood is almost always criticized for the wrong things. Take the Production Code—our so-called "self-imposed censorship." I think it's a necessary evil. It gives us at least some protection from the pressure groups, the minorities of all kinds and colors, the police officials in search of a distracting stink and those wanton little groups of women who hate their homes or have none—the self-appointed custodians of everybody's morals. They invoke the magic of Mom and The Church and Protecting Our Youth, and they've got us at their mercy. And, of course, there's the Legion of Decency. They have the literal power to decide what pictures will and will not be made. Now I don't believe that any Catholic should be forced to see *The Miracle* or that any Jew should be forced to see *Oliver Twist*. But when Catholics or Jews try to tell other people what they can and can't see, I think that's intolerable.

PRODUCER: Joe is very verbal. I admire that. He can express himself. Some of these directors, they're incoherent. Joe can always tell an actor what he wants and make him understand.

LINDA DARNELL: Joe never shouts on the set, he never even raises his voice. He comes over and talks to you, just to you, so nobody else can hear. And he never says, "That's wrong"—only, "Maybe it would be better this way."

CELESTE HOLM: He starts out by assuming that you're a professional and that you have at least reasonably good sense. Then, if you make a mistake, he corrects you. He seems to know actors and to understand what it's like to be an actor, although he's never been one, so far as I know. . . .

PAUL DOUGLAS: He's a friend. I couldn't wait to get to the studio in the morning—it was like meeting up with an old chum. And he shows great humor at all times. You know, I'm a sweater. He brought me out here for *A Letter to Three Wives*: it's my first part in a movie, and I was scared. I showed up sweating that first day and I sweat through three shirts. Finally I'm sitting over in a corner quietly going to pieces. Joe comes over with his photographer, Artie Miller—used to be a jockey. Joe knows I'm a horse player, so he talks to me in my own language. He turns to Artie and says, "Shall we put an exercise boy on the son of a bitch and dry him out?" That did it. From there on I was all right.

THELMA RITTER: Take some directors. A director with that monocle and riding-crop style, pretty soon you get into the act. After all, you're an actor, it's irresistible. But here's Joe, he's a working guy. With him you'd feel pretty silly getting temperamental. And the way he handles you. He saw me in that bit in *Miracle on 34th Street* and decided I was right for the maid in *Letter*, so he came to New York and interviewed me. I walk in nervous, and besides I cut my finger and it's all done up in bandages so it sticks out like a barber pole. Joe looks at me, looks at the finger, and says, "Did you have it wrapped for a gift?" So of course I fell in love with him. He's for you all the time and with you, but you have to sense his approbation. He doesn't tell you. I was anxious and went up one day after the rushes and says, "Was I all right?" He says to me, "What's the matter—you're a manic-depressive?"

MANKIEWICZ: I work with people on their own terms. It's like the story of the lost cow. The man found it by asking himself, "Now let's see, if I was a cow where would I go?"

CRITIC: Mankiewicz is a good director, no doubt; probably in the first half dozen. However, his real brilliance is as a writer. His dialog is among the best that is being written in any medium. His situations are convincing and his characters are real: they're motivated people and, moreover, such different kinds of people. He moves from the domestic comedy of Main Street in *Letter* to Negro family life and psychopathic white slum dwellers in *No Way Out* to high comedy and extremely sophisticated people in *Eve*—all with equal authority. He writes as if he had been a New York newspaperman—someone who had knocked around from the police courts to the drama page, started writing for the theater, and come to Hollywood that way. Yet actually he is a product of what he calls this Ivory Ghetto. It is that contradiction that fascinates me.

WRITER: So much movie writing is done in pure blacks and whites— the villain a complete symbol of evil, the hero a symbol of ideal good.

But in *Eve* Joe showed that he knew how to handle the gray zones, which is where people really live, you know. He had the courage of his insights: he let his characters do what potentially they might do—so that although you were often surprised by them, you always believed in them. And he wrote without snobbishness, although he learned to write in Hollywood, the most snobbish school in the world. Like that story of the little girl, the daughter of a producer, who came home one day with a story she had written in school. Her father asked her to read it, so she began, "Once there was a very poor family. The father was poor, the mother was poor and all the servants were poor." But the thing that impressed me most about *Eve* was the thing without which no writer can be great, the quality of pity. Compassion. The town is full of false pity, the trees drip with false sentiment; but his compassion is real. How and when did he acquire it?

NARRATOR: Mankiewicz's father's ancestors lived in Posen, a border area that was sometimes under German, sometimes under Polish or Russian, hegemony. The Polish name stuck, and it was kept even after his late forebears moved to Berlin. The Blumenaus, his mother's family, had lived in Latvia; a pogrom sent them also into Germany. Frank Mankiewicz and Johanna Blumenau both had emigrated to America, and they met and married in New York. They had three children: Herman, Erna, who was four years younger, and Joseph, eight years younger than she. Joseph was born in Wilkes-Barre on February 11, 1909.

ERNA: Pop was a marvelous man. He was a professor, the absent-minded type. Details like names weren't important to him. Once he was out in Hollywood and Jimmy Cagney came up to him in the Brown Derby. Jimmy had been one of his students—and he was just then at the height of his fame. Pop recognized him all right as a former pupil but drew a blank on everything else. Finally Jimmy caught on and said, "I'm James Cagney." Pop said, "Of course, how nice to see you again. What do you do these days?" But Pop was deeply interested in people. Our house was always full of strays he'd picked up and befriended. Everybody called him Pop. He had a real contempt for money and the things money could buy. You could make $1,000 a week and that didn't impress Pop. It was what you were inside—what you had learned that day, had you done something kind or worth doing, had you done something well. All of us kids were precocious. Joe got out of grammar school when he was eleven, high school at fifteen and Columbia at nineteen. That sort of thing didn't impress Pop either. He'd say, "To brag about being smart is like bragging about having blue eyes. It's just a characteristic. It's what you do with it that matters." He'd never praise us. He was proud of us—he'd tell other people, but he'd never tell us. Joe would come home from school with a 97, say, and Pop would say, "What happened to the 3 percent?" Joe might say, "But *Pop*, nobody else got more than 90." And Pop would say, "The boy that got 90, maybe it was harder for him to do that than for you to get 97. It's not good unless it's your best."

HERMAN: Pop was a tremendously industrious, brilliant, vital man. A father like that could make you very ambitious or very despairing. You could end up by saying, "Stick it, I'll never live up to that and I'm not going to try." That's what happened eventually with me. Joe was fiercely ambitious as a kid. He was bright, gifted, gay, charming. But Pop didn't see much of him. He had done all sorts of things, mostly newspaper work, before he took up teaching, and then he went into that like an earth-moving machine. Night school, summer school, student tours, home courses, working at the same time to support his family. He ended up with his Ph.D. and as a professor at C.C.N.Y. But when he wasn't studying he was working. By necessity Joe spent most of his time with our mother. She was a round little woman who was uneducated in four languages. She spoke mangled German, mangled Russian, mangled Yiddish, and mangled English. She raised Joe—Pop had no time for him.

JOE: The Mankiewicz family had color. I was so much the youngest that to me all the others seemed huge, violent. And we kept moving. Always new neighborhoods, new gangs of kids, new adjustments. I became skillful at taking on the color of my environment without absorbing it, at participating in almost everything without becoming part of anything. I acquired an awareness of people the way an animal knows the woods in which he lives. I made no friends. I have no contact today with anyone who knew me as a child. I escaped into fantasies—thousands of fantasies. It isn't surprising that I ended up as a writer and in show business.

But I started out to be a psychiatrist. I took a pre-med course at Columbia. Then came the part where you disembowel frogs and earthworms, which horrified and nauseated me. But what really finished

me was physics. I got an F-minus. There is no such grade. I went to
Professor Farwell and protested. He said, "I feel that I must distinguish
between mere failure and total failure such as yours." So I switched to
straight liberal arts and got my A.B. in 1928. Afterward I went to
Germany to visit some relatives. I worked for a while for the Chicago
Tribune and later as a title translator at UFA, the German studio. In
January I came back and started to look around. Things weren't too
promising, so I came on out here, because of Herman.

PRODUCER: I used to see a good deal of Herman. He'd got into newspaper work, covered all sorts of things, and finally became a dramatic
editor for the New York *Times*. That got him into writing for the
theater—he did skits for things like the *Follies* and *Scandals* and the
Little Shows, and a couple of plays. He had terrific talent; but beyond
that, he was a Personality. He was a great arguer and a great talker, a
brilliant, savage wit. There were giants in those days: Robert Benchley,
Dorothy Parker, Alexander Woollcott, Ring Lardner, Wilson Mizner—he
was in that league. He came out here on one of those six-month deals
to pick up some easy money. He kept intending to go back to New York,
but he never did.

HERMAN: I'm one of those who never got reconciled to this place. Of
course, it's a hell of a time to be thinking about that after twenty-five
years.

NARRATOR: Herman was so successful as a Hollywood writer that
B. P. Schulberg and David O. Selznick, the heads of Paramount, asked
him to make trips to New York and bring back some of his writing
friends. It was through him that such people as Nunnally Johnson and
Robert Benchley first came to Hollywood. On one trip he brought back
Joe, freshly home from Europe and needing a job. He came to work as
an apprentice writer at sixty dollars a week.

FRIEND: Joe was the kid brother all right. Herman rode him, patron-
ized him, did everything but send him out for cigarets. Well, that was
understandable. Herman was a god among the writers, Joe was strictly
nobody. Even people who knew him, when they bumped into him
around the studio, would say, "Hello, Herm—I mean Joe." One day Joe
said, "I know now what will be on my tombstone. It'll say, 'Here lies

Herm—I mean Joe—Mankiewicz.'" But at the same time Herman did a lot for him. He showed him the ropes, gave him advice, steered him around, did all sorts of things. He was really more like a father than a brother to him, sort of a substitute father.

HERMAN: I suppose—in fact, I'm sure—I've been an influence in Joe's life, but it's been mostly negative. Like Shaw said, "Parents should be a warning to their children instead of an example." Nobody can deny I've been a good bad example. Otherwise I make no claims. I helped him at first, but he learned fast.

JOE: Those were the last days of silent pictures, when the continuity man and the dialog man worked together on a script. One did the action, the other did the words, the "subtitles." They matched me up with several of the oldtime continuity men to teach me the business. They were awful hacks, in a literary sense; they couldn't have written a decent letter in words, but they were real writers nevertheless in their own medium. I remember one old guy sitting there and explaining to me the thing he called "the-what-they-didn't-know-was. . . ." "For instance," he'd say, "there's an heiress, Mary Brian. She's afraid somebody is going to marry her for her money, so she runs away from home and gets a job as a waitress. So she's walking along the street one day and there's a guy, Richard Arlen, crawling out from under his taxi. He's been fixing it, he's all covered with grease and dirt. They see each other. Now *what-she-didn't-know-was* that he is really the Archduke Ferdinand of Baden-Wurst, who is over here in disguise to find a girl who isn't marrying him for his title and his money. So you've got a situation—take it from there. . . ." Of course it's as old as *Oedipus Rex*, but it's fundamental. I learned a lot about writing from those men. For that matter, the whole framework of *Eve* is a *what-they-didn't-know-was*.

Block bookings were still the practice then: the studios would say to the exhibitors, we'll sell you four Clara Bows, two Gary Coopers, three Jean Harlows, and so forth, as a package, and with the following titles. They'd sell the star and the title and *then* make the picture. One of the Clara Bow titles coming up was *Saturday Night Kid*. So I sat down and in a couple of weeks' time wrote six completely different stories to go with that title. B. P. Schulberg called me and said they all stank, but that he liked some of the dialog. I told Herman, and he convinced David O. Selznick that I should have the chance to do some "additional dialog" on a Jack Oakie picture, *Fast Company*. The picture made Oakie a star. So I was put to work on a whole series of Jack Oakie–Skeets Gallagher pictures. Then in 1930 I did the screen play for *Skippy* and got my first nomination for an Academy Award. I was twenty-one.

It wasn't long afterward that, as it must to all Hollywood writers, there came the time when I served my stint at Metro. I wrote a couple of successful films—*Forsaking All Others* and *Manhattan Melodrama*—but what I really wanted was to be a director. I was told, "You have to learn to crawl before you learn to walk," and they made me a producer. I've never heard a better definition of the average producer. I started off with *Fury* with Spencer Tracy. It didn't do much business, but it was a critical success and established me as "an important producer." Then came all sorts of things: *The Three Godfathers, Love on the Run, Double Wedding, The Bride Wore Red, The Philadelphia Story, Woman of the Year, Mannequin, Three Comrades, The Shopworn Angel, The Shining Hour, The Adventures of Huckleberry Finn, Strange Cargo*. Some hits, some runs, mostly errors. *Philadelphia Story* was my first big smash hit, and I followed with *Woman of the Year*, also a hit. On most of them I did some writing, but without screen credit. I never stopped thinking of myself as being really a writer. I never have stopped.

NARRATOR: Thereby furnishing the basis for a literary *cause célèbre*. One of the writers who worked on the screen adaptation of the Remarque novel, *Three Comrades*, was F. Scott Fitzgerald. Joe rewrote a great deal of the dialog, and Fitzgerald took it hard. He wrote Mankiewicz a letter eloquent of wounded pride. Later Fitzgerald related the incident and said that it marked the end of any hope he had of getting real satisfaction from working in Hollywood.

JOE: I didn't realize at the time that Scott was so upset. After all, as he said in his letter to me, it wasn't the first time such a thing had happened. I'd forgotten about it until, long afterward, I was named as his literary Judas and people began calling me. I ought to say something, they said, I ought to make a statement. Some explanation. Or expiation. I didn't know what to say. Scott was one of my idols. I hired him for the picture, and I had to fight to do it; everybody else at the studio said he was washed up, why take a chance with him? So he did the script—and incidentally, it wasn't all his; he had a collaborator, Ted Paramore—and the dialog just wasn't "dramatic dialog." It was fine novel dialog, it read, but as dramatic dialog it wasn't good. I changed it. And then the ironic thing—when the picture was released the critics all loved the "F. Scott Fitzgerald dialog."

CRITIC: The word "producer" covers all the known sins and some of the virtues. A producer can be somebody's nephew who draws his pay for signing his name to things, or he can be an important creative and catalyzing agent. There never was any question about Joe's creativity—but there was about his critical judgment. A producer—a good one—is above all a man who takes responsibility. He selects a story, selects the actors, supervises the sets and costumes and music and all the complex elements that go into making a picture; and he takes a couple of million dollars of somebody else's money and bets it on his judgment. This you don't do lightly. I think it gave Joe a discipline that he needed. Naturally also it gave him a rounded view of the techniques and problems and possibilities of picture-making, and this shows in the way he works now. Without all that producing experience he wouldn't be nearly as far along now *as an artist.*

NARRATOR: He was in his early thirties then, and by all the conventions of Hollywood was a living success story. He was a Big Producer, with all the perquisites of that high office. His salary was $3,000 a week. In 1934 he had married Elizabeth Young, actress and New York society girl; two years later they had a son, Eric; and the next year they were divorced, the mother retaining custody of the child. But at least one bad marriage was an accepted part of the Hollywood pattern. In 1939 he married Rosa Stradner, a beautiful and gifted Viennese actress who had been "imported" by M-G-M. They have two sons, Christopher, ten, and Thomas, eight.

ROSA: To me then he was everything I had read about the ideal young American male. He was full of confidence—even rather cocky—optimistic, energetic, taking everything in stride. He was so sure of himself that he was even rather lazy. Now he is not lazy at all, and he is less optimistic.

FRIEND: He was a boy wonder, of course, a phenomenon, and absolutely brimming with gall. He used to sit at the head of the writers' table—by what authority I don't know, but these are subtle relationships—and settle the affairs of the day. Someone would bring up a subject, and Joe would listen a minute and then move in. Everybody was a New Deal Democrat. So he was a Willkie Republican. One way or another he was the center of attention.

JOE: I was completely uncomfortable as a producer. I felt useless and sterile and pretentious. And since I was about as emotionally immature and mixed up as anybody can be at that age, I got myself into all sorts of troubles, some of which wouldn't get through the U.S. mails. I was a neurotic gambler, and what I didn't throw away I spent on boats. At one time I was supporting both a sixty-foot sloop and an eighty-seven-foot schooner. I hadn't made less than $2,500 a week for years, and yet I was broke. I dislike water, I almost never swim, I can't bear to be in cold water; but I was never happier than when I was on one of my boats sailing out over the ocean, heading away from shore. The only other time I felt that way was on a set. There I was boxed in, protected, away from it all in the land of make-believe where nothing really existed.

FRIEND: I knew Joe pretty well in those days, and I suspect that several things were bothering him. A really bad first marriage, and then having the child taken away. The frustration about writing. And also, perhaps, becoming aware that he was a Jew. The family was typically intellectual-class German. Joe was very much aware of his German cultural heritage, and I don't think it had really occurred to him that he was Jewish. And then along came Hitler, and somehow, through nothing he had done, Joe found himself suddenly set apart from a lot of the rest of humanity.

And then, of course, there was Herman. A long time back Herman had begun to throw it away. He was a fantastic gambler and drinker. He had always been the most argumentative man in the world, but it seemed as if he began to insult studio executives just for the pure fun of it. I suppose he was really *trying* to fail so he'd have to go back to New York and the life there he missed and talked about so much. And eventually things began to catch up with him. There was a new escapade a week, and finally something pretty close to total ruin, health and all. Joe was around helping to pick up the pieces. Herman is doing all right now. He works, and there's no question about his talent. But someplace along the way, you see, the two brothers passed each other, one going up, the other going down. What that may have done to Joe's heart—and his ego—is something to think about.

JOE: Having started out to be a psychiatrist in the first place, I'd kept an interest in the subject, and I'd done a lot of reading in the field. Finally I had enough insight into myself to realize I needed the complete works. I decided to be psychoanalyzed. It was a major operation.

PSYCHIATRIST: I did not have Joe in treatment, so of course I can speak about him only from the point of view of a friend.

Perhaps there were several reasons why he went into analysis. Here in Hollywood the life of most people is built around the frantic avoidance of being alone, because this requires one to think, even to think about oneself. But Joe is essentially a solitary man. He has a natural introspective interest in himself. Furthermore, analysis would help him to understand people, to see them free of the distortions of his own neurotic attitudes toward life. And he has used this understanding superbly well. He writes now from the psychologically sound principle that character is the same as fate—that what happens to people and what they do is usually in a final sense the result of things within themselves. Thus his stories are not the usual Hollywood childlike mechanical stories of external action; his plots take place within his characters.

In the same way he himself was not satisfied with the external symbols of his success. On the one hand he enjoyed money and prestige; on the other, for some reason his big salary made him feel rather guilty, and fundamentally he was not deceived by his prestige. He was unhappy and wanted to find out why.

JOE: I left Metro before my contract was up. I went to work at 20th Century-Fox with a raise and a promise that they'd let me try directing. I've always felt that directing his script is the other half of the writer's work. So in the beginning I directed everything I could get my hands on, to learn the trade. *Dragonwyck*—on which I did the screenplay too—then *Somewhere in the Night, The Late George Apley, The Ghost and Mrs. Muir,* and *Escape.*

With those behind me I felt really ready to take a story all the way through as writer and director. I'm not good at "originals." The only original story I ever sold to the movies was *Million Dollar Legs* back in 1932. I have to start off with something, some plot or situation; then I rework it in my own language and my own form. After I'd finished *Escape,* Sol Siegel showed me an adaptation Vera Caspary had made of a novel called *A Letter to Five Wives* by John Klempner. I read it and knew

I had looked upon the Promised Land. I wrote the screenplay about four wives; Zanuck, in an almost bloodless operation, excised one, so we ended with *A Letter to Three Wives*. Then I made another try at directing somebody else's script in *House of Strangers*. I liked the idea so well—a father and son relationship—that I couldn't resist trying it. It was a flop. Then came *No Way Out*. Lesser Samuels had done an original I liked. I reworked it and we shared the screen credit; I directed. Then *Eve*. I'd had the general idea in mind for a long time. But I never had a middle, a second act. Then our New York office submitted a short story by Mary Orr called "The Wisdom of Eve"—later a radio script—and I had found my second act. I did the film and here we are. The time is the present.

   Incidentally, Zanuck deserves some credit for what has happened. He's the only studio head in town with the courage and intelligence to try new things. I don't think I could have made these last few pictures on any other lot.

DARRYL F. ZANUCK: I take no credit for *Eve*. That was Joe's picture. Yes, the only credit I'll take is that I had faith in Joe. I felt—I *sensed*—I *knew* that Joe had a big talent. His greatness is just beginning; yes, it is just beginning. I knew that it was a matter of his finding himself—and of finding the right story. Actors, sets, direction, camera work—that is *all decoration*. There must be a story. Now Joe has found himself and he has found his kind of story—things like *Letter* and *Eve*—what I call "bitter comedy."

CRITIC: Whatever you call it, it is his own. And to generalize, that is the main significance of Joe Mankiewicz vis-à-vis Hollywood. For many years—since the passing of the great individualists like David Wark Griffith—the industry has worked on the principle that too many cooks improve the broth. The result was that most movies sank to the least common denominator of safe mediocrity. But now comes television. People won't go out any more just "to see a movie." They can stay comfortably at home and look at the same kind of tripe that is playing at the local Bijou. The only answer is quality. So now, in order to protect their huge investments, the studio owners and executives increasingly are being forced to take the risk of giving people like Mankiewicz a chance to do their stuff. He isn't the only one. George Seaton, Billy Wilder, Robert Rossen, Leo McCary, Frank Capra, John Huston are some of the others. Gradually these creative people, mostly writer-directors or writer-producers, intelligent men with broad experience, are getting control of their own products, stamping them with their own personalities. This is the single most important development in the movies since sound. It just happened that Joe was ready for it when it came.

JOE: Things have worked out for me. All those years of sweating in the vineyard, getting experience; the analysis; coming to Fox; finally growing up; everything pulled into focus at the right time.

PRODUCER: It's a very encouraging thing to some of the rest of us, what Joe has done. He proves that if you keep working along, learning and doing your best, trying to do better, you can beat the machine. But he's in a highly vulnerable position just now. There are hundreds of people sitting around waiting for him to fall on his face so they can say, "Yeah, *Eve* was good, but boy, did you see his last one?" This is a town where the only thing two people can agree on is the other guy's bad picture.

JOE: This next picture, *The Doctor's Story*, is something I've wanted to tackle for a long time. It's based on *Doktor Praetorius*, a German play and later a German film. I'm hoping to be able to say a few things about the cant that permeates my first love, the medical profession. But I'm afraid it won't come off right. It's one of those situations—the studio could get Cary Grant on a certain date, and that's the date we start shooting. I just don't have time to do the writing. Anyway, after this one is laid away, I'm going east. I'm going to sell my house here and move my family out there, and that will be our home. I'll make one picture a year, but I'll write it in the east and come out here only when I'm directing it. It's a ten-year deal with Fox. The rest of my time I'll be writing and directing plays, and maybe even doing a couple of books. I'd like to do something on the "great American Mom" and on organized religion. I've got strong feelings about both.

PRODUCER: That's an old story. People are always talking about getting out of what I call this "gold rut." Maybe he'll do it, maybe he'll be happy; but I doubt it. He's had no practical experience in the theater. He's used to the unlimited financial and technical resources of the movies; he'll be like the woman who's used to Bergdorf Goodman and suddenly finds she has to do her shopping on Third Avenue under the El. Besides, what's the point? He can write his own ticket here, do anything he wants. Why leave?

CRITIC: If you ask me he's stage-struck. *Eve* showed that—it was full of surface cynicism about the Theater, but fundamentally it was a poem to Thespis. That's one reason it was good: he was absolutely fascinated by his subject matter.

JOE: I want to leave this intellectual fog belt. Los Angeles summed itself up for me a while ago. The *Mirror* had a straw poll to decide who was the city's most distinguished citizen of 1950. First place went to the football coach of U.C.L.A. God meant Los Angeles to be a desert, and its existence as a city is a defiance of His intention. Someday someone will turn off the necessary faucets, and it will return to a state of grace. I want my kids to be exposed to books and to people who can talk about something besides pictures. I want Rosa to have a chance to act again on the stage. She's a fine actress and an intelligent woman, and she's wasted out here. To be the mate of a Hollywood big shot is like having an infectious disease: he or she is the person the rest of the people wish you hadn't brought to the party. I want to make my pitch for the theater. I'm not predicting anything. I may flop, but I think I may have something to contribute to the stage. So far all the traffic has been from Broadway to Hollywood. I think it's time it began to move the other way.

FRIEND: Motivations? He's in the motivation business—he should know. But I suspect that he'll try to find the life he never had in New York—the life that Herman had. He would be the center of a new charmed circle. That might be a very special satisfaction, a unique double-switcheroo. And suppose he really writes a play for that great cultural medium, the Broadway stage? A serious play that even Brooks Atkinson liked? I don't say he will—I doubt that he can—but suppose he did? Then at long last he could stop asking himself, "What happened to the 3 percent?"

Joseph Mankiewicz: Putting on the Style

DEREK CONRAD / 1960

SHEPPERTON STUDIOS had two of the big pictures for this
winter on the floor. One was set in America's Deep South, the other in
Cuba's capital. Journalists were welcome to meet the stars of Reed's *Our
Man in Havana* and there was no bar to them browsing around the
sound stages while production was in progress.

The publicity department of *Suddenly, Last Summer*, on the other
hand, were given very different and very firm instructions. No interviews. No studio trips. There was one exception. I happened to be it,
representing *Films and Filming*.

So suddenly last summer I found myself in a fast studio car, speeding
through the bright sunshine of a perfect July to meet director Joseph
Mankiewicz in an American mental home of the 1920s.

The mental home occupied one of Shepperton's largest sound stages.
It was designed by Oliver Messel who, as *Suddenly, Last Summer*'s production designer was responsible for one of the most fantastic, most
expensive sets ever to be built in an English studio. This was the garden
of Violet Venable's home in New Orleans. I found Mankiewicz browsing
between a coleus gloriosa and a funkia giagantium.

Joseph Mankiewicz is a soft-spoken man of fifty. Dressed in dark grey
slacks and navy blue sports shirt, swell built and continually puffing his
beloved pipe, he was a picture of a quiet American. He at once escorted
me through dark green passageways, past the office of neuro-surgeon
Doctor Cukrowicz (Tennessee William's hero played in the film by
Montgomery Clift) and past barred windows which looked onto the

From *Films and Filming* (January 1960).

bare sound-proofed walls of the studio, into his small portable dressing room tucked away in a corner.

I asked him why he was directing a film that he hadn't written, which is unusual for him. (*Suddenly, Last Summer* was adapted from the Williams one-acter by Gore Vidal.) "My reasons for doing this one are purely personal. My wife died about a year ago and I wasn't doing any writing. Then this script came along and the play had fascinated me . . ."

Summer was originally presented with *Garden District*, another of Williams's one-act plays. It concerns a young girl (Elizabeth Taylor) who is believed to be mentally sick as a result of the death of her husband, Sebastian. Sebastian was idolized by his mother, Violet Venable (Katharine Hepburn) who, until Sebastian married, accompanied her son everywhere. When the wife reveals that Sebastian was, in fact, homosexual, and his death was at the hands of his victims—an irate gang of beach boys—Mrs. Venable attempts to persuade a young surgeon (Montgomery Clift) to perform a leuchotomy on the girl's brain to obliterate her memory.

"I am playing *Suddenly, Last Summer* as I meet it, I think. I have a great admiration for Tennessee's writing. I don't know whether it's poetry or drama. I think it is a strange mixture of poetry, drama and analytic free-association. It isn't real, it isn't unreal. It doesn't happen, but it doesn't not happen. I think it has to be played as Tennessee writes—a little larger than life and with an eye and an ear to effect rather than veracity."

The dressing room was becoming like a hot house. I asked Mankiewicz whether he felt that *Suddenly Last Summer* is Williams commenting on psychiatry. A smile crossed the rough hewn features. "Tennessee's concept of psychiatry and psychiatrists is far more bizarre vis à vis reality than his concept of cannibalism. You are more likely to encounter cannibalism than you are to encounter psychiatrists who behave as Tennessee has them behave. He has a *grand guignol* concept of psychiatry: you either accept it or you don't. But I don't think anyone should, or could, look upon *Suddenly, Last Summer* as a comment upon psychiatry."

Mankiewicz has had an astonishingly successful Hollywood career. At twenty-one he was nominated for an Academy Award for his screenplay *Skippy*. During his first years in the film city he wrote the scripts of among others, *If I Had a Million, Manhattan Melodrama, Alice in*

Wonderland, and *Forsaking All Others.* Later moving to M-G-M he produced *Fury, Three Godfathers, The Philadelphia Story, A Christmas Carol,*
and *Woman of the Year* . . . and many more.

"I was very unhappy as a producer." The remark surprised me. But I
said nothing, and he went on, "There is an anecdote connected with
this period of my life which is one of the greatest comments on
Hollywood and on one of the men who did as much to destroy the
American film as any man ever did—Louis B. Mayer.

"I had always wanted to direct. I had come to M-G-M as a very
young writer. Mr. Mayer had his eye on me as a producer because at
Metro at that time, and indeed until very recently, the producer was the
highest form of human existence. M-G-M was known as the producers
studio as Fox was always known as the directors studio.

"Well, I went to see Mayer to tell him that I wanted to direct; and
telling me he wanted me to produce, he made this classic remark—'You
have to learn to crawl before you can walk.' He didn't realize the brilliance of his definition."

From Metro-Goldwyn-Mayer Mankiewicz moved over to the "direc-
tors studio," Twentieth Century-Fox. The change of air did him good.
He became the only film-maker in the history of Hollywood to win four
Oscars in two successive years. (In 1949, for writing and directing *A
Letter to Three Wives* and in 1950 as writer-director of *All About Eve*.)

"My stay at Metro were ten of the unhappiest years of my entire
career. I produced a great many films which I am embarrassed to have
associated with my name."

At Fox, Mankiewicz made the Mankiewicz film : sparkling dialogue,
witty, sophisticated, abounding with clever situations and superbly
written parts that most actors would give their eye-teeth to play.

"I am afraid my kind of film might have had it. The French refer to
me as making what they call *le théâtre film.* I write plays for the screen.
Eve was a play. So was *A Letter to Three Wives.* I write essentially for audiences who come to listen to a film as well as to look at it."

He betrayed a half-smile and I suspected he was getting at me. "This
may account for some of my intolerance toward 'the long hair' concept
of film as something that is done in terms of quick cuts, montages and
synchronizations. I think film is a medium for the exchange of ideas
and exchange of comment as well as purely visual effects."

It was lunch-time. The artists and technicians made their way to one of the three canteens (you choose the price-range you can afford). Montgomery Clift, after a grueling morning's work made his way to his dressing room for a sandwich lunch specially prepared each day for him by the Savoy Hotel.

We eat quickly . . . and in silence, everyone seemed to be thinking about the afternoon's work. I made my way back to the mental home and Mankiewicz. The studio was quiet although crowded with technicians. Clift paced the floor restlessly, pondering his approach to the next scene. For his role he is on call for forty-three days as against Liz Taylor's twenty-nine and Katharine Hepburn's twenty-three.

Elizabeth Taylor dressed in black and looking quite beautiful listened to her director as he quietly explained what he wanted. Mankiewicz is rarely given to displays of temperament—if ever.

We talked again. Our conversation got around to Chaplin. Mankiewicz recalled a television programme he had seen recently on *The Art of Charles Chaplin*: "This idiotic programme said that Mr. Chaplin 'refused' to give up the great medium of the silent film and talk. He refused because he b . . . well couldn't talk.

"If there was ever a commercially-minded genius it was Charlie Chaplin, who stuck to the best he knew until he couldn't any more. He's made talking pictures and they have been simply b . . . awful.

"I have no complaints about Charlie at all in politcal terms, or in any other way, except that I wish he wouldn't pretend that the collapse of his career was due to anything but the fact that when he spoke it came to be nothing more than a dull, monotonous Cockney which had nothing to do with the little man in the funny shoes and the cane. It's a great pity it happened to him . . . but it happened to a lot of others as well."

Mankiewicz is quick to defend his own type of picture from the purists among critics. "The talking film, once it did talk, and I think I am in a great minority, should say something. I think I have proved with some of my films that an audience can be held by talk as well as the fellow shooting the other fellow on the empty Western street. I, being a writer and having a great deal to say some of which is palatable and some that is not, want it to talk.

"Of course there's an excess of bad talk (even in two reelers) but I don't think there can ever be an excess of good talk."

Mankiewicz left Fox in 1952 and returned to M-G-M to make *Julius Caesar*. With a good natured smile he told me, "Of course on *Caesar* I just did a polishing job. So much of it was full of *cliches!*"

He is justifiably proud of *Julius Caesar*. "I didn't cut or add anything. It was Mr. Shakespeare to the syllable." Mankiewicz became suddenly serious as he told me of *Caesar*'s treatment by various film festival selection boards.

"There is a very interesting anecdote. It has to do with one of my pet abominations: film festivals. Their approach is very often so esoteric as to have no connection with the realities of making films. Or as they are in the case of Cannes and Venice festivals, purely the utilization by hotel keepers of rather gullible and naive film-makers to stimulate a tourist season."

The director took a puff on his pipe and warmed to his theme. "I haven't permitted any of my films that I had any control over to be submitted or shown at any festival. The only picture that I directed that was submitted to a film festival was *Julius Caesar*. It was rejected at Venice because it was not up to the 'artistic standards' of the festival. This was an official rejection. Their reasons were that only a 'Hollywood' director would commit such a gaffe as to have Brutus read a book, as to have clocks strike, as to have various things which any semiliterate person knows are the fascinating and famous anachronisms which Shakespeare committed in his play.

"What I thought was a particularly beautiful touch of irony was that my film was rejected and, in its place, meeting the 'high standards' of the Venice festival, was a film called *The Kentuckian* directed by and starring Burt Lancaster."

After *Julius Caesar* Mankiewicz formed Figaro Inc., in 1953 his own production company which releases its pictures through United Artists. For his first film as an independent he filmed *The Barefoot Contessa* starring Humphrey Bogart, Ava Gardner, and Rossano Brazzi. The film told the story of a film producer (Bogart) who discovers a girl (Gardner) and makes her world famous as a Hollywood star. Later she retires from the screen to find what she believes to be real happiness for the first time in her life by marrying an Italian Count (Brazzi). On her wedding night she discovers his impotence, the result of a battleground injury. She takes a lover in order to give the Count an heir. The Count discovers her deception and shoots her dead. Some hokum!

"It was a transitory piece. This was on my way into a slough of ill-humour. It was almost a good film but there were too many stories; I was angry at too many things. I tried to cover too many aspects of that particular world. I still want to do a film about the wastrel international set, but in *The Barefoot Contessa* I tried to do a film about that and a film about the type of woman whom I know only too well: the self-destructive, beautiful woman.

"I tried to do a bitter Cinderella story. The Prince should have turned out to be homosexual but I couldn't go quite that far. Some people think I went farther! I felt myself losing my sense of humour about these people and that is why it was a little too much for a lot of people. They resented the vitriolic quality of the film."

Mankiewicz added: "You see, you cannot point the truth out too relentlessly otherwise it becomes effective to the point of creating a defense within the people who hear it. They find themselves called upon to defend rather than to admit."

I felt that Joe Mankiewicz's recent scripts had betrayed a certain bitterness, which had not characterised his former work. I asked him whether he would describe this period of his work as his "tragic phase."

"*The Barefoot Contessa* was a tragedy. Even the very bad film I made during a very muddled part of my life, *The Quiet American,* was. During this unhappy phase I became a sort of Angry Old Man. I was bitter. I think I started using a club where I previously used a very sharp knife on things that upset me. I got angry at them rather than exposing and ridiculing. The result, whenever you do a thing like that, particularly in high comedy on the screen, is that you are in great danger of losing what high comedy has to offer . . . which is audience identification.

"My work has always strongly relied on somebody nudging somebody and saying, 'Just like you' or 'That happened to me.' Whether it was *People Will Talk* on the idiotic practises of doctors and nurses who wake patients up to give them sleeping pills, or the theatre in *All About Eve*."

It was time for me to go. The next set-up had been lit. The actors went through their lines. Mankiewicz, as apparently unpeturbed as always, inhaled his pipe and stood quietly watching. I ventured one more question. "As for the future," Mankiewicz was saying: "I want very much to return to the type of social comment and satire that I love to do. If I do anything well, I think I do that well. The type of pictures like *Five Fingers, A Letter to Three Wives, People Will Talk,* and *All About Eve.*

"As my next picture I may do *John Brown's Body,* the Stephen Vincent Benét epic poem about the Civil War. It could be the definitive film about the period because of its scope covering every level of American life at that time. It might well be the one film that the rest of the world might be interested in seeing about America."

Mankiewicz returned to minister to his artists. "Put up the red" I heard the assistant director shout. Quietness gradually settled over the studio. The heavy sound-proof door swung to silently behind me. A bell clanged in the corridor. The sign above the locked studio door read "Shooting in progress." *Suddenly, Last Summer* was well on its way. I wondered, would Mankiewicz be on his way, too, for that fifth Academy Award?

Mankiewicz of the Movies

ANDREW SARRIS / 1970

"I'M JUST ABOUT the oldest whore on the beat," Joseph L. Mankiewicz told me as we relaxed in his reconverted barn in Bedford, New York. A huge portrait of his late father brooded over the mantelpiece on which reposed four Oscars, two of which had been earned for the writing and directing of *A Letter to Three Wives* in 1949, and two for the writing and directing of *All About Eve* in 1950. Also on the mantelpiece was the Sarah Siddons Award that gilded trophy—more brass than gold—presented by Walter Hampden to Anne Baxter in *All About Eve* as a fictitious prize of theatrical excellence. But apparently the Sarah Siddons Award was no longer fictitious.

"This thing"—Mankiewicz gesticulated at the bogus bauble, "I invented as a basic symbol in a satire about prize-giving; now there's some outfit in Chicago actually promoting a Sarah Siddons Award every year, and people like Helen Hayes go out there and make tearful acceptance speeches."

I took one of the Oscars in my hand simply for the experience, of course. (The Oscar is much heavier than I imagined.) But I couldn't help thinking that life *did* imitate art in the way Mankiewicz's films always seemed to suggest. Here I had been only a few minutes in a movie director's home, and already I was fondling his trophies. From a certain point of view, that is to say, from a certain camera angle, might it not seem that I was reenacting the final mirror-multiplied envy of Barbara Bates as she posed narcissistically with Anne Baxter's Sarah Siddons Award in the last frame of *All About Eve*? I quickly banished the

From *Show Magazine* (March 1970). Reprinted by permission of Andrew Sarris.

analogy from my mind. I was merely doing an interview for *Show* with the blessing of Warners, distributors of *There Was a Crooked Man*, Mankiewicz's latest movie, with Henry Fonda and Kirk Douglas, from a script by Benton and Newman of *Bonnie and Clyde* fame. "An ironic fairy tale" was my host's description of this, the nineteenth film he has directed and we didn't pursue the subject, inasmuch as I hadn't seen the movie yet, and we were both too old to gush over the unknown and untested.

Besides there were so many other things to talk about. Like "Rosebud" in *Citizen Kane*. It came up quite unexpectedly. Thinking about the mirrors in *All about Eve* made me think about the mirrors in *Citizen Kane*, and the link between *Citizen Kane* and *All About Eve* is the fraternal link between the late Herman J. Mankiewicz, co-scenarist with Orson Welles of *Kane*, and his younger brother, Joe, who followed in his footsteps. (I remember James Mason telling me once when we were trapped together in a film festival in Argentina that Joe Mankiewicz had been profoundly, perhaps traumatically, influenced by his older brother.)

"I saw an interesting movie your brother wrote—*Ladies' Man*—1931, I think. William Powell, Carole Lombard, Kay Francis. Magnificent ending but not too well directed. Lothar Mendes."

(Later in the interview, Mankiewicz quipped that Mendes talked like Ernst Lubitsch, but directed like Frank Tuttle.)

"The strange thing is that the ending of *Ladies' Man* reminded me that your brother had worked on the script of *Kane*, and probably had more to do with the wild romanticism of the movie than most people realize. . . ."

"Do you know what 'Rosebud' was?" Mankiewicz cut in.

I shook my head, feeling suddenly like an archaeologist about to unearth the missing arms of the Venus de Milo.

Mankiewicz puttered in the kitchen a few moments to let the suspense of the scene build.

"It happened when he was growing up in Wilkes-Barre. Herman had always wanted a bicycle, and one Christmas he got one with 'ROSEBUD' printed on the frame and two days later it was stolen. Toward the end of his life, when he was drinking heavily, he'd often mumble 'Rosebud.' He never got over it."

Mankiewicz was well aware that he seemed to be challenging one of the reigning deities in the contemporary cult of film directors, and he went to great pains to disclaim any derogatory intent toward Welles in the "Rosebud" revelation. "Herman wrote the script of *Citizen Kane*. Orson, in my opinion, could have been the greatest film director of our time, had he not insisted on acting and even writing."

I wondered why the "Rosebud" story had never been told before, and I decided that no one had bothered to ask. Film history is a vast jigsaw puzzle, and we shall never have access to all the pieces, but we have to keep searching just the same. Now at least one of the pieces had fallen into place, and Herman J. Mankiewicz took his place with Jean Prévèrt as one of the poets of the screenplay.

And what of Joseph L. Mankiewicz? What would film historians say of him? I glanced at the credit sheet in front of me from *The Dummy* in 1929 to *There Was a Crooked Man* in 1969, a period of forty years that took in virtually the entire history of the talking pictures in America. Joseph Leo Mankiewicz was born 11 February 1909 in the aforementioned Wilkes-Barre Pennsylvania, received an A.B. from Columbia College in 1928, worked briefly in Berlin as a correspondent for the Chicago *Tribune* before quitting to do English subtitles for German films, returned to America in 1929 to join his brother on the writing staff at Paramount, worked on titles for silents, then dialogue for talkies, and finally screenplays. He became a producer at MGM in 1936 and a director at Fox in 1943.

"I wanted to be a director at Metro, not a producer, but L. B. Mayer insisted I start off as a producer. 'You have to crawl,' Mayer explained, 'before you can walk,' which is about as good a definition of a producer as any."

The films that stand out from Mankiewicz's Paramount period are *Skippy* (1931), *If I Had a Million* (1932), and *Million Dollar Legs* (1932). Mankiewicz received an Oscar nomination for *Skippy*, but *Million Dollar Legs*, which he once described as a surrealist satire, still has a preeminent place in his affections. Curiously, it is a W. C. Fields film that almost never pops up in Fields retrospectives, perhaps because Lyda Roberti is so much more memorable with her joyously professional bumps and grinds on the hallowed field of Olympic sports.

Mankiewicz's shiniest Metro credits include *Manhattan Melodrama*
(1934), the movie that cost Dillinger his life; *Fury* (1936); *Three Comrades*
(1938); *The Philadelphia Story* (1940); and *Woman of the year* (1942). I
asked him about Fritz Lang.

"I first met Fritz right after he had come over to do a movie for
Samuel Goldwyn. I admired *M* as everyone else did. I was assigned to
the Selznick film as a writer. After that project fell through, I was made
a producer, and sold Mayer on Lang to direct my film, which was *Fury*.
Fritz was a strange man. He was a terrible tyrant on the set. At noon-
time an assistant would come in with a shot of brandy and a pill, and
that was Fritz's lunch. The performers and the crew would continue working until Fritz was ready to let them have lunch. But Spencer Tracy wasn't
having any of that. When Fritz refused to call a lunch break, Spence simply wiped off his make-up and yelled, 'LUNCH!' The crew cheered!"

"Tracy was something special," I suggested.

"That's because he was already formed before Hollywood got him."

This was an idea that Mankiewicz kept returning to over and over
again in one form or another: the perniciousness of the Hollywood
system, but Los Angeles in particular.

"Actually, Hollywood was even worse for the kids who grew up on
the studio lots than for the adults, who at least had had a childhood in
a real world."

"But what's the difference between sitting here in a barn in Bedford
and sitting in a mansion in Beverly Hills? You're surrounded by your
things here, your memories and memorabilia, your work and your
loved ones just as you would be there. Is one place so much different
from another?"

"Well, here I look out the window and I see snow. The seasons
change. I'm aware of living—in Los Angeles, time stands still and
suddenly you're old."

At one point in the interview, I thought I had caught Mankiewicz in
a moral contradiction, or, if not a moral contradiction, at least a contradiction in roles. We had spoken previously of his troubles with Zanuck
on *Cleopatra* and *All About Eve*, almost classic confrontations between
director (Mankiewicz) and producer (Zanuck). Suddenly we were back
in 1936 at a Pasadena preview of *Fury*, and the audience was howling at
the ghosts (Furies?) pursuing Spencer Tracy down the city streets.

Mankiewicz, then the producer-scenarist of *Fury*, cut out Lang's ghosts, and the German director screamed that his film had been butchered. I asked Mankiewicz if he was aware of the irony in his reversed roles vis-à-vis Lang and Zanuck. In short, had Mankiewicz not acted as Lang's Zanuck?

Mankiewicz shrugged his shoulders. "I never thought of it that way. Back then, both Lang and I were workers in a factory. We were enclosed within the same system. Actually, I was ordered to make the cuts— which, however, should have been made. It was nothing in those days especially at Metro, for one director to do retakes on another director's movie. We were hemmed in on all sides by studios censors . . . I've actually seen a memo from the Hays Office removing the tits from the cows in Mickey Mouse cartoons."

When I asked about Mankiewicz's current opinion of Zanuck, the director was reluctant to rake up all the old headlines from *Cleopatra*. Mankiewicz seldom grants interviews, is almost never seen on talk shows, and has actually gotten through life without a press agent. Such an independent attitude carries with it certain handicaps. For one thing he is ill-equipped, indeed, to wage warfare in the gossip columns with a studio head armed automatically with legions of publicists. But I gathered that what galled him most about the whole *Cleopatra* debacle was that he had lost the opportunity to do *Justine*, a Mankiewicz dream project to end Mankiewicz dream projects, a twentieth-century literary work of the first magnitude systematically embellished with all the appurtenances of ambiguity and multiplicity of viewpoint to which its ideal director had dedicated himself time and again in his films.

"Like the point-of-view cuts in *All About Eve*?"

"Even there Zanuck had final cut and he got bored with the same scene shot from different points of view even though that was the whole point of the intricate flashback structure."

I asked Mankiewicz about his run-in with F. Scott Fitzgerald in the late '30s. A *Times* book reviewer gave all the best of it to Fitzgerald in reprinting an excerpt from *The Letters of F. Scott Fitzgerald*, edited by Andrew Turnbull: "I'm a good writer—honest," Fitzgerald had written to Mankiewicz. "To say I'm disillusioned is putting it mildly. For 19 years, with two years out for sickness, I've written best-selling entertainment, and my dialogue is supposedly right up at top. But I've learned from the script that you've suddenly decided that it isn't good dialogue and you can take a few hours off and do much better."

Mankiewicz stood by his guns. The script was for *Three Comrades*, and Fitzgerald's dialogue was literally unspeakable. "Writing dialogue for a novel and writing dialogue for the stage or screen are two different crafts. Margaret Sullavan couldn't read most of Scott's lines, and I rewrote them. That's all. It happens all the time, and it doesn't cast any more of a reflection on Fitzgerald's novels than the bad plays of Henry James cast on his great novels.

"An indication that Fitzgerald couldn't write good acting dialogue was the screen version of *Tender Is the Night*. All the critics jumped on the dialogue, and it was taken almost literally from the novel. It was very literary dialogue, very novelistic dialogue. A very important issue was involved here, actually more important than the fact that I once had the temerity to rewrite F. Scott Fitzgerald. I once wrote an article for the *Journal of the Screen Writers Guild* in which I explained very clearly the essential identity of screenwriting and directing. Every screenwriter worthy of the name has already directed his movie when he has written his script. While he has been writing, he has been visualizing as well, dictating by the point of view of each scene almost every camera set-up. Conversely, every director worthy of the name has written a movie when he has finished directing it. Writing and directing are over-lapping functions of a single creative process. There are no tensions fundamentally between the functions of writing and directing, merely between the various individuals, two or more, who may be involved with the same creative process at the same time. The tension on *Fury* was not between a writer-producer and a director but between a man named Mankiewicz and another man named Lang. The novelist has an entirely different relationship with his reader than the screenwriter (or playwright) has with his audience. With a book, the relationship is between the printed page on the reader's intellect. The response is cerebral. On the screen (and the stage) the dialogue is heard, there is no time for cerebration—the response is to the rhythm and sound of the speech almost as much as to its content."

I agreed completely with Mankiewicz on this point, but I couldn't help feeling that he was caught in the middle on this particular issue. Here he was being savaged not by the West Coast slobs, but by the East

Coast snobs. Thus, the same book reviewers who took Mankiewicz to task for trifling with Fitzgerald's dialogue quoted approvingly Fitzgerald's moralistic comments on the film industry: "Advertising is a racket, like the movies and the brokerage business. You cannot be honest without admitting that its constructive contribution to humanity is exactly minus zero. It is simply a means of making dubious promises to a credulous public."

Did the book reviewer ever see the script in question? Probably not. He didn't have to. The legend of Hollywood as the Great Corruptor of literary talent was too firmly established by then, and even now only a perceptive debunker like Leslie Fiedler has had the cultural audacity to suggest that Hollywood did not so much corrupt serious writers as accommodate in luxury their creative decline. But Mankiewicz doesn't fit comfortably into either cultural bag—Atlantic Coast or Pacific Coast. He was always too New York for Hollywood in temperament and always too Hollywood for New York in training. And so he has been sniped at by sports-shirted slob and turtle-necked snob alike, and yet he still retains his sense of humor and, more important, his serious-minded liberalism.

"People are always talking about the 'swimming pool Stalinists' and 'swimming pool Communists' and 'swimming pool liberals' of the '30s—seems they've forgotten about the 'swimming pool Fascists.' If Hitler had not attacked the Jews, he would have represented every illiberal, undemocratic, philistinish value most of the studio heads stood for—and he would have had their support. The things the studios did to break unions, to elect Merriam over Sinclair, to make up blacklists require the kind of mentality we associate with the Reichstag Fire. As late as 1938, Louis B. Mayer screened *Three Comrades* for the German consul in Los Angeles and asked if there were anything the consul wanted cut from the movie so as not to offend the Nazi regime. Why? Metro was the only studio that was still distributing its movies in Germany in 1938, and they wanted to protect the market."

Mankiewicz still found it absurd that the film industry was so dominated by the pitiful tastes and perverted bookkeeping of the theater owners. Back in 1949, he hot-footed theater owners around the country by ridiculing them as "real estate operators whose chief concerns should be taking gum off carpets and checking adolescent love-making in the balcony."

While we were talking about other directors, I gathered that Mankiewicz deeply admired Lubitsch, and deprecated the pomposity of the "Antonioni School of Obfuscation."

"There's nothing new about the director with the jacket draped over his shoulders and the pseudo-philosophical cop-outs: 'What do you mean, where are the tennis balls? Life is a tennis game without tennis balls.'

"Back in 1928," Mankiewicz recalled, "a Romanian director named Buchowetski came to Hollywood on the Chief, and the newspapermen were there, and they cornered him as he stepped off the train, and there he was with the jacket draped over his shoulders and the hired lackeys, and somebody asked him about his philosophy or point of view or something, and he drew himself up and declared, 'Life is like a camera,' after which cryptic comment he swept into the Paramount limousine with the Paramount press agent, who was a little desperate, because he knew that the press would want some amplifications on a remark like 'Life is like a camera.' So the press agent asked the Romanian director to explain what the remark meant, and the director gave him a withering glance and said: 'How should I know what it means? I'm a director, not a philosopher.' He, too, couldn't be bothered to explain the invisible tennis balls."

Still, Mankiewicz had somewhat mixed feelings about the old movie moguls he had known too well. "They were complete monsters, and let's not get sentimental about that, but one quality they did possess was dedication to their factories. They acted in the firm conviction that their studios would live on for a thousand years. They were like feudal lords, and their subordinates and technicians were like their serfs, buying up homes around the studio grounds so that eventually Hollywood resembled a cluster of fiefdoms, Metro here, Warners there, Paramount there, Fox there, and the studios did provide a brutish form of noblesse oblige. But the real villains are the new breed of studio bosses, the creatures of the conglomerates, the carpetbaggers, the looters. They go out to Hollywood and assure the frightened old retainers that everything is going to stay as it was under the old regime and everyone will be taken care of, and then they sell the studio grounds right out from under the pathetic wretches who have planted their roots there. And now Hollywood resembles Appalachia far more than it does Eldorado."

Though Mankiewicz sheds no tears over the imminent demise of the old Hollywood system, he is not at all heartened by many of the "modern" attitudes toward film. He's turned down several projects because they were, in his phrase, "stupid and simple-minded." He finds most of the fashionable new movies less engaged with the complexities of human relationships than were the old studio movies. Have we indeed replaced L. B. Mayer and his chicken soup for monosyllabic motorcycle riders and the New Philistinism of the Young? Mankiewicz was not sure. He possessed the old liberal's faith that people, contrary to Barnum's maxim, were getting smarter all the time, and thus seeing life from more and varied points of view. He was suspicious of the over-dependence upon the optical trappings of modern films. Except for the invention of a few new lenses including zoom, Mankiewizc felt, nothing essentially new had been added to film technique since 1928. And even the lenses were mixed blessings, hardly adequate compensation for the lack of observation of man, his manners and his morals. These latter concerns define Mankiewicz's own role as a moviemaker. He believes there is an important place for words on the screen (however much critics like this interviewer might deplore the limitations of his visual style). Young people, the director feels, are too one-dimensional in their attitude toward moviemaking. They don't want involvement with plots and characters, even ideas. They want merely to stand behind their finders and let life happen in front of the lens. That way they can remain voyeurs, and voyeurism is more the spirit of the age than commitment.

I found myself responding to Mankiewicz's attitude more than I had thought I would. Possibly, the times had become so unexpectedly brutish, that what some people dismissed to old-fashioned liberalism in the '60's may be the last hope of mankind in the '70s. Perhaps, also, an unconstructive cynicism had become the opiate of the intellectuals, and all that this cynicism had to show for itself was Nixon, Agnew, and Mitchell. Suddenly a man who believed in amelioration rather than annihilation did not seem quite so much out of it as the deep-think seminars imagined. As I looked over a list of the films he had directed, I saw emerging a pattern of intelligence, charm, and subtlety that I had tended to take too much for granted in the days I thought that intelligence, charm, and subtlety would always be with us.

I find even the apprentice films—*Dragonwyck, Somewhere in the Night, The Late George Apley* (all 1946), *The Ghost and Mrs. Muir* (1947), *Escape* (1948)—relatively civilized and complex entertainments. (Indeed, *Somewhere in the Night* seems even better than Mankiewicz himself gives it credit for being.) Then came the break-through films: *A Letter to Three Wives* (the movie in which Mankiewicz, in between attacks on national priorities which price radio soap operas higher than education, proved that Linda Darnell could act) and, that same year (1949), *House of Strangers* (a movie that becomes more memorable with each passing year, at least partly because of Susan Hayward's toughly American brand of emotional intelligence and Richard Conte's Italian-American, a blend of brashness and moral discernment almost comparable to John Garfield's Jewish-American). And, then, in 1950, *No Way Out*, the first black-power movie ever, but so far ahead of its time that it flopped at the box office, and even the learned sociology journals ignored the precedent-shattering victory of blacks in a race riot to concentrate on the invidious effect of hearing epithets like "nigger" and "coon" on the immaculately liberal screen. Followed by *All About Eve*, with Bette Davis spawning a new generation of camp lines and female impersonation routines (through no fault of her own, of course) and exchanges almost worthy of Wilde or Congreve:

"Do they have auditions in television?"

"That's all television is, my dear—auditions."

And who could forget breathless Marilyn Monroe ("a natural star if ever I saw one"—Mankiewicz) patiently explaining to George Sanders that she wanted a drink and she couldn't call the butler "butler" because his name might be "Butler" and so she called him "waiter" instead, to which George Sanders replied, "You have a point, my dear, an idiotic one, but a point. . . ." Or Monroe again: "A girl could make sacrifices for a coat like that," to which Gary Merrill replies wearily, "One probably has."

Then came *People Will Talk* (Cary Grant against medical quackery, and oil depletion allowances in the context of an adult love story involving a girl (Jeanne Crain) who has become pregnant by another man; all in all, too much of a liberal fantasy even for the effete East); *Five Fingers; Julius Caesar; The Barefoot Contessa; Guys and Dolls; The Quiet American* (another film ahead of its time in probing the personality aspects of political prejudice); *Suddenly, Last Summer; Cleopatra; The Honey Pot;* and imminently, *There Was a Crooked Man.* Time and again, Mankiewicz has produced performances of emotional intelligence: from Jeanne Crain in *People Will Talk,* from Danielle Darrieux and James Mason in *Five Fingers,* from Ava Gardner and Humphrey Bogart in *The Barefoot Contessa,* from Jean Simmons in *Guys and Dolls,* and from Rex Harrison, Cliff Robertson, and Maggie Smith in *The Honey Pot.* Mankiewicz has paid a high price for the literate quality of his scripts, and for disdaining subjects and genres that lent themselves to facile mythmaking. He is obsessed with that civilized realm in which characters are conscious of the roles they play and examine them with the very gravest humor. Joseph L. Mankiewicz is playing a role like the rest of us, the role of rational intelligence, constructive iconoclasm. What makes him truly admirable as he sticks to his guns in his converted barn in Bedford, New York, is his defiance of a historical process that in its viciously simple-minded way is striving to make intelligent liberalism obsolete in a world sinking into the chaos of aimless absurdism.

Cocking a Snook

GORDON GOW/1970

SOME PEOPLE might be inclined to take *There Was a Crooked Man . . .* seriously. Such is the opinion of its director, Joseph L. Mankiewicz; and it's all right by him if they do. There were many who took his *Five Fingers* (1952) seriously, he reminded me; and I remarked that certain audiences had been known to preserve straight faces throughout the James Bond films, too. "As you say," he concurred.

Five Fingers had been based on fact, of course: the notorious and hilarious case of the spy "Cicero" (James Mason) who operated smoothly in Ankara during the Second World War. It is a movie that sticks in the mind as both suspenseful and amusing, as well as making a worldly comment on the dangerous absurdity of nations in conflict.

Mankiewicz enjoys "cocking a snook." "I'm doing that again in *There Was a Crooked Man . . .* you see. What I like to do is put my tongue halfway into my cheek. Here I'm having a little fun with the mythology of the Wild West." The screenplay is by David Newman and Robert Beaton, the *Bonnie and Clyde* writers, and the characters are a whole clutch of crooked men in an Arizona prison in the 1880s, among them Kirk Douglas as a big-scale thief, Burgess Meredith as a train-robber long since gone to seed, and Henry Fonda as a sheriff who gives the proceedings their ultimate cynical twist.

This is the first time Mankiewicz has directed a Western: "It's been a chance to try some muscles I haven't used before. Although, of course, I wrote a lot of Westerns in the old days. The old, old days." His words conjured up an impression of antiquity that his cheerful face denied.

From *Films and Filming* (November 1970).

But his Hollywood career dates back quite a way: "I'm either the eldest statesman or the oldest whore on the beat."

He began as a writer, and among the first to appreciate his brand of humour was W. C. Fields, for whom he provided some choice repartee in *Million Dollar Legs* and *If I Had a Million*. "In those days a comic set great store by owning his material. And, I remember Bill coming up to me one day and offering to buy the dialogue I'd written for him and Alison Skipworth in one of the episodes of *If I Had a Million*. It was full of bird terms: my little tomtit, and so forth: and Bill seemed to like this ornithological touch. So he offered me fifty dollars for it. I told him he didn't need to buy it, because it was already paid for by Paramount. But he insisted that I was the writer and he was making a purchase from me, and he put a fifty dollar bill in my hand. So later on, these bird terms kept coming back in W. C. Fields movies—*My Little Chickadee* and so forth."

Mankiewicz became a director in 1945 with *Dragonwyck* for 20th Century-Fox; Gene Tierney and Vincent Price had leading roles in this screenplay by Mankiewicz himself, based on a romantic novel by Anya Seton. Since than he has combined the assignments of writer and director so frequently that he qualifies in the strictest sense for the title of *auteur*—unless anybody feels inclined to quibble about *Julius Caesar* (1953). He smiles at this recent addition to movie terminology: "A wonderful laudatory word. But, of course, I can't think of any first-rate director who isn't also a writer—not necessarily with words." His mind flicks back to the heyday of Ernst Lubitsch; "I was his protégé. Mr. Lubitsch could do more with one shot of a woman going up to a door and opening it than any present-day director can do with all his discotheque effects. He couldn't put it on paper. Nor could a lot of other directors. It's like this: the writing of a screenplay can be the first part of a director's work, and the actual directing of a film is the second part of the screenplay writer's job. When you write a screenplay, you have virtually directed it by the time you have finished writing. You bring a woman into a room, say. And there's a sense of tempo and mood and lighting in what you write. Then it's turned over to the director, who imposes a second interpretation. There aren't many directors now who will just pick up a script and start right off, as some did in the old MGM days when they'd give it to him on Saturday and tell him to begin shooting Monday."

From the late 1920s and throughout the first half of the 1930s, Mankiewicz wrote screenplays to be directed by other men. First at Paramount, and then at MGM. Among these was the celebrated *Manhattan Melodrama* (1934), with William Powell, Myrna Loy, Clark Gable, and Mickey Rooney as the Gable character when younger, directed by Jack Conway and W. S. Van Dyke. This was the film Dillinger liked so much that he sat through it a second time, since the screenings were continuous; the police received word that he was in the movie house, and gunned him down as he emerged.

Enough of the directors who worked on screenplays by Mankiewicz were of the creative kind he favoured in principle. But, almost inevitably, as a writer "I felt the urge to direct because I couldn't stomach what was being done with what I wrote." This stands to reason, of course. And yet it's a kind of paradox, to which the only solution is for one man to be both writer and director, if possible. In the case of Mankiewicz it was possible, but not easy: "I went to Louis B. Mayer and told him I wanted to direct, but he said that first I must become a producer for a time. The way he put it was, 'You have to learn to crawl before you can walk.' I said to him, 'That's the best definition of producing I've ever heard.' And then came my blackest years at Metro, a young writer who wanted to direct but had to produce."

In this capacity as writer-producer he began with a modest version of *Three Godfathers* (not to be confused with the later John Ford film of the same name). The stars were Chester Morris. Lewis Stone, and Walter Brennan, and the director was Richard Boleslawsky, trained in the Moscow Arts Theatre. A man of some distinction in the Hollywood of the 1930s, Boleslawsky also directed Garbo in *The Painted Veil*, the Barrymores in *Rasputin*, Laughton in *Les Misérables* and Dietrich in *The Garden of Allah*. From their association on *Three Godfathers*, Mankiewicz remembers him as "an unhappy man who never quite dug the American environment. He was very dedicated in the old Russian way, very traditional. But he had a wonderful visual sense."

After this came *Fury* (1936), with Spencer Tracy and Sylvia Sidney. The director, making his American debut, was Fritz Lang who was internationally famous by then for his *Nibelungen* films, *Dr. Mabuse*, *Metropolis*, and, of course, *M*. Mankiewicz began work on the script with Lang: "I remember he had pieces of paper on his office wall, marked in different colours to distinguish each character. The story of *Fury* came from an idea Norman Krasna had for a play. He told it to me and said that he thought I could write it better. This was just after there had been a lynching in northern California, which was unusual because evil things mostly happen in southern California. Anyway, he based his plot on that, and some time went by, and one day I told the story to Louis B. Mayer who said he'd let me make it. He said also that he would spend as much money on exploiting it as he was spending to exploit *Romeo and Juliet*—the Norma Shearer and Leslie Howard one, just to prove to me that even with all this publicity *Fury* could never be a big smash hit. Well, Fritz Lang was on the point of leaving MGM, because he'd been brought over and had been around for some time with nothing to do. So he was about to go back to Germany. But he stayed for this. And I think it was the best of all his American films. He did a brilliant job. I'd been an admirer of his work for a long time. It was funny, though, when they phoned Krasna to buy the story. He'd forgotten what the story was. I had to dictate it as he'd told it to me, so that he could sell it to MGM. Then from my story outline Bartlett Cormack wrote the screenplay, and of course Lang sat in with him."

Mankiewicz continued at MGM as producer and writer until 1943 when he went to 20th Century-Fox to produce *The Keys of the Kingdom* with Gregory Peck, directed by John M. Stahl from a novel by A. J. Cronin. From this he progressed a year or so later to the status he had wanted for so long, director—and often writer as well—beginning with *Dragonwyck*, and following up handsomely with *The Late George Apley* in which Ronald Colman gave one of his most polished performances, notably supported by Edna Best, Richard Haydn, and Richard Ney who had attracted some attention previously in *Mrs. Miniver*.

It was Philip Dunne, however, who provided the screenplay for *The Ghost and Mrs. Muir*, leaving Mankiewicz to operate on that "second interpretation" which a script undergoes in a director's mind. The result was remarkable for a period when Hollywood ran knee-deep into any- thing sentimental. The notion of a fragile widow in a house where the ghost of a charming seadog was wont to lurk (Gene Tierney and Rex Harrison), fraught with potential goo, became instead a thing of light- ness and grey charm. A love which penetrates the barrier of death was nothing new under the Hollywood arc-lights, but Mankiewicz, who "wanted to know more about the technique of directing" (which was why he left the writing to somebody else in this case), came through with a mood of tenderness and mystery, an astringent romanticism, with an apt ozone that could almost be sensed in gently brooding passages by the seashore, while the repeated manifestations of the benign spectre had both wit and an underplayed sorrow: tricky stuff, excellently done.

A couple of films later, in 1948, Mankiewicz wrote and directed *A Letter to Three Wives* which took an Academy Award for its screenplay: "I won my first cap." At the time of writing it, however, he didn't feel he was making a giant step forward: "I felt no different than I did back in the days when I was writing my episodes for *If I Had a Million.*" A fairly tough satire on suburban gossip-mongering, the story is of the upheavals in three marriages caused by a mean-minded woman with a poisonous pen. Among the sufferers were Jeanne Crain, Ann Sothern, Linda Darnell, Kirk Douglas, and Paul Douglas. Although primarily a film of words, given their due and deserving it, *A Letter to Three Wives* carried its wit over into visual contrasts for the three households.

By 1950, the Oscars came threefold for *All About Eve*: best film, best screenplay, best director in the Academy's view, which isn't always everybody's but was shared on this occasion by many critics in a year fairly rich in quality for Hollywood. It was the time of Wilder's *Sunset Boulevard*, John Ford's *Wagonmaster*, Henry King's *The Gunfighter* and *Twelve O'Clock High*, Huston's *The Asphalt Jungle*, Wyler's *The Heiress*, and Clarence Brown's *Intruder in the Dust*. Amid such splendour, *All About Eve* had a diamond glitter, and a hardness to match. Based on a novel by Mary Orr, *The Wisdom of Eve*, the screenplay flashed with Mankiewicz *mots*, savoured to the full by Bette Davis as the Broadway actress who befriends a deceptively wide-eyed girl (Anne Baxter) bent upon using the elder woman to further her own young dream of theatrical fame. A bitter study in ascendancy; complemented by acid wit from a drama critic played by George Sanders and by the cute vapidity of his current girlfriend, also aspiring to a career on the stage (Marilyn Monroe). Balancing these showy but highly credible figures with intimations of normality amid the giddy and cut-throat life such thespians lead, Celeste Holm played a nice woman easily deceived, Thelma Ritter a down-to-earth servant who sizes up the ambitious Eve at first glance,

Gary Merrill a weary Broadway director, and Hugh Marlowe a bedev-
illed playwright. It certainly went further than most attempts to prove
that showbiz glamour is a brittle surface, easily cracked to disclose
something raw and primitive. But Mankiewicz did it with high style,
disenchanting and yet delightfully wry.

The same year had seen his contribution to the growing number of
Hollywood movies on the "colour" problem: *No Way Out* marked the
initial film appearance of Sidney Poitier as a black doctor more likeable
by far than the whites around him. Then came another comedy, *People
Will Talk*, with Cary Grant; the aforementioned spy lark, *Five Fingers*;
and a conscientious but curious film of Shakespeare's *Julius Caesar*
which abandoned from the start any hope of ensemble playing by
bringing within the stones of Rome both Marlon Brando and John
Gielgud. Taken as separate considerations, Brando's instinctive Antony
was impressive if rough with the metre, while Gielgud's Cassius was
vocally eloquent and visually the very image of one who thinks too
much. Admirable each: but not to be cast in the same Shakespearean
work—elsewhere, with material that calls for a strong contrast of styles,
perhaps: it would be interesting to see. Bridging the gap, as it were,
James Mason played a coolish Brutus, but his argument with Cassius in
the tent scene really kindled excitement, as it so often will, giving
Gielgud something to illuminate his art.

Mankiewicz has directed Brando in two of his far-reaching excursions, the other being *Guys and Dolls*, neither more nor less than a
movie of a musical from Broadway, nicely enough endowed with Jean
Simmons and Frank Sinatra and Vivian Blaine (just the girl to deliver
the lyrics Frank Loesser wrote). Brando sang. But then, once upon a
time, Garbo laughed—and so what? It wasn't a film a director could
be expected to infuse with any of his own individuality. But it was
popular.

The Barefoot Contessa, which preceded it, was not. "I missed," says
Mankiewicz. Ava Gardner and Rossano Brazzi starred with a suitably
sour Humphrey Bogart in what was intended to be "a cynical fairy
tale." The original thought was to make the Brazzi character a homosexual; but on account of the prevailing Hollywood codes in 1954, he
wound up as merely impotent; "Even then you wouldn't believe the cir-
cumlocutions I had to use before I could do that. There was nothing

like the freedom that writers have today. But they don't use it. Today there's too much reliance upon the camera, rather than depth of human comment."

Bones of contention were rattled when Mankiewicz filmed Graham Greene's *The Quiet American* in 1957; realistic in appearance, sometimes verging on an appropriate newsreel-rawness, it had Audie Murphy as the young Harvard graduate and Michael Redgrave as the middle-aged Englishman who meet and clash, over politics and other things, in Indo-China. Mankiewicz changed the ultimate balance to give a more sympathetic impression of the American: "I heard Graham Greene was upset about that, and I'm sorry, because I admire his work." Numerous critics weren't exactly jumping for joy, either; but Mankiewicz takes solace in the fact that Jean-Luc Godard rated it the best film of its year.

A brave and variable, but continually absorbing work was the expansion of a Tennessee Williams exercise in oblique horror, and intensified psychology, *Suddenly, Last Summer*, with a screenplay by Williams himself and Gore Vidal. Making the horror a little more explicit, and cinematic, Mankiewicz devised visual impressions of a young woman's hapless vacation tour with her homosexual cousin, who was ritualistically eaten alive. The images, while good, were outshone by the words, which were brilliant, although Elizabeth Taylor had yet to reach the vocal and dramatic command that would be hers in Albee's *Who's Afraid of Virginia Woolf?* and more especially in another Tennessee Williams script, *Boom* (from *The Milktrain Doesn't Stop Here Anymore*). *Suddenly, Last Summer*, with a neatly contained portrait of a brain surgeon by Montgomery Clift, was dominated by Katharine Hepburn as the dead man's overbearing, wild-minded mother, gaining every nuance of terror from the great symbolic speech in which she recounts her son's vision of "God" on a beach where carniverous birds descended upon baby turtles. An impression of torment, its value was obviously appreciated to the full by Mankiewicz, but probably it was a little ahead of its time for the cinema.

Cleopatra, which followed, was a salvage operation—which is all I feel necessary to say about it here. All Mankiewicz says is "We don't discuss it."

When breath had been drawn, he made another comedy, *The Honey Pot*, a Venetian scamper, lightly related to *Volpone*, with Rex Harrison,

Maggie Smith, and Cliff Robertson on hand. For that he also wrote the screenplay; but now, *There Was a Crooked Man . . .* is another of his interpretations of work he has not written himself. "It's difficult for me to find material I can write quickly. If I write *and* direct a film, it takes me the better part of two years." This one he describes as "funny and frightening. Not broad burlesque. Satirical."

He concedes that his own kind of cinema is very much orientated to dialogue: "My particular type of writing is concerned with the manners and mores of our time, and it demands an audience which is patient with *the word*. I guess that's out of favour at the moment. Audiences are conditioned to having their eyeballs jabbed.

"I don't disapprove. But we're on a voyeuristic kick. This is a spectator society. I guess television has contributed a lot to it. The audience in the cinema, by and large, comes to be titillated by colour and effects. But the so-called innovations of recent years—indeed since the end of the war—haven't emanated from directors, but from the laboratories and the lens-makers.

"In the early days, Pabst—and in the USA, Lubitsch or John Ford— did everything that could be done with the camera. They didn't have the telephoto or the zoom. A good thing, probably. Because too many over-inflated directors are more interested in that, than in what they can get out of an actor, or how they can express the nuances of human behaviour. The director's responsibility is to put life on the screen, rather than just a kaleidoscopic effect. But the pendulum will swing. The audience will begin to demand more contentment, instead of these easy optical trappings."

More About *All About Eve*

GARY CAREY/1972

TO GET TO JOSEPH L. MANKIEWICZ'S home in Pound
Ridge, New York, nondrivers take the Harlem-Central Line from Grand
Central Station to the Mt. Kisco stop. That first day I went to visit
Mankiewicz was dreary with rain; the train's windows were dirty and
cracked; there was too much heat; and the seats were so arranged that
everyone had to ride facing backwards. The unsavory background further unsettled my already anxious mind. I was worried that the train
would be late and that the tape recorder wouldn't work (it didn't), and I
was frankly apprehensive about meeting Mankiewicz. He has a distaste
for interviews in general—and, in particular, for interviewers who paraphrase what he has to say and then quote him directly in language
which is not his own.

(He recalls with particular dismay an extensive one he granted
the French magazine *Cahiers du Cinema*. I later discovered that this
interview, originally published in the French edition, had been given
in English, translated into French, and then, for the American edition,
retranslated from the French into a pidgin English which lost all of
the director's conversational flavor, distorted most of his meaning,
and resulted in what he describes as "incoherent gibberish. Shrdlu,
in fact.")

As I looked over the Harlem-Central timetable, I noticed that the
final stop was Brewster, which in *All About Eve* is the locale of Lloyd

From *More About* All About Eve, by Gary Carey and Joseph L. Mankiewicz (New York:
Random House, 1972). Reprinted by permission of Rosemary Mankiewicz.

Richards's "little place just two hours from New York."[1] Consequently, this might have been (particularly from the look of it) the very train Margo missed that eventful night Karen drained the Richards' coupe of its gas. I was visiting Mankiewicz to find out all about *All About Eve* from genesis to *fait accompli,* and being superstitious, I regarded this mental double exposure of Margo and me on the same train as some kind of good omen.

The train pulled in to Mt. Kisco only about five minutes late and Mankiewicz was waiting to meet me at the station; a stocky man with an open, friendly face who looks a good deal younger than his years. He has the gift of putting people immediately at their ease; as we drove from the station to Pound Ridge (about a twenty-minute drive), the conversation was relaxed, and although it served the purpose of feeling each other out, there was nothing tentative about it. I was to find out that "tentative" was applicable to almost nothing about him.

When we reached the driveway of his home, Mankiewicz stopped the car to fetch an enormous stack of manuscripts, books, and letters from his mailbox. Never a notably prolific director, Mankiewicz has made only three films in the past ten years. Much of that unproductive time he rather bluntly attributes to a deliberate and depressed withdrawal from creative activity due to the brutalization by its releasing company of *Cleopatra,* a film which Mankiewicz rarely refers to by name and has deleted from any filmography of his work over which he has control. Still, judging from the pile of letters to be answered, scripts and books submitted for his approval, his current disenchantment does not seem to be regarded as irrevocable. (Nor is it; Mankiewicz has his plans for the future, although they do not presently include writing for the screen. The only directorial project he speculated about, probably because it was the one least likely to come to fruition, was a film version of *Macbeth* which would star Marlon Brando and Maggie Smith.)

The Mankiewicz home is a former dairy farm, an unpretentious and charming conglomerate of tiny white buildings, rolling fields, and duck ponds. Mankiewicz beeped the horn as we drove past the small main

---

1. The Brewster station was also the opening vista of *A Letter to Three Wives,* establishing the suburb with "those horrible chain stores that breed like rabbits."

house, but did not come to a halt until we reached what had formerly been a cow barn, now converted into a study-workroom. The conversion had been done with taste: white plaster walls, beamed ceilings, and an imposing, rough-hewn stone fireplace. Four Oscars, an award from the New York Film Critics, diplomas, scrolls, and figurines from England, France, Italy, Japan, even Cuba—from "those organizations which proliferate all over the world, smugly designating the best of everything"—covered the mantel and walls. Nonetheless, there was none of the vainglorious ambience which overruns a prizewinner's trophy room. This was a warm and friendly workshop, lined with bookshelves whose contents showed a wide diversity of interests, all of which were extensively covered—and the books had obviously been read.

After lunch, provided by his attractive wife, Rosemary—described by Mankiewicz as "possibly the only Englishwoman with an awareness that coffee is more than just any brown liquid, heated"—we discussed how to proceed on this account of the making of *All About Eve*. A process which Mankiewicz described as "having, somehow, the flavor of a posthumous undertaking." I suggested that we work chronologically, which I presumed started with his coming upon Mary Orr's short story, "The Wisdom of Eve," the basis for the film. Mankiewicz attempted to oblige, starting at the point I had given him, but to ask Mankiewicz to start at a chronological point is to ask him to flash back. The flashback is to him not at all a device; it is "an omnipresent part of 'now' in time—that part of the past which is in everybody's present." So, with a quick cut, we were deep in Mankiewicz's past. (We were to remain in Mankiewicz's past for our next two meetings, and he was to linger even longer as he subsequently reworked and expanded upon those portions of the interview which quote him directly.)

It all really began with Mankiewicz's lifelong dedication—"a calling, really," in his words—as a theatre buff. Particularly, his almost obsessive interest in the "inhabitants of the theatre—those who cause it to exist—its creative commune." This affection is readily apparent from his library. Two entire walls of his study are lined with theatrical books: biographies, more biographies, encyclopedias, yearbooks, an extremely comprehensive collection of published plays from Aeschylus to Albee. But even without this ambience, one would sense it from the added warmth and fervor in Mankiewicz's voice whenever the conversation turns (as it invariably does) to the subject of the actor, his craft, "the quirks and frailties, the needs and talents of the performing personality." Once, after tuning up to the subject for ten minutes or so, Mankiewicz concluded: "I often wonder why serious students of the human psyche look to anything *but* theatre-folk for most of the answers they seek."

The genesis of *Eve* lay in this enduring fascination. "I imagine it surfaced for the first time," Mankiewicz said, "when I was about eight years old. I saw my first film—I think it was my first—in a lower Second Avenue movie theatre; could it have been called The Casino? Anyway, the film—which was entitled *Hock The Hun* or *Hock The Kaiser*, that should date it—starred Jane and Catherine Lee. Two little girl actresses, precursors of Shirley Temple, who—apparently to this day—nobody but me has ever heard of. The movie was a First World War two-reel comedy in which these two little American girl spies were hiding from the Germans and a bee was about to sting one of them on her bare bottom—and betray their whereabouts to the brutal Huns. The suspense nearly destroyed me. But—most importantly—I remember that after the film was over I got up, walked down to the screen, and insisted upon looking behind it. I was convinced the two little girls would be there. I have never, since that day, been completely certain that actresses on the screen were altogether unreal—or that, off the screen, they were altogether real."

This inquisitiveness never waned, although his professional and personal proximity to theatre folk in his later life would seem to have been more than sufficient to engender both disillusionment and satiety. Mankiewicz had begun his career at Paramount Studios in 1929 as a title-writer (for "talking pictures," which were being released in the thousands of theatres still without equipment for sound projection), graduating to writing comedy scripts for Jack Oakie and W. C. Fields (including his original screenplay for the memorable *Million Dollar Legs*—and four episodes for the equally famous *If I Had a Million*, in one of which he created for Fields the "My Little Chickadee," "My Little Tomtit," etc., syndrome that Fields continued to utilize in later films). In 1931, at the age of twenty-two, he received his first Academy Award nomination, for the screenplay of *Skippy*.

In the mid-1930s he moved to MGM, where he first wrote *Manhattan Melodrama*—a Gable-Powell-Loy film "most noteworthy for having lured John Dillinger to his entrapment and death at the hands of the FBI." This was followed by two screenplays for Joan Crawford, *Forsaking All Others* and *I Live My Life*—successfully typical of the "madcap-young-heiress and brash-young-reporter film cycle of that Hollywood era." Then, refused an opportunity to direct by Louis B. Mayer, he was cajoled by that same "Great Cajoler" into a lengthy period of producing films for MGM's vast stable of female stars—innumerable vehicles for Miss Crawford, Margaret Sullavan, Katharine Hepburn, Myrna Loy, and Rosalind Russell, among others—a period he refers to as his "black years." His writing, which he contributed liberally to most of his productions, went uncredited due to the stringent regulations of the Screen Writers Guild (of which Mankiewicz had been a founding member and officer a few years earlier)—and he loathed having his creative identity restricted to that of "producer." (He still bridles at being referred to as a movie producer. Yet, among his productions at MGM were such vintage favorites as *Fury, The Philadelphia Story, Woman of the Year*, and *Three Comrades*.)

In the early 1940s he moved to Twentieth Century-Fox, having been contractually granted the opportunity to direct. After writing (with Nunnally Johnson) and producing *The Keys of the Kingdom*, finally, in 1945, under the aegis of Ernst Lubitsch—who had been Mankiewicz's "friend, guide and preceptor" since his earliest junior-writer days at Paramount and of whom he still speaks with reverence—he directed his own screenplay of *Dragonwyck*. (Mankiewicz, by the way, dismisses as "utter fantasy" the scuttlebutt legend that he took over the direction from Lubitsch due to the latter's ill health. "For some time—ever since his heart attack during the shooting of *A Royal Scandal*—Ernst had not felt up to the physical demands of directing. Accordingly, he decided to function for a while only as a producer. Fox purchased the Anya Seton novel, *Dragonwyck*, for Lubitsch's production schedule—and he asked me to write the screenplay and direct it. Ernst is not credited on the screen—there is no producer's credit on *Dragonwyck*—but he did, in fact, produce it.")

By now, Mankiewicz's protean career had already spanned some fifteen years. "Hollywood, at the time," he commented, "was a small strangely remote enclave on the outskirts of Los Angeles—professionally and socially inbred and self-preoccupied—a weird mixture of goldmining camp and ivory ghetto. One knew almost everybody else casually and an ever-changing small group intimately. The major studios were separate duchies—and somehow one's contract implied an exclusivity not only of professional talents but of one's private and social life as well. By and large, those one worked with during the day became one's companions at night. Accordingly, during my ten years at MGM my Paramount friends, even my intimates, had inevitably grown remote. And now, as a subject or citizen (of serf, if you will) of Fox—there were new faces, new personalities, egos, and idiocies with which to cope and work and fraternize. Not different—mind you—just new."

During those first fifteen years, Mankiewicz had written and produced for, and was presently also directing, most of the current stars—the "great and near-great; the young not-to-be-denied; the aging scrambling-to-hold-on—and that vast mass who never quite fail but never quite succeed but who also never quit." The actor's persistent drive for success is, of course, an important theme of *All About Eve.* I asked him how he would define it. Mankiewicz pulled at his pipe:

"The definitive answer, I think, would be different for each individual ego. But there are some basic common components. For one—what amounts to an obsessive need for the young actress/actor to acquire a substitute identity. A personality-proxy, really, wherewith she can attain acknowledgment, acceptance, even love and/or its many equivalents, from a society in which she is usually unable to function successfully as just herself. Or what she considers herself to be, or not to be—which is the same thing.

"For another—possibly an even more acutely obsessive need for the no-longer-young actress to ensure, at the very least, *survival* for that substitute identity which had for so long sustained her. To each and all of them, you know, there arrives that one last time when the make-up comes off—to stay off. Leaving him, leaving her—as what? With what?"

Mankiewicz grinned. "I have no intention of relating chapter and verse of *The Actor: The Origin and Continuing History of the Species.* That's just one of the many books I've promised myself to write before my Exit into That Great Green Room Above—but which I most likely

won't. Let me present to you, though, a valid capsulized concept of
how the actor could have come to be—and how his place in society
could have evolved . . ." He took another long drag on his pipe. He has
been a pipe-smoker for forty-five years—smokes them unceasingly—
about a pound of Barking Dog tobacco every ten days—and is inordi-
nately proud of his ability to keep his pipe from going out.

"A minor talent—keeping my pipe lit—but one of my few remaining
competitive social aptitudes. Back to the actor. It is my belief that, historically, the actor could have predated fire, the wheel, the axe, the
priest—every major manifestation of human creativity, really—except
possibly killing and making noise.

"Let's fade in, then—or 'iris in,' which is earlier—upon a particular
occasion in the dim prehistory of what we call, hopefully, *Homo sapiens*.
One pleasant evening, herded together by the earliest stirrings of a gregarious instinct, a gathering of our forebears was sprawled listlessly on
some sheltered slope, temporarily safe from attack by the many larger
and stronger and more resourceful animals which customarily and
casually ate them.

"They, our forebears, in turn, had just finished their own feeding—
gorging themselves beyond saturation with whatever could be pulled
from the earth or hit by a rock—already committed to probably one
of the earliest and certainly most enduring of human rituals: The
Evening Meal.

"And there they sat—then, as now. Bellies distended, eyes glazed by
gluttony, acutely aware of visceral discomfort and mentally aware of
nothing at all—the dreary silence broken only by an occasional belch
or break-of-wind. Incapable of communication with each other—and,
in any case, with nothing to communicate. Then, as now. Facing, with
apathetic resignation, that most empty and most frightening time of
the human day as *Homo sapiens* has created it for himself: the few hours
that stretch endlessly between mankind's Evening Meal—and
mankind's Bedtime.

"How indescribably intolerable they must have been, those evening
hours during our earliest existence. With literally noting to distract
our forebears from the stultification of their—then, as now—spiritual
emptiness and lack of resource. Incapable, yet, of conceiving the
wheel much less TV and the movies, gin rummy, booze, pool, pot,

pornography—some of the countless more or less successful distractions whereby we, the ultimate refinement of *Homo sapiens, can* make it from dinner to bed. Some of the time.

"But, on that particular pre-historic evening whereof I speak, something happened. Something that broke into the seemingly hopeless lethargy like a thunderclap—and changed the very nature of living for those stuffed witless human creatures. For suddenly one of them jumped to his feet (as I picture it, he'd been sitting off to one side, not really part of the pack, maybe smaller and weaker than the rest) smeared some birdshit over his face, shoved a big feather up his ass, and began to prance up and down waving his arms and making noises like a roc or some equivalent prehistoric chicken. And at that precise moment, my friend—Curtain Time, Make-up, Costume, and the Actor simultaneously came into being.

"The others stared at him for an instant; then intuitively roared with pleasure. The first Belly Laugh. They yelled for more—and got it, I'm sure. The first Encore. That poor bastard with the feather up his ass must have pranced and danced and cackled himself into total exhaustion that first First Night. When—we mustn't forget—the Audience, too, was born.

"But what also resulted from that particular occasion was—the nature of the actor's place in the Audience's world. Because the next night, as they sat around with their swollen bellies, they called for him to get up and do the same thing. Which he did, of course. Again and again, night after night—until, after a while, they stopped laughing at the chicken bit. They'd seen it too often. They went back to belching, scratching, yawning. So the actor got himself a fancier feather, maybe a bearskin or a dinosaur's tooth—maybe some other misfit came to him with a suggestion; but that's how Gag Men came to be, and that's a different story—and they laughed again. One time he hid behind a rock, imitated thunder or the roar of a lion, and frightened them. Thus he discovered the Audience liked to be afraid almost as much as to laugh—provided they knew it was make-believe. He was learning that every aspect of the Audience's world had its counterpart in a make-believe world which, it seemed, was the actor's private domain—and that revealing it was his private skill, his talent—and that this revelation, if successful, could ensure him acceptance within the tribe, within society.

"That may well have been why he shoved the feather up his ass in the first place. Possessed of the same, perhaps even greater, appetites and ambitions as the others, he had never before found a way—as *himself*—to attain that acceptance, let alone the share of leadership and adulation he craved. In terms of physical endowment, as I've postulated, he was probably ill-equipped (Did you know that Garrick, Booth, Kean, among many other greats, were under five feet six inches tall?) to compete in a very physical world. He was a lousy hunter, a pitiful warrior, given to daydreaming, pushed around or ignored, relegated to the remnants of food and least appetizing of the women, probably considered expendable in case of hostilities.

"But now—ever since that First Night—living was different for him. He now moved among his fellows with assurance, ate well, slept securely inside the cave—probably knocking off any number of tasty broads, in whose eyes he had suddenly acquired that strange special sexuality which women so often ascribe to men engaged in other than traditionally masculine pursuits. Why? Why that difference in his status when he *himself* was no different—when, by the reality-standards of the society in which he existed, he *himself* was every bit as insufficient as before?

"Simple. Because each evening, and maybe even on rainy afternoons, as *somebody or something else*, he had ministered to the basic need of that enduring human entity—the Mass Audience—to be beguiled and distracted when forced back upon its own inner resources which were—and are—nil. And that Mass Audience, in turn, had gratefully rewarded him for satisfying that desperate basic need with approval and applause. With a sense of belonging and having purpose within the tribe—with, at long last, an acceptance.

"Imagine. All that. Just for shoving a feather up your ass and making like a chicken. How infinitely more gratifying it must be today—how much more prideful, even ennobling—when that identity proxy can be Oedipus or Hamlet or Medea, St. Joan, Eliza Doolittle, Camille, even Auntie Mame. For that matter, even Margo Channing. Even *Eve*."

While his intense preoccupation with "the theatre historically, and its inhabitants in terms of the inner 'alarums and excursions' which motivate them" never waned—and still hasn't—Mankiewicz in 1949, wrote and directed the first of his manners-and-mores films, *A Letter to Three Wives*, which won for him the first two of his four successive Academy Awards for writing and direction. Mankiewicz has never had a personal press agent and he has never, as has become usual in the Oscar sweepstakes, indulged in any form of promotion in order to better his chances. Nor was he particularly shocked when he was informed by Darryl Zanuck himself that Twentieth Century-Fox had no intention of backing his film—that the studio was putting all of its advertising and publicity resources behind another nominee, *Twelve O'Clock High*, personally produced by Zanuck.

Mankiewicz, who enjoys referring to himself—as far as the realities of moviemaking are concerned—as "the oldest whore on the beat," took particular delight in winning his Oscars as an untouted dark horse. Even more, he became increasingly interested in "The Award" itself, as a symbol. Or as he puts it:

" 'The Award' as also a totem. Its implications as a sort of cocka-maimy immortality. Together with the conniving and soliciting and maneuvering that goes on for the acquisition of it—and, in the end, the strangely unenduring gratification it provides. Award-winning can often be followed, almost reactively, by a period of depression—not unlike suddenly going off amphetamines. Anyway, I found myself pondering these and other ramifications of 'The Award' syndrome; it would make an excellent frame, I thought, for a film—or play or book—about the theatre, the theatre-folk, those motivating 'alarums and excursions' I've been talking about."

The "pondering" was not a search for dramatic material; what Mankiewicz still needed was what Alfred Hitchcock has called "the McGuffin": the hook or gimmick upon which a plot hangs and by which it is triggered. This he came across in a short story, "The Wisdom of Eve," written by actress and sometime playwright Mary Orr.[2]

This story, which first appeared in *Cosmopolitan* in 1946—some three years before it came to Mankiewicz's attention—is reportedly a lightly fictionalized account of an incident in the career of Elisabeth Bergner,

---

2. Miss Orr's greatest success as a playwright was *Wallflower*, a domestic comedy she wrote in collaboration with Reginald Denham in 1944. She also appeared in its original Broadway cast.

the famous Austrian actress. "The Wisdom of Eve" concerns a stage-struck girl, Eve Harrington, who plays upon the sympathies of an aging and happily married Broadway actress Margola Cranston (sic), becomes her understudy, and then ruthlessly attempts to replace her both on stage and in her husband's affections. Though Eve fails in this attempt, she does win the lead in a new play written by Lloyd Richards, Margola's favorite playwright, and eventually steals Mr. Richards away from his wife Karen, also an actress, who happens to be Margola's best friend.

Miss Orr's story was little more than an anecdote, but it had the ring of true theatrical scuttlebutt as told out of school, and attracted enough attention to be adapted as a radio drama. At that time, however, the story departments of the major film companies were extremely diligent in their search for potential material, and "The Wisdom of Eve" came to the attention of James Fisher, then head of Twentieth Century-Fox's story department. As was standard procedure, Miss Orr's story was mimeographed and then sent to the studio's various contractual producers, writers, and directors.

Mankiewicz showed me the memo from Fisher which accompanied the story, suggesting that it was "something unusual" and adding as possible encouragement that the rights could be obtained at an extremely reasonable price. There is nothing about the memo to suggest that Fisher knew of Mankiewicz's interest in doing a theatrical film—it reads like a routine story department coverage. But the story hit home: it gave Mankiewicz the "McGuffin" he needed.

II

Mankiewicz began writing *All About Eve* (or *Best Performance*, as it was then called) in the early fall of 1949, in the peace and quiet of a ranch near Santa Barbara. The treatment[3] took three months to complete; the first rough draft of the screenplay, six weeks. The shooting script was delivered in mid-March. According to Twentieth Century-Fox's records,

---

3. A treatment is technical jargon for an outline, usually sketchy, but which Mankiewicz invariably constructed in great detail before going into screenplay, in which the story is broken down into scenes, the dramatic continuity is constructed, and the characters are developed.

Mankiewicz's services as writer (for accounting purposes) terminated on March 24, 1950.

Anyone who has the opportunity to compare the original story with the subsequent treatment and screenplay will realize the extent to which Mankiewicz rewrote and re-characterized those characters who have counterparts in Miss Orr's story. Addison DeWitt, Bill Sampson, Birdie Coonan, Max Fabian, Miss Caswell, and Phoebe are entirely of Mankiewicz's creation.

But the greatest change from the original was wrought upon the character of the famous actress. In the story, Margola Cranston is happily married and as Miss Orr has someone say of her: "If she ever sees forty-five again, I'll have my eyes lifted." Well past forty and happily married were exactly what Mankiewicz did *not* feel were characteristic of the actress he wanted to portray; actually, what he wanted to dramatize was:

"The trauma and terror with which so many of them approach *both* age forty *and* the transition from married actress to just married woman. The transition of their main performing arena from stage—to home. And the rapid narrowing of roles available, down to the ultimate two: wife and/or woman.

"Let me digress a moment to get a definition straight. I'm talking about *actresses* (and actors, too, of course, except they're men and infinitely luckier and less complicated and less intriguing—to me, at any rate)—women who, since almost their earliest awareness of themselves, have been *compelled* to act in order to *be*. I am *not* talking about that vast remaining spectrum of those who appear on stage or screen (some successfully, at times, for a time) with all the emotional involvement of trained seals playing cornet solos. To wit: the big-titted sex symbols, the city-type cowboys, the country-type shitkickers, the once-and-future stuntmen, the TV transplants, the New England tawny-types, the Bennington dropouts who invariably make the cover of *Life*—you can supply the names as well as I. No, Margo, *the actress*, was—and is—none of these. She was—and is—a woman whose need to act equates with her need to breathe. Who, when she isn't 'on'—just isn't, at all.

"Forty years of age. Four O. Give or take a year, the single most critical chronological milestone in the life of an actress. Look, I *knew* these women. I'd been in love with some—I'd worked with many of them. In the 1930s I'd watch them roll into Paramount and Metro at six thirty in the morning on their way to hairdressing and make-up. Drive in usually with the top down, their hair all blown by the wind, no lipstick, their own eyelashes, wearing anything from a poncho to a polo coat—and I'd think Percy Westmore should be arrested for so much as touching a powder puff to their loveliness. Well, by the late thirties they were driving with the top up. Then, in the forties, they started wearing scarfs—and, by 1950, large hats. The pancake was getting thicker, the makeup took longer, the cameramen started using specially built little banks of "inkies" to iron out wee bags and sags.

"Fortyish. You know, there's an old cue that never fails to stimulate some bitchy theatrical wisecracks—just drop the name of the current fortyish actress who is having to decide for the first time whether to play the mother of a late teenager. The jokes may be funny, but don't laugh. It's a bitterly sad point of no return for an actress. It usually means that a wide range of stimulating and gratifying identity proxies—particularly those that reflect and sustain the metaphor of youth—would, from now on, be inexorably unavailable to her. That the personality-aliases left for her to assume would now become inevitably character roles and—if she was unlucky enough to have to go on and on and on—caricatures. Four O. Fortyish. For the actress, a kind of professional menopause, really . . .

"Well, so we'd grown up together, my generation of them; they were pushing forty—and so was I. But I was a writer and director, just beginning to formulate what I wanted to write and what I wanted my films to be about. And, lucky me, even if I'd been an actor, a male. There was—and is—the theatrical rub. Women's Lib has quite a point to make here: about a society which can evolve and foster a set of standards by which, at roughly age forty, the female actress is required to forswear the public projection of romantic and/or sexual allure—while the male actor carries on blithely.

"Gary Cooper was 'getting the girl' (a felicitous phrase, equating the female with a vice-presidency, a touchdown, or maybe the clap) after he was sixty; Gable was sixty, or close to it, when Marilyn Monroe (in *The Misfits*) wanted into his bed. Wayne, Fonda, and Cary Grant are well into their sixties; Kirk Douglas, Mitchum, Lancaster are among those in the middle fifties—hell, even Paul Newman and Brando are on the other side of forty-five. It'd make a fascinating sociological study: why our American morality considers it indulgently 'G' for Cary Grant to make love to, say, Ali McGraw (in her twenties) and would react with 'X' outrage at Ryan O'Neal (in his twenties) bedding down with, say, Ava Gardner (in her late forties). Me, if I were O'Neal, I'd choose Gardner any time.

"But that's how the career crumbles with the female of the theatre-folk. And that was one of the facets of the actress I wanted to explore. With Margo, I complicated and compounded the problem by having her—at age forty—in love with Bill. I couldn't have given her a more threatening love object. For one thing, as a director, he worked in the same profession which had provided her with a lifelong sustenance—from which she was about to undergo the involuntary weaning I've described. Bill could, and would, go on forever in that profession; her share of its sustenance, however, would depend upon whatever he happened to bring home with him at night. Would that, that—shared ration—be enough? She'd had her own, all of it, for so long. She'd been, don't forget, the only angel on the head of the pin. Would she grow to resent being, as it were, on some sort of ego-sharing welfare program?

"Another curve I threw the poor woman was to make Bill eight years younger than she. I've told you about how theatre-folk have their own arithmetic; not a new but a very old math, indeed. Margo describes it in the screenplay: 'Bill's thirty-two. He looks thirty-two. He looked it five years ago, he'll look it twenty years from now. I hate men.' And, later, to Karen: 'Those (eight) years stretch as the years go on.'

"Most importantly, I guess, I wanted Margo to dramatize, if even briefly, my concept of the actor and his/her early flight into the 'identity-proxy' or 'personality-substitute' or 'ego-alias' or whatever the hell else I've dubbed it. His/her subsequent measure of success in coping with society behind the mask of that 'proxy-substitute-alias.' And then, inevitably with the actress, the traumatic reemergence of that inner *Self* she had decided so long ago was inadequate to attain even acceptance. An inner *Self* from which she had hidden behind those magical protean masks, or—as in the most tragic of instances—a *Self* she had never really known at all . . .

"When you're Judy Garland, say. And at age *three*[4] you're shoved onto a stage into a spotlight to sing 'Jingle Bells.' And from that moment on, you're told and told and *told* by everyone—audiences that cheer you in that spotlight when you sing, to a draconian mother who drills the unshakable conviction into you (you'll carry it with you until you die)—that *only* in that spotlight, singing as loud as you can (didn't Mummy have you billed as 'The Little Girl with the Leather Lungs'?), were you even acceptable to society, much less attractive in any way at all—how the hell can you possibly, for the rest of your life, know *who you really are*? And offstage, offscreen, with the spotlights and arc lights dark, when all through childhood and puberty you were never spared the acute awareness—in endless crowded studio conferences—that your waist was unusually high and your shoulders unusually rounded ('humped,' they were often called in your presence), and that *other* than your singing there was nothing about you that would merit a second glance or second thought from anyone—wouldn't that substitute-identity, the identity that existed only in a spotlight, become pretty goddamn important to you? Wouldn't it, in fact, become the one and only source of acceptance, of security and salvation, in a society which apparently considered you otherwise worthless?

"And with the passing years and accumulating fat and the deteriorating effect of the pills and drugs and booze that had somehow kept you going—kept you unaware, anesthetized as it were, in between spotlights—wouldn't the approaching finish, the approaching *blackout* of that spotlight-identity terrify you almost beyond reason, drive you to a despair of being capable even to go on existing without it? Roughly, that was Judy. She was the most terrible loss of them all, and probably the greatest of the talents lost that way. Not that the pattern of her tragedy was unique. Not by hundreds, maybe thousands. From the most celebrated to the most unwept of the unclaimed identity-unknowns . . .

"There was Marilyn, of course. The symptoms, the sources of infection were different, but the syndrome was the same. More mawkish horseshit has been intoned and written about how 'Hollywood destroyed

---

4. The screenplay places Margo's stage debut at age four when she entered, "stark naked," as a fairy in *A Midsummer Night's Dream*.

Marilyn Monroe.' Her particular pattern of self-destruction had been completed long before she ever heard of Schwab's Drugstore. But the movies—and her sudden, staggering, inexplicable movie stardom—did shape the finish for her, and hurry it. And cushioned it, in my opinion— in a strange way made the end easier for her. With the fantastic miracle of her 'career' already a shambles ten years ago, can you imagine Marilyn Monroe today, alive—existing as what? Where? How? Think about it.

"There were so many, many others—variations, all of them, on one tragic theme. Just some that come to mind: Olive Thomas, Lupe Velez, Jeanne Eagles, Thelma Todd, Carole Landis—why draw up lists? I could fill your cassettes with them. Strange, though, isn't it, how few men come to mind? There were plenty, of course. As noted, however, they usually went on so much longer before they ran out of masks. John Gilbert, for one. James Murray—remember him in King Vidor's *The Crowd?*—reportedly drowned himself. Milton Sills—big star, as big in his day as Gable—drove his car off a cliff, it was said . . .

"Lou Tellegen's reputed finish was, if nothing else, the most perti- nent I've ever encountered. He was another great star of the early days—played Essex to Sarah Bernhardt's Elizabeth, I believe—married to Geraldine Farrar and costarred with her. Well, in the mid-thirties, Lou Tellegen committed suicide. Apparently they found him surrounded by his vast collection of scrapbooks, crammed with clippings of the only life he had found tolerable, innumerable three-sheets (small posters) of his innumerable triumphs, and countless photos of himself as all of his 'proxies.' He was nude. It was said he'd committed hara-kiri. Not by means of a samurai sword, but with a pair of gold scissors—engraved with his name—the same pair he'd used to trim all those clippings, doubtlessly. Pertinent, don't you agree?

"Back, once more, to Margo. To the nature and ramifications of the actor's original, inner Self (really the *ego*, in psychiatric terms; one doesn't dare refer to it as such because, in common usage, the word has acquired so many other irrelevant meanings). Margo wasn't any of the above, of course. Nor was *All About Eve* about them. They, poor souls, were—and are—from another part of the Garden. Damned even before sinning. And their punishment, when the time came, or comes—with the stripping of the masks—is a total absence of any *ego* at all. Literally, an inner vacuum. With which, obviously, even mere existence becomes impossible.

"No, Margo's problem wasn't a—say—a 'void' behind that public identity which had for so long, with her permission and connivance, usurped her private identity. It was more: 'I wish I knew what the hell, after all these years of exile, my Self will turn out to be.' Putting it simplistically, of course. Margo could accept that Bill was in love with what the spotlight picked up. But when that spotlight turned off (and stayed off) how would Bill then feel about—*what*? She couldn't even guess. She knew only that it would be female—and eight years older than Bill. It wouldn't cook, surely, keep house or take second billing. Given to infantile tantrums, probably, for which there'd now be no ducking the responsibility. The angers would be hers—Margo's—no longer Medea's. It would be her bitchiness, now—not Becky Sharp's. She would be growing old—not Elizabeth the Queen.

"Not, I submit, the well-known, well-worn problem of the career woman playing tug of war with career and marriage. Not this one. 'I'm forty and maybe a bit more—I have had a highly successful and gratifying public identity which, since age four, has also functioned as my private identity, but which is not me—and when that public identity, that alias, ceases to exist, which will be any day now, I just don't know what the hell will be there in its place—and I love a man who, in turn, can love only the identity which I am about to lose because he has never known any other as me.' This is a very special problem, believe me. Indigenous to the female of the theatre-folk."

In creating Eve, Mankiewicz set out to portray a more universal type, a female whose ambitions and machinations are not uniquely indigenous to the theatre:

"There are Eves afoot in every competitive stratum of our society, wherever there's a top you can get to from the bottom. Eves are predatory animals; they'll prefer a terrain best suited to their marauding techniques, hopefully abundant with the particular plunder they're after. But in default of that happiest of hunting grounds—they'll work any beat at hand.

"Watch little girls. Certain little girls, that is. Eve's the one who always seems to wind up at the head of the line for cookies—she'll make or steal her own gold stars to take home if teacher can't be conned into giving her one—she'll throw fits, even run up fake fevers, if the prize is worth it to her. Eve is the one who must inevitably attain Daddy's assurance that he loves her more than he loves Mummy—and then goes after the identical assurance from Mummy.

"Full-grown, in the workaday world, Eve is everywhere. Corporations great and small, department stores, magazines and publishing houses, advertising companies, even—as in the script—breweries. Secretarial pools breed Eves like guppies.

"In the theatre, in the movies, in show business, she's there because there lies the particular loot she's after. 'Loot' may be an inaccurate word; it implies money. Of course there are hustler 'actresses' after money—but they, almost always, are after nothing else. And with no discernible talents out of the hay. They operate usually on the fringes of Broadway, TV, and the movies—drift back and forth to what used to be called Café Society and/or the Jet Set—but their true habitat and trade, however vaguely legitimized by publicity puffs and multiple marriages, is essentially whoredom. Eve is anything but a whore.

"Nor is she the proverbial wet-lipped starlet who makes all the Gala Openings wearing two shoelaces over her tits and a glaze on her eyes. Some cheap-jack agent has told her that'll do it for her. It won't, it never has. Jayne Mansfield's neck-to-navel probably made more magazine covers than J. Kennedy Onassis *plus* Audrey Hepburn, drew mobs at supermarket openings and roller derbies—and emptied theatres. Oh, of course screwing your way into a bit part of screen test can be so often more persuasive than reading for them—but I can think of no instance in which a truly important role, a demanding and significant one, has been 'cast on a couch,' to coin a cliché. Anyway, none of this has to do with Eve. This has to do with commerce, not ambition.

"Eve is essentially—in the theatre, *Harpers Bazaar*, *Vogue*, I.B.M., or wherever—the girl unceasingly, relentlessly on the make. Not necessarily for men; as a matter of fact, only rarely. A particular man, perhaps, or series of men—or women—may be the means to an important end, but almost never the ultimate goal. That goal—toward which Eve is fanatically and forever at full charge—is no less than all of whatever there is to be had.

("I know I seem to be indicating that the Eve *drang* is exclusively feminine; it's not, of course. It is a deeply rooted obsessive male/female need, an insatiably greedy one, to acquire more and more and more— but *not* necessarily money or possession; indeed, very rarely tangibles of any kind. And its manifestations appear no more frequently in one sex than the other. Eve has to do, after all, with much of what also made Sammy run.)

"That insatiable need and greed. You will remember that they become even more intolerable to Eve, in the end, than they have been to us all along. Because she is confronted in the end—as all Eves must be, and are—by an acute awareness that, in fact, ever since the beginning, she has been servicing a bottomless pit. A void. Her ego? That Self, without which nobody is anybody? The Eves—male and/or female—have none. Just an inner emptiness they can never fill—but must continue to feed, merely to exist. Such, exactly, was the human condition of our heroine when we first came upon her in my film.

"Gertrude Slescynski (the name and person Eve had discarded) had rendered herself literally nonexistent. Not one facet of Gertrude's previous life or personality did she consider worthy of inclusion in the Eve Harrington she fabricated for the wooing of Margo and the others. Gertrude/Eve was of course unaware, consciously, that she had no more depth of identity than a cartoon. How could she have been aware? When her existence up to that point had undoubtedly been a montage of hundreds of such fabrications?

"Actually, I clobbered Eve with self-knowledge long before her co-predators are forced to face it, as a rule. Usually it hits them only after the pickings have grown thin. When they're getting on. When the dissembling has come to require more effort, the lying become less intuitive and the lies less valid. When the equipment's grown old or outmoded—or they've just gone as far as they're going to go. From that point on they sulk a lot, drink a lot, scrounge for small favors—but it's downhill to nothing, and they know it. You gather I don't like Eve? You're right. I've been there. I've seen what they can do to living people, the scars they can leave. The most virulent Eve I've ever known was the production head of a major studio.

"Nobody (I'm back to my film, now) could have 'told' Eve Harrington what she was. Or wasn't, if you will. Honest insight into one's self is rarely acceptable from external sources; there are simply too many compensating equivocations available to an even minimally resourceful neurotic. No, it has to come up from within one—explode, more often than not—and has to be an experience of self-confrontation that cannot be evaded or transformed into a more tolerable substitute. That's why it was only under the relentless pressure of Addison's devastation of her masquerade—only after he had thoroughly sealed off every possible escape route—that I felt justified, at the very peak of her hysteria and terror, in having Eve give voice to her first acknowledgment of the emptiness she was and had always been: 'I had to say something, *be somebody!*'

"I'm sure you understand by now—God knows I've gone on long enough about it—that it was Gertrude Slescynski who blubbered those words up at Addison, not Eve. Gertrude, who had been nothing, justifying her creating of Eve—who would be everything. And now that the breakthrough had happened—it could not unhappen. Eve would never be altogether Eve again. And as her self-awareness increased, so the others being 'on' to her mattered less.

"I made that clear, I think. At the end, after the award ceremony, for instance. Eve's listlessness, almost a numbness, one type of the 'post-award depression' I spoke about earlier (a sort of reverse alchemy: the gold, as you hold it, turns into shit). Her vague searching for drink, her sulky unwillingness to go to the party in her honor. Addison, completely aware, remonstrates patiently: 'Max has gone to a great deal of trouble, it's going to be an elaborate party, and it's for you.' Eve holds up, and refers to, the Award: 'No, it's not. It's for this.' Addison couldn't agree more: 'It's the same thing, isn't it?' 'Exactly,' says Eve.

"Even more pertinent to my point, I think, was to make it evident that Margo now knew all about Eve. And that Eve knew she knew. Witness Margo's 'congratulatory' remark to her upon the same occasion: '. . . nice speech, Eve. But I wouldn't worry too much about your heart. You can always put that Award where your heart ought to be.' That about sums up Eve, I think."

All About Eve has usually been regarded only as a satire preoccupied with the New York theatre. Actually, Mankiewicz places it within a series of consecutive films (*Letter to Three Wives*, 1949; *House of Strangers*,

1949; *People Will Talk*, 1951; *No Way Out*, 1950; *Five Fingers*, 1952) in which he attempted "a continuing comment on the manners-and-mores of our contemporary society in general, and the male-female interrelationship in particular." In fact, as he discusses his characters, it becomes clear that this latter aspect was as important to Mankiewicz as was giving the low-down on the dog-eat-dog world of Broadway. Though these relationships may be somewhat atypical because they are set against the extraordinary background of the theatre, they still have wider application. Margo's identity problems are not only to be found in the theatre and, as Mankiewicz has said, there are Eves in all professions of life. Similarly, while the emotional problems of the third major female character, Karen Richards, are also spotlighted by her involvement with the theatre, they are the most universal, for her sole career is that of wife.

Karen is another great variant upon her counterpart in the Orr story. In the original, she is an actress, not quite first-rate (or so it is implied), and she has a tongue as cheap and acid-tipped as Clare Boothe's characters in *The Women*. Mankiewicz, however, had a much different concept he wanted to explore with this character, set off from the others by her nonprofessional standing:

"Of all the females that inhabit the society of theatre-folk, the one for whom I have always felt the greatest compassion is she for whom, in that society, only one role is available: that of 'wife to ———.' As in the *dramatis personae* of Elizabethan plays, her billing (i.e., tribal status) is far down the list. With luck, she will be identified as a specific 'wife to ———.' (As in 'Calpurnia, wife to Caesar'; 'Margaret, wife to Mayer'; 'Virginia, wife to Zanuck'; 'Legion, wife to Rooney,' and so on). More often than not, she is lumped anonymously among: 'Courtiers, Lords and Ladies in attendance, and gentlewomen-in-waiting.'

"They're in waiting, all right, these 'wives to ———.' Day and night, increasingly as time goes on—waiting. For the axe, the heave-ho, the marital pink slip. For that increasingly foreseeable tumbrel trip to the divorce court. (For some reason I've never asked about, movie people usually divorce themselves in Santa Monica, California, a community otherwise notable only for a little-known statue of Myrna Loy at the foot of Wilshire Boulevard—and a teeming ghetto of rather elegant homosexuals, cashiered to the Pacific from their origins elsewhere within our Great Silent Morality.)

"Anyway, before that court she will produce evidence of irreconcilable incompatibility; the property settlement having already been negotiated by professionals trained in the *quid pro quo* of how-much-money for how-much-misery. The interlocutory decree of divorce will be handed down, a ritual every bit as impressive as being slipped a baggage check. She will then return to a house of which she may or may not have been granted custody—stripped of a marriage which had totally absorbed anywhere from ten to forty years of her adult existence. An ex- 'wife to ———.' Very much alone.

"As an alien among the native citizenry of theatre-folk, resident only by virtue of marriage to one of them, her 'visa' remains valid for only the duration of that relationship. Once it's over, she becomes a foreign body and quick removal is indicated. Sometimes they won't accept that premise, these ex- 'wives to ———.' They've made 'friends of their own' among the theatre-folk, they insist, sharing interests other than the last play, the present film, the future commitments to stage or studio or TV. They're wrong, they haven't. There arc no other interests, in fact, among theatre-folk.

"The activities generated by these 'wives to ———,' which, hopefully, will sustain for them the illusion that they have found 'lives of their own'—or that they contribute importantly to the careers and lives of their mates—may include political activism, community affairs, and the pursuit of self-improvement (Let's hear it for those extension courses at U.C.L.A., Columbia, and The New School). No matter. These and other efforts, however assiduously pursued, are invariably regarded by theatre-folk to be nothing more than the hobbies and diversions to which the nonprofessional must turn to pass time. Like masturbation and billing, of real concern only to those immediately involved.

"To be sure, if her body has retained sufficient attraction—and sometimes even if it hasn't, even if she just makes it available—the most recent ex- 'wife to ———' may attract some early action in bed. For one thing, among theatre-folk, there's that corps of strange studs—their motivations have always fascinated me—who specialize in servicing, sexually, the newly widowed and newly divorced female. As quickly as possible after the fact of the funeral or divorce decree.

I imagine it's a sort of vicarious necrophilia; probably the one they're really 'screwing' is the dead, or departed, husband. Certainly not, I think, the confused and despairing woman who has quite naturally overreacted to an indication of affection.

"The studs move on, though, as swiftly as they moved in. The kids, if they're grown up—and they might well be—extend the proper assurances, go through the proper motions, and then go about living their own lives. Quite rightly. What next, then? For this woman, no longer young by the standards of a society that sets a stringent early limit upon the female right to youth and its benefits—now cut adrift at age anywhere from thirty-five to fifty-five—suddenly a stranger and afraid in a world she never made and thank you, Mr. Housman . . . ?

"About Karen. When I wrote Addison DeWitt's capsulized summary of her as: '. . . the wife of a playwright, therefore of the Theatre by marriage. Nothing in her background or breeding should have brought her any closer to the stage than row E, Center.'—actually, I was stacking the circumstances in her favor. Those who are of the Theatre only by marriage, or other emotional attachment to one of its native citizenry, usually have neither the intellectual capacity nor the emotional stability of a Karen. Yet she, too, was a foreigner, an émigrée from what a producer's wife once described to me as 'private people.' And in common with all other 'wives to ———' among the theatre-folk, Karen, too faced an ultimate probable expendability.

("I don't know why I feel I must periodically point out that these theatre-folk types exist in both genders. Of course there are 'husbands to ———,' as well. But, as always, the male is luckier and has many more disguises available for camouflaging his inferior status. And usually, among theatre-folk, the Wife of Importance will actually connive at the masquerade of her schmuck husband; witness the prevalence of 'general managers,' 'executive and/or associate producers,' 'creative consultants,' and other smoke-ring designations for the husbands of theatrical Wives of Importance. He can carry her make-up kit right on the stage and retain his *machismo*. The 'wife to ———' rarely dares so much as a visit to the theatre-folk at their work. Not if she has even an instinct for survival, she doesn't.)

"But when had this female of the 'private people' been essential to the male of the theatre-folk who married her? At what point had she been so desperately needed—under what circumstance was functioning without her so impossible for him—that marriage became a necessity? When they were both very young. When she needed him—and he needed his needs. When they spoke love, which is a very imprecise language—and not at all a specific emotion. Just about everything that anybody has ever demanded of anybody else—has been called love. But that's different cassette.

"She wasn't 'wife to ————' back then, No, sir. Back then she was—right out of the catalogue—wife. Meaning also: mother; cook/laundress; childbearer; accountant; partner and professional consultant; whipping post (with understanding: 'an Artist has to take it out on somebody,' right?) for his frustrations and failures; sexually, whenever and whatever he wanted (her own pleasure relatively unimportant: 'a Man needs relief,' right?) for his tensions and insecurities. And he? What was he, where was he? A couple of generations ago, out in his junkyard, maybe. Or looking up from cutting gloves and shirts—perhaps from collecting fares on a trolley car—to stare at that movie nickelodeon on the corner. To dream of owning a factory to supply it with 'product.'

"Or—in a later generation—on another, more creative level. Auditioning, 'making the rounds,' more auditioning, blowing the rent money for classes in acting and/or directing. Those 'classes.' Usually conducted by actors and/or directors whose qualifications to teach acting and/or directing seemingly go unchallenged except by those who have successfully acted and directed. Or—that tiresome but nonetheless valid cliché—asleep by day and up all night, at the kitchen table, typing at the play or the book—posting the fat envelopes, haunting the mailbox for skinny replies. But always, in all these instances, her mission, her reason for being: to sustain hope for them both, to make do with what there was, and, above all, to keep fixed his position as the shining center of the universe.

"Those, although she couldn't know it at the time, were the best years she would ever know. Especially when they were ultimately culminated by that Moment, Day or Night of Triumph. (We speak, after all, of the Successful. The Failures, that vast majority—they just went on with their limited lives and long marriages of mutual recrimination.)

"So witness our heroines: a generation or so ago, the junk dealer's/ glover's/trolley conductor's wife on her first ride to the West. That drawing room aboard the Twentieth-Century Limited, the layover at the Blackstone in Chicago with its marble bathtubs and cattle-baron elegance, and then the Santa Fe Chief for three night and two days— luxuriating by day, only half-listening to his endless planning with his new partners—movie retailers all—at long last on their way to build factories in California for the manufacture of 'product.' And at night, after a dinner she hadn't had to cook, being humped in a bouncing berth she hadn't had to cook, being humped in a bouncing berth she hadn't had to make up, enjoying it even, permitting herself the hope that, at long last, her life would include joy.

"And now a quick cut to that later, other generation. (We used to utilize dissolves for a time lapse that long, quite rightly—anywhere from eight to twenty feet. European film labs made lousy dissolves then, so bad they couldn't be used, and European directors fumed and fussed but were forced to make do with the straight cut. Then discovered, to their utter amazement, that early U.S. cinéastes were hailing them for having developed a new editing technique. But now that the film labs abroad are by far the best in the world . . . but that, too, is a different cassette.)

"However we get there, let's make the setting obvious and to the point. It's that Night of Triumph at—you guessed it—Sardi's. The critic of *The New York Times* has just been observed still dancing on Forty-fourth Street. The TV reviewers, unanimous raves, have been permitted to usurp as much as fourteen seconds of the weather outlook for Northern Greenland, thus extending to almost two full minutes their thoughtful appraisals of a work representing possible two years of the creative lives of many artists. But 'they've made it.' The playwright-husband is now 'a new and vigorous talent—a witty and trenchant observer of the current scene.' The director-husband is no longer 'professional, capable and sound'—tonight 'he created that inter-play of movement and mood and dramatic impact that make for magic in the theatre.' And the actor-husband—this night 'he came gloriously into his own, master now of his techniques, drawing upon a now richly matured and bountiful talent.'

"As for their young wives—awash with champagne and blissful tears—there never was, never would be, another Night such as this. They were being rewarded with the most that any vicarious participation in glory ever provides: a happy conviction that their years of self-denial, of drudgery and devotion, had made a very real contribution to this Great Moment. As, indeed, they had. There might, during that Night of Triumph, even be public acknowledgment of that contribution: 'her night as much as mine . . .' 'her faith in me, the times I was ready to just quit . . .' all to be heard from the lips of Don Ameche and Ty Power on the Late Show, but none the less valid. And later that Night, at home alone in ecstatic privacy, he might even whisper it just to her: 'We've made it, you and I. We've made it.'

"But *they* haven't, of course. Not among the theatre-folk. *He* has. Remember those services she'd performed as wife—so desperately needed by the Artist, so essential to his functioning at all? 'Mother'? The Mass Audience will replace her, there. They'll give suck to him, spoil, scold, cuddle, and reject him in a variety of ways beyond her power even to imagine. Cooks and house-cleaners will be hired now, of course, and come and go as they do, and her domestic duties will become that of personnel manager for backward delinquents.

"Childbearer? Oh, she'll want children rather soon if she doesn't already have some. If for no other reason than as a reassurance, to herself, of her physical presence—as a sort of sea anchor to control her drift. Then she'll discover that, among theatre-folk, children become almost always the sole responsibility of the non-performing parent; there is almost always too large an area of competition between the child and the performing parent.

"What else? Partner—wailing wall—even whipping post? Forget it. What with producers, packagers, lawyers, agents, business managers, publicity men, secretaries—his professional life and income will become so compartmentalized and overstructured that he, himself, will rarely know what they are. Annually, she will sign a joint income-tax return where designated. At specific intervals, regular deposits will be made in what is called her 'household account.' She as far as her contribution to her husband's life is concerned, will become one of the smaller moving parts in a mechanism.

"Sex? No need to go into that, why belabor the obvious. It's not surprising, really, the readiness with which the 'wife to ———' adjusts to sexual infidelity by her spouse. After all, he does come home; her visa does remain valid.

"What she does dread, lives in terror of, is—serious emotional involvement on his part. It could happen any day. Her man doesn't leave of a morning, after all, for a corporate structure in which he merely fills a niche. No, this husband goes off to a fun fair where he's the brass ring on the merry-go-round; a nonstop Miss Universe contest and the one he smiles on goes into orbit. He's fair game every minute he's away from home. At the studio, the audition, the rehearsal—it can happen while waiting for a traffic light to change. That involvement. An Eve in the car alongside. Meanwhile, back at home, the 'wife to ———' can do nothing but wait. And play out her role, that of being 'in-waiting.' For as many years as she lasts.

"You know, I've written about a lot of women—most of the time not as truthfully or perceptively as I would have liked to, for various reasons—and I've speculated about hundreds. They're my favorite humans. Pondering men, by comparison, is staring at alphabet blocks. And I can't think of, I couldn't dream up, a human being more truly helpless than the 'wife to ———,' at this point, among the theatre-folk.

"She is completely helpless. Without weapons. Her physical attractions are faded; at their best, they were no match for those, the best in the world, that now beguile her husband relentlessly. His former dependence upon her has been fragmented and distributed among those whose profession it is to keep him dependent. He no longer needs her. Not at all. Nor has she allies; after all, she can do nothing for anyone. Not even herself. Except hope for him to come home—and prepare for the time when he doesn't. She is a civilian casualty, unwept and unsung, among the theatre folk.

"Yes, I liked Karen more than any of the others. She was more aware—less ignorant, rather—of what the theatre, and she in it, was all about. So witness her musing—when she recalls the night Lloyd left her to go to Eve: 'It seemed to me I had known always that it would happen—and here it was. I felt helpless, that helplessness you feel when you have no talent to offer—outside of loving your husband. How could I compete? Everything Lloyd loved about me, he had gotten used to long ago . . .'"

In conception, Karen is the film's most original character. Mankiewicz's admiration for her is evidence by the writing of the part; she is the most intelligent, dignified, and warm person in the story.

"I endowed Karen with intelligence and taste," Mankiewicz recalls, "because to the extent that they possess those virtues, the disquietudes and frustrations of women become ever move complex—and fascinating. And because the well-bred and well-spoken have become a dwindling minority in a society in which, too often, witless rudeness passes as a badge of merit."

Just as in many other Mankiewicz films, the female characters are more vividly drawn than the men in *All About Eve*. When I asked him if it were fair to say that as a writer, he was more attracted to women and their problems, he answered:

"Fair? I'm well-nigh besotted by them. Writing about men is so damned . . . limited. They're made up, for the most part, of large, predictable, conforming elements. Men react as they're taught to react, in what they've been taught is a 'manly' way. Woman are, by comparison, as if assembled by the wind. They're made up of—and react to—tiny impulses. Inflections. Colors. Sounds. They hear things men cannot. And, further, react to stimuli men either can't feel or must reject as 'unmanly.' 'Unmanly.' Whatever the hell that means. Of a kind with 'virtuous,' I suppose. Part of the dogma set down by a manly and virtuous society to which our evolving genders must adhere. A surprisingly large proportion of females do not. A shockingly large proportion of males do. And you'll find that the rules of 'manliness' restrict the writer about men almost as much as they do the male who submits to them.

"It would be fascinating to do a film about a man in rebellion against 'manliness.' (Not necessarily a homosexual. There's another of our society's rigidities: you're either 'manly' or queer. The simplistic Agnewistic black-or-white ploy—if you're not with us, you're against us—America and 'manliness'—love 'em or leave 'em. Homosexuals—male and female—are constituents of a thoroughly viable third sex. Within it, the chances of success or failure in personal interrelationships need be neither more nor less than within any other. *If*, that is, our 'virtuous' and 'manly' society drops its vendetta against them.) Anyway . . . the film about the man in revolt against 'manliness': I'd like to tell it by suggestion, by nuance and mood, by utilizing all of the subjective techniques and material you're supposed to eschew in portraying the male on stage or screen. Why the hell, for instance, shouldn't a man burst into tears? Or lose badly? Or be indecisive—or be irrationally afraid of the unknown or unseen—or smell good—or want peace?

"No, the 'man's role,' as presently in vogue, doesn't interest me very much as writer and/or director. He is invariably expected to pit himself physically against his adversary: to me, the least imaginative and interesting form of confrontation. His goals are usually restricted to, variously, conquering or amassing things. A fortune of money, an enemy country, a chain of factories, a series of broads—one or more loathsome children who, quite understandably, find him equally loathsome—in short, acquisitions. His conflicts, overt and incomplex all, are resolved by physical action, usually violent.

"Far-fetched generalization? Not all that much. Examine the recent spate of so-called 'youth-oriented,' 'anti-establishment' films. When, ever, were the creative spokesmen for a generation granted such an extensive platform from which to expound and clarify the substance of its objectives? Name those films—count them on your thumbs—which reflected the slightest vestige of inner conflict, the emotional strains and stresses of cerebral decision, cerebration of any kind, for that matter. Name those in which the opposing forces were not 'stacked' with childish simplicity on a par with that which used to put black hats on Noah Beery and his nasty rustlers—and white hats on Tom Mix and his true-blue cowboys. *Strawberry Statement, Getting Straight, Zabriskie Point,* countless other revolutionary potboilers before and since. (And I do mean 'pot.') What struck me was how far back they reached—to the very beginnings of film-making—to resolve the presumably complex problems they posed. In the last reel, the White Hats simply kick the shit out of the Black Hats. And everybody goes home happy. Just like the good old days.

"I'm quite aware that what we used to call 'heading 'em off at the pass' is now known as 'confrontation' or, even less to the point, 'happening.' But even the reality 'happenings'—and certainly the films about them—seem to have no more intellectual implication, and little more pertinence, than the old-time dynamite blast in the mine shaft. Blowing up a college is not an answer to educational inequities or idiocies. It doesn't solve the problem; it merely blows it up. Pissing on a church is hardly a valid comment on the medieval restrictiveness of organized religions; it's a cheap and infantile substitute for thought. If the writer and/or director is incapable of the latter, he must not be permitted to piss away our time and attention on the former. Confine him to a projection room, make him run the films of Federico Fellini over and over and over—and study his craft."

Mankiewicz cited this "preoccupation with externals" as one of the reasons he didn't think he would be writing films for a while:

"Besides which, women are rarely represented on the screen these days, except as tits. Do you want to make a million dollars? Discover the biggest Star of all time? Be the first to come up with a beautiful girl with square tits. It seems to me that's what they must be searching for. Why else should the female mammary gland have replaced the ringing telephone as the movies' most photographed insert?"

All About Eve does, however, contain one dynamically drawn male character, Addison DeWitt, the acerbic critic who gives Eve her comeuppance. According to Mankiewicz:

"Addison's essential motivations and instincts are those of a collector. True, an acceptable male objective, the acquisition of possessions. But the items he collects are the most subjective imaginable: the secret fears, the private peccadillos of other people. His ultimate goal, of course, is dominance over them—and their work. As a critic-commentator among the theatre folk, as a noncontributive bystander—it's as if all of their lives were somehow a continuing auction, and he empowered always to bid highest. Note, please, that his superiority to his antagonists is cerebral; he doesn't blow them up. And note also that Addison DeWitt, as an inhabitant of the Theatre, is a greatly exaggerated character. His component parts exist—and have existed—in reality. But not the sum total of them. Not nearly."

(The scene between Addison and Eve in the New Haven hotel room is sex-as-politics—a startlingly modern idea for a film made in 1950. One in which 'killer' meets 'killer'—Eve 'steps up in class'—and Addison proves himself, as he had warned Eve, 'champion.')

"To a certain extent, in some of his externals—his 'asides,' as it were—Addison is me," Mankiewicz continued. "His comments on the nature of the actor, for instance, and also those on the pontifications of the elder statesmen of stage and screen." This rather eyebrow-raising admission was mitigated as he continued. "There's always a character—sometimes more than one—that is me in the films I've written. Why should that surprise you? I'm a film-heretic—anathema to those who find it so much easier to point a camera than direct an actor. I'm known to be committed to the heresy that the word can be at least as contributive to the non-epic film as the lens. I am also known to prefer actors trained in speaking to those who just grunt through hair. My films talk a lot—hell, *I* talk a lot; have any cassettes left? At best, I suppose, hopefully I've been, at times, a witty and perhaps trenchant commentator on the manners and mores of our society. At worst, a describer, let's say, of various aspects of the human condition and the social background against which it endures. At the very worst—a bore. But, then, simply because my talents may not live up to my standards is certainly no reason to abandon those standards."

It has generally been assumed that Addison was based on George Jean Nathan, the acidulous theatre critic whose reviews between 1920 and 1950 were considered by many to have been more outrageous than accurate. There are certain similarities between Nathan and DeWitt: the acerbic tongue, the fastidiousness of dress, and the dramatic cigarette holder. Also, some aspects of the relationship between Eve and Addison suggest a parallel to the friendship between Nathan and his various protégées, as, for example, Julie Haydon.[5] When I asked Mankiewicz to confirm this supposition, he replied, "In his mannerisms and posturings, I suppose Addison reflects some of those of George Nathan—but not to the exclusion of many others on the periphery of the creative community." But certainly, I pointed out, Addison's anti-Hollywood bias was drawn directly from Nathan's vitriolic stance on America's film-making capital. Mankiewicz concurred only in part:

"That 'vitriolic stance' of Nathan's, as you put it, was probably, to a large extent, as much of a façade as the 'Hollywood' against which it was directed. You must bear in mind that even critics—especially

---

5. Nathan first met Julie Haydon when she was making the Hecht-MacArthur film, *The Scoundrel* (1935). He was instrumental in getting her her first important lead on Broadway, *Shadow and Substance* (1938). Miss Haydon's most famous role was as Laura in the original production of *The Glass Menagerie* (1945).

critics—have their personality-aliases. Today more than ever, I would say, now that criticism is quite obviously on its way to becoming just one more of the performing arts. Actually, I look to the emergence of a new form of criticism—one which will render impersonal, unimpeachable critiques of the performances of our contemporary critics and their pseudocritical shenanigans.

"Critics have acquired all of the managerial trappings of performers, you know; their tradition is no longer so much that of William Winter[6] as William Morris. Their writings, even their opinions, are too often obviously intended either to establish or enhance their individual 'box-office draw' as 'personalities'—with a dismayingly canny and commercial eye on the public marketplace. (Ah, those juicy fees for speaking tours amongst the community-culture circuits. So rewarding to both ego and pocketbook, especially if immediately preceded by a well-publicized, mercilessly witty savaging of a major new work by some—preferably native—author, playwright, or film maker. Or, increasingly popular these days, the mercilessly witty savaging of another critic. Have you noticed how, more and more, they seem to be writing for, about, and against, one another? Today's proverbial Gentle Reader, in search of objective and qualified opinion about a new play, film, or book, more often than not winds up being told more than he wants to know, really, about the deficiencies of another critic.)

"You know, I've never been quite sure of what the qualifications are for, say, a film critic. Surely not just the experience of having looked at, and digested, thousands of movies. By that criterion, half my class at college would have qualified. But I can stipulate one essential prerequisite for the present-day critic who would attain that ultimate of critical attainments—the power to affect the popular acceptance or rejection of a creative effort. He or she had damn well better be photogenic and without lisp or stutter. Therein—to the degree to which he possesses

---

6. William Winter (1836–1917). Dramatic critic of the New York *Tribune* from 1865 until he retired in 1909. Highly esteemed by the world of the theatre, considered the dean of dramatic criticism in America. In 1916 a unique memorial was tendered him, signed not only by most of the leading contemporary actors, actresses, and playwrights but also by President Woodrow Wilson, Theodore Roosevelt, and William H. Taft among other prominent public figures.

equipment hitherto essential only to the performer—may well lie his ultimate critical status. His verdict either accepted as unquestioningly as is the laxative commercial which follows it, by millions of television viewers—or relegated to the negligibly few, haphazardly interested readers of *Women's Wear Daily, The New Leader,* and other consumer guides.

"Back to George Nathan and his fellow 'Hollywood' baiters of the thirties and forties. (After the early fifties—after Television folk inundated the area—using 'Hollywood' as an epithet became a critical cop-out, really. Some critics still do, of course. When they can't, or won't bother to, analyze their dislike for a film or its creators. Calling something 'Hollywood' today is just a cheap shot. Whipping a horse that's not only dead but disintegrated.) But back then, in what has now come to be known as 'The Golden Age' for reasons which escape me, Nathan and many other professional denigrators of 'Hollywood' spent more time out there than you might think.

"Harold Ross, for one. Founder, editor, and czar of *The New Yorker.* Harold was famous for the edict that he cared not who his film critic was, as long as he hated movies. I have always been of the opinion that one of the most contributive elements to Harold's intense dislike for Hollywood was the fact that so many of his friends, over the years, deserted New York—and *The New Yorker*—to go out there. He was a gregarious man (with a chosen few), and resented the great inconvenience of having to travel three thousand miles to visit with the wit and talent he had been accustomed to find in an adjoining office—or certainly no further away than the Algonquin. But Hollywood was where they were—and Harold came out. Often. As a matter of fact, Harold Ross was chiefly responsible for one of the few bastions of good taste ever to endure in Southern California: Chasen's Restaurant.

"Ross had known Dave Chasen ever since Dave had been Joe Cook's top banana in Vaudeville and on Broadway. (Chasen and Joe Cook, along with Ted Healy, Frank Tinney, Bobby Clark, Leon Errol, and Frank Fay—just for starters—were some of what made people laugh before *The Beverly Hillbillies*.) Chasen worked with a red wig and a blacked-out tooth, and came out with Joe Cook to do a film for Columbia. Frank Capra directed. It was called *Rain or Shine*, I believe, and Joe Cook never made another film as far as I know. Financially, he had no problems; he'd saved a lot of money during the fat years on Broadway. But Dave

Chasen had nothing to fall back on but the red wig and the blacked-out tooth—*and* a talent for making the best chili and barbecued spareribs this side of anywhere—*and* many good friends that ranged, socially, intellectually, and financially from Ross and Nunnally Johnson to Jock Whitney. So, with Harold Ross as godfather and chief backer, Dave Chasen opened what was, to begin with, no more than a glorified chili, spareribs, and hamburger joint, in the mid-1930s, exactly where it is today—ever an oasis for the unassimilated Eastern palate exiled to the land of The Prime Rib.

"The activities of George Jean Nathan, and others of his ilk, were less gastronomical. George enjoyed, shall we say, the company of extremely beautiful young women with extremely limited mentalities—who would listen. He was not a lone prospector, believe me. For the intellectual on the prowl, Hollywood, at the time, was a veritable Klondike. The place was chock-a-block with ravishing young females, many of international renown, hungry to be appreciated for qualities they had not. Like the nothing-but-rich who want to be loved for anything but their money, these babes would genuflect before anyone qualified to endorse their claim to even the faintest glimmer of cerebral capacity. The awesome physical attributes of the young Adonises who swarmed about these beauties like suntanned ants, attracted them not at all. If anything, their steel-muscled, flat-bellied male counterparts were irritants: they tended to emphasize the anatomical hollows and protuberances upon which their own fame rested. Barely capable of spelling out the screenplays they were enacting, they wanted so much to be sought after as more than just one cute ass or two sun-kissed tits—oh, if only they hadn't dropped out of high school and if only they could remember whether it was George Eliot or George Sand who was really a woman . . .

"The cultivation of these minuscule mentalities was a game that George Nathan and many other marauding *litterateurs* delighted in playing during their occasional sojournings out there. Almost the most successful sexual ploy in Hollywood during the thirties and forties (far more productive than the fox cape or diamond anklet) was, quite simply, a list of books which the visiting—or resident—intellectual would draw up for the edification and education of the culture-hungry screen beauty. (For some reason, *Zuleika Dobson*—'Max must have had you in mind when he wrote it . . .'—was on all the lists. Another favorite was the collected verse of Edna St. Vincent Millay, which the lip-reading cuties would underscore heavily, usually with eyebrow pencils, as giving precise voice to their own troubled hearts.) Whether or not they actually read the books, they bought all of them; merely acquiring the complete list provided for them the equivalent of an intellectual mink coat they could wear proudly and publicly. (What greater legacy, after all, could Scott Fitzgerald have left to Sheilah Graham than her delusion of literacy?)

"At any rate, whatever the relationship between illiterate Beauty and lettered Beast it was merely one of the relatively undamaging, and for the most part enjoyable, fringe benefits to be garnered on the outskirts of the theatre-folk corral out there. I certainly didn't intend to equate the Addison–Eve alliance—an unholy one, of mutual mistrust and manipulation—with any of those I've been nattering about. Eve was no starry-eyed babe in search of a mind to improve. Nor is there, as I've already pointed out, any substantial basis for a serious identification of Addison DeWitt with George Jean Nathan.

"I think it was probably Addison's unashamed and overt theatricality that attracted you so much to him as a character. It was intended to. Whenever your villain becomes a bore, whatever you're writing—play, film, whatever—wrap it up, abandon ship. Conversely, first-rate villains very often, by the mere reflection of the infinitely greater attractiveness and scope that villainy has over virtue, will endow the most numbing of dullard heroes and heroines with an appeal they couldn't possibly attain on their own. From Mephistopheles to Rupert of Hentzau. It's my guess Will Shakespeare found Iago a breeze to write compared to Othello; and that he sweated more over Brutus than Cassius. No further resemblance intended, or even hinted at, of course.

"I hurry to throw that in because once, in defense of my position that the offstage or offscreen moral and/or political propensities of creative talents should not be applicable to a judgment of their work, I used Michelangelo as an example. I said that I doubted very much whether anyone gazing for the first time at the ceiling of the Sistine Chapel had ever been repelled by knowing that its creator had been a pederast. Nor, as far as I knew, had it been of concern to Pope Julius II who must have been aware of Signor Buonarroti's sexual nuances but who nevertheless hired him to do the job. My remarks were passed on (second-handedly, by his own admission) to Dwight Macdonald, a whilom critic whose judgments, while oozing papal infallibility, rarely stooped to clemency. Mr. Macdonald promptly handed down the pronouncement (from the pages of whatever magazine then served as his pulpit), in evaluating my involvement with the most absurdly traumatic experience of my professional life, that I had quite seriously compared myself to Michelangelo! So—I must be forgiven a certain amount of apprehension when, in the course of being interviewed or otherwise saying what might be repeated or printed, I allude, while making a point, to artists and works of a quality of genius which is, as yet, many light-years away from the furthest horizons of film-making."

I indicated to Mankiewicz that I had found the remaining male characters in *Eve* sketchily drawn. It has been conjectured that Bill Sampson, the young director with whom Margo was in love, was based in part upon the young Elia Kazan. He and Mankiewicz have long been good friends; they share similar views about many aspects of both the theatre and film-making. For example, Sampson's no-nonsense attitude towards both the theatre and working in it (as illustrated in his sounding-off to Eve in Margo's dressing room) is, Mankiewicz admitted:

"Not unlike Gadg's own non-horseshit approach to his profession. In his case, it sets free his great talent. However, too many of our steadily employed colleagues have unhappily too little talent to set free. Accordingly, they keep on applying layer after layer of 'theatuh' bushwah—like house paint. It seems to work, horseshit being a basic commodity in both 'theatuh' and 'cinemah.' It abounds throughout the entire spectrum of American theatrical activity; from our most pretentious, oversubsidized, and calamitous attempt at repertory (here in New York City)—up or down to the innumerable 'Drama Schools' on the university level, where the instillation of 'theatuh' is prescribed by curriculum and the damage begun."

I continued to argue the point that in my opinion Bill wasn't really fleshed out enough to become an interesting character. That, in fact, I found him rather bothersome. After that initial characteristic aria to Eve, he's defined almost entirely by his soothing effect on Margo's tirades, and his endless good sense and babying eventually become patronizing. Similarly, it seemed to me that Lloyd Richards had very little personality or existence beyond what was demanded from his reaction to the other characters and the action. Actually his plays, which, it is indicated, derive from the Tennessee Williams school of Southern depravity, struck me as better defined than he was. Mankiewicz disagreed with my criticisms of both Bill and Lloyd:

"Perhaps you found Bill not 'interesting' and Lloyd wanting in 'personality' because of the absence of overt theatricality in their private and professional behavior. (Even so, not a total absence: Lloyd does have his screaming playwright–actress confrontation with Margo, ending with his 'It's about time the piano realizes it has not written the concerto!' And Bill, in a temperament tantrum, does walk out on the rehearsal of Lloyd's new play.) On the whole, they're what I intended them to be: two talented craftsmen, one a director and one a writer, who have worked hard and long and responsibly at their craft within a theatre which they love—and within which they earn their livelihoods.

"Lloyd relates the production of his plays to his personal financial concerns, as well he might. As a playwright, he is not, as he points out, 'an oil well operator.' Therefore he is not preferentially treated by a society which refuses to concede that a human talent is either as important, or as subject to depletion, as a geological deposit. He is well aware of the contrasting demands of the make-believe world in which he practices his craft—and the very real one he encounters as he steps out of the stage door. He lives expensively. A snazzy duplex in town; also a country home. He and Karen dress well, eat well, probably travel and entertain a lot.

("By the way, your analogy to Tennessee Williams—except for the fact that Tennessee was, at the time I wrote *All About Eve*, both headmaster and head-of-the-class of an entire school of writers about Southern sexual proclivities—is not otherwise even remotely applicable. If you must have a frame of reference for Lloyd, I could suggest many candidates: Phil Barry, Bob Sherwood, Moss Hart, Sam Behrman, et al.—all eminently talented, highly successful, and partial to the good life.)

"When playwriting is your only profession, your only source not just of gratification but also food and shelter and covering for your nakedness—whether in the theatre, film or, the Saints preserve us, television—you learn very quickly that the successful craftsman must be responsive to more than just capturing, on one hundred and twenty pages more or less, the freewheeling fancies of his Muse. He must be aware of, and understand, and face the workaday practicalities of making his living in the theatre, film or, the Saints preserve us, television.

"Art? Yes, I have studiously avoided using the word. If it has slipped out, it's been by inadvertence, believe me. Art—with a big, A, to set it apart from its general connotation of highly developed skill—is a designation I'm extremely chary about using. Another one is: Genius with a big G. We live in a time of instant coffee, soup, cake mix, copulation—also instant Genius. They carry the label but neither the content nor the quality of the original, more slowly arrived at, product. They're ersatz. Our language has the largest goddamn vocabulary in the Western world, and the lack of selectivity with which we use it appalls me.

"Year in and year out our creative talents turn out a few first-rate books, plays, and films which reflect, at most, superb craftsmanship—and of which too many are frivolously, even casually, hailed as Works of Art. (I once witnessed, on what I believe is called Educational Television, the resident *cinéaste* quite seriously extolling the texture of a wall, in front of which Monica Vitti—I think—was posing in an—I think—Antonioni film, as being subtly contributive to the aesthetic purpose of the Master. Now, I had personally utilized that same wall—or its exact duplicate—in at least two of my own movies. The plaster shop at Cinécittà turns out that particular wall, in that particular texture, by the mile.) Antonioni—and Art? What epithets do we set aside for Aeschylus, Aristophanes, et al.?

"Film—as Art? It's too soon to say, by several generations, I think. Of course film is presently an art form, with a small *a*. But then, so is pavement painting—and it's been around a lot longer. I'm not prepared to list two, twenty—or any—films to which schoolchildren will be exposed, say, two hundred years hence. They'll bloody well be absorbing the miracle of Shakespeare, though. And who knows? Absorption may be by then, literally the medium. The *Hamlet* pill; the *Titus Andronicus* suppository.

"Film itself, the physical commodity, already being superseded by video tape, with increasingly insubstantial substitutes already on the horizon, may actually cease to exist sooner than we think. A couple of hundred years from now man, in search of diversion, may simply settle back in some sort of electronic easy chair, adjust a pair of computerized stimuli to either side of his brain—and conjure up whatever pleasing fantasies occur to him at the moment. These, or course, will be instantaneously and faithfully transformed, by the magic of electronics, into a continuing flow of imagery projected upon a small screen which he will hold in his hand—as we now hold a book. At that point—what price Film Immortality?

"Bill Sampson's 'babying' of Margo—which struck you as becoming 'patronizing.' He doesn't really, you know. She wouldn't stand for it, not for a minute. 'Babying' the Margos of the theatre folk is a waste of effort. It's almost the first technique used in manipulating them professionally; very early on, stars learn that ass-kissing is almost always a form of negotiation."

There are remarkably few changes from first draft to final shooting script in the (only two) versions of the *All About Eve* screenplay. Mainly, it seemed to have been a matter of editing and refinement—from the former to the latter—culminating in what was still to be a very long (one hundred thirty-eight minutes) film for its era. The eliminated material merely elaborated points that the audience could quickly pick up from the subsequent action. The dialogue of the first draft, oddly enough, is almost as polished and precise as those aphoristic speeches heard from the screen. Such sure-handedness, at so early a stage, with what is usually the most reworked and rewritten aspect of any script, not only recalls Mankiewicz's early specialization as "dialoguist." It serves also to underscore his enduring high repute as a writer of what Vincent Canby describes as "urbane, sardonic comedies" and, to continue Canby's evaluation: "The sort of taste, intelligence, and somewhat bitter humor I associate with Mr. Mankiewicz who, in real life, is one of America's most sophisticated, least folksy raconteurs." The quality— and, at times, overabundance—of Mankiewicz's dialogue has, in fact, led many critics to regard his talents as essentially those of a theatre playwright who has somehow diverted his writings from stage to screen. (Only recently, writing approvingly of Mankiewicz in *The Guardian*, Derek Malcolm wryly dubbed him: "Old Joe, the Talk Man.")

The major difference between the scripts and the released film version lies in the narrative structure. The dramatic construction of the scripts is more complex. There it is clear that we are getting a composite

portrait of Eve, as seen from three different points of view—those of
Addison, Karen, and Margo. Even the shooting script keeps cutting back
to each of these three narrators at the Sarah Siddons banquet as each
relinquishes one segment of the story, and another picks his up. The
total effect was to be, according to Mankiewicz: "A composite mosaic-
like structure in which several characters, while narrating their remem-
brances of still another, construct not only a portrait of the character in
question but inadvertent self-portraits as well."

Another technique utilized by Mankiewicz in his final screenplay was
the repetition of the same scene as witnessed from two different points of
view. In the shooting script of *Eve*, this technique is used only once, but
to great effect. In the sequence showing the party given by Margo for Bill
Sampson's homecoming, Eve's speech about the meaning of applause
("Imagine, to know every night that different hundreds of people love
you . . .") is presented to us first from Karen's point of view—and later
from Margo's. From the scenes that precede each point of view (i.e.,
Karen's, followed by Margo's) we gain a clearer understanding of both
women's reactions to Eve and of their subsequent behavior to her.
Although the sequence was shot as written, it never reached the screen.

All About Eve is structurally an extremely elaborate use of one of the
basic forms of film storytelling: the flashback. Anyone searching for a
common narrative approach among Mankiewicz's films, as widely different in genre as they are, might begin by examining his use of this
technique. The flashback and its advantages in characterizing human
behavior—"summoning up not only the effect of the past upon the
present, but also the degree to which the past *exists* in the present"—
have made it Mankiewicz's favorite form of dramatic construction.
Somewhere in the Night (1946) concerns an amnesiac's attempt to trace
his lost identity; *Letter to Three Wives* (1949) recalls the marital memories of three women who are informed that one of their husbands is
about to run away with another woman; *The Barefoot Contessa* (1954),
which presents the director's "most unimpeded" use of the "mosaic"
construction, begins as a group of mourners gathers around actress
Maria Vargas's grave and recalls, each in turn, Maria's tragic life. (Here,
too, Mankiewicz utilizes the technique of repeating the same scene as
different characters recall it, thus "providing a single narrative episode
with varying dramatic connotations." This time, Mankiewicz having

approval of the editing, the scenes in question remained in the released film.) *Suddenly, Last Summer* (1959), tells the story of a girl who has been severely traumatized by a past experience. (Gore Vidal and Tennessee Williams wrote the screenplay, based upon the latter's play.) It is worthy of note that here Mankiewicz utilizes, long before it became a fairly common film technique, the device of the "subliminal recall": the climactic scene in which the girl, Catherine, struggling to remember, manages to summon up to her memory only a flash or two of the past—and then loses it.

Mankiewicz's most ambitious, and hopefully "definitive," involvement with the flashback was to have been *Justine*, his adaptation of Lawrence Durrell's *The Alexandria Quartet*. He says of this unrealized project:

"It became necessary for me to withdraw from *Justine*, and I consider that the greatest disappointment of my career. The fact that it was preceded by, and resulted from, the most humiliating experience of my career didn't help much, either. I was ecstatic about the film possibilities of the *Quartet*; within them lay the most difficult, but potentially the most gratifying, challenge I had ever faced as a writer-director. I had been working on it for many months (there are still, in my files, a couple of hundred pages of screenplay Fox never even requested to see) when I was urgently approached by Spyros Skouras and my (then) agent Charles Feldman. Would I suspend my work on *Justine* to take over a very expensive, very sick movie Fox had just closed down in London? Mark you, they didn't hold a gun to my head—there was a very large amount of money involved—it was, on my part, knowingly an act of whoredom—I was handsomely paid. And, in the end, in turn, I paid. Most unhandsomely indeed.

"You see, I had solved the two major problems of incorporating all four volumes of the *Quartet* into one viable film-structure. (All four were, after all, essential components of Durrell's single entity. Not one was expendable. It was either all—or nothing. I haven't seen the film that eventuated, called *Justine*, but apparently, based upon what I've heard about it, they settled for nothing.) The problems were those of the two continua: the time continuum and that of narrative content. I had written an exhaustive, detailed screenplay-treatment. Just as with *All About Eve* and my other screenplays, this was the most difficult and time-consuming aspect of the entire project. Except that *Eve* and the others were as the New York *Daily News* crossword compared to Ximenes of the *London Observer*. Talk about 'mosaic' structuring; this was my answer to Daedauls and that simple little labyrinth he whipped up for the Minotaur.

"My screenplay-treatment was ridiculously long, I was well aware of that, but footage had not been my chief concern while structuring the film. Editing the treatment to a realistic length would not be easy, but certainly feasible; as a matter of fact, I was progressing nicely toward that end while writing my aborted first-draft screenplay. The treatment, how-ever, did have one peculiarity that was probably considered outrageous: the content of it would be unintelligible to anyone who had not read all four volumes of *The Alexandria Quartet*. I placed a warning to that effect on its title page. This, of course, decimated the potential readership on the Twentieth Century-Fox lot. At first-hand, I know of only one who did read it: young Richard Zanuck. He was most enthusiastic and, up to the bitter end (and I do mean bitter), encouraging and anxious for me to complete the project. I shall always wish him well.

"The other reader of my *Justine* screenplay treatment that I know about was Lawrence Durrell. I sat opposite him in a hotel room in Paris, keeping him from food and drink and even the toilet, until he had read it from start to finish. Larry expressed his delight; he was most congratulatory. I suppose, eventually, I shall have to make do with that much; not, after all, inconsiderable praise. But I do wish it had all been otherwise—and that I'd been able to finish *Justine*. I cannot help feeling that if ever I were to summon up enough talent to make a definitive film about anything, this would have been it—for me, at any rate—about a woman."

(The "humiliating experience" Mankiewicz refers to was, of course, *Cleopatra*, particularly its aftermath. This is the one film in his lengthy career which he steadfastly refuses even to refer to by name. Mankiewicz had conceived of *Cleopatra*, and wanted it so released, as two separate films, to play simultaneously in separate theatres, each to run about two hours and twenty minutes. The studio management refused even to consider this concept, and emasculated the footage—in particu-lar, according to Mankiewicz, the performance of Richard Burton—into one film, lasting a little over four hours. It has since been hacked into varying shorter lengths. Almost, according to Mankiewicz, "to suit the whim of each individual theatre manager or projectionist. There's a good chance that it may wind up as a handful of the world's most expensive and beautifully photographed banjo picks." At any rate, during the result- ant brouhaha Mankiewicz was fired by the new management of Fox— and removed from any further connection with *Justine*.)

   Mankiewicz is something of a rarity in American film in that for the most part he has written his screenplays in addition to directing them—a duality of responsibility that was rare in the assembly-line pro- duction methods of Hollywood. Long before he had the opportunity of putting the theory into practice (as far back as his MGM days, when he pleaded with L. B. Mayer for the chance to direct his screenplays), Mankiewicz was convinced that directing and writing for the screen were far from mutually exclusive:
   "You know, one of the many frustrations which will increasingly confound our film historians will be a baffling inability not only to identify new techniques and concepts, but even to establish accurately when those presently employed were innovated—and by whom. The concept of *film auteur*, for example, presently the subject of so much intra-critical haggling (as if over the custody of an only child)—and which some believe to have been sired, in the late 50s, by the critical pantheon of the *Cahiers du Cinema*. Not so.
   "Not even close. In 1946 Jean Benoit-Levy (*La Maternelle, Ballerina, et al.*) devoted much of his book, *The Art of the Motion Picture*, to a discussion of the nature, functions, and responsibilities of the *film auteur*—supplying, even, a rather ingenious chart which demonstrated his relationship to other components of the film-making process. Benoit-Levy used the epithet, *film auteur*, quite casually, as if it were common usage to describe a film maker so; certainly not as if it were a newly designated status, or one which he was originating. The following May (1947) I reviewed the book in a critical essay for *The Screen Writer* (a damn good film monthly published, at the time, by the Writers Guild of America). As the title of my essay I used its theme: '*Film Author! Film Author!*' Let me 'put into the record,' as presidents and lawyers say, a couple of paragraphs of what I wrote

twenty-five years ago—presenting a point of view I consider equally valid today:

"I wrote then: 'An examination of the aforementioned chart (Benoit-Levy's, mentioned above) would indicate that an American equivalent of the *film author* would be our writer-director. That is, the *film author* works in immediate contact with a producer and his business organization; the original work from which he develops his script; his creative and technical associates, such as cameraman, set designer, cutter, composer, production staff, et al. However—and here is the very essence of his role in film making—the contribution of the *film author* is an uninterrupted process which begins with the development of the screenplay, and ends with the final editing of the film.'

"Next paragraph: 'Writing and directing moving pictures, then, are—and should be—the two components of that hyphenated entity, the *film author*. Put it as you will—that the direction of a screen play is the second half of the writer's work, or that the writing of a screen play is the first half of the director's work. The inescapable fact is that a *properly written screen play has in effect already been directed*—in his script, by the trained screen writer who has translated the visual and verbal concept of his film into descriptive movement, sound and spoken word. Thus the size of the image, its duration of the cut, the tempo of movement and speech, the nuances of interpretation, the need and nature of musical punctuation—in short, *the film* must unfold before the screen writer's eyes and in his mind as he writes. It seems to me to follow in natural creative sequence, then, for that same mind to direct the process by which this translation of his visual and verbal concept is realized upon the screen.' End of my quoting me, as of 1947.

"It shouldn't be stated that simplistically, of course. Especially against the background of commercial film-making in Hollywood when it was still getting away with the pretense of being an 'industry.' Would it interest you to know that the vast majority of American films turned out in the thirties and forties were shot by directors who were handed their scripts anywhere from two to ten days before the starting date? Scripts already cast from the studio stock company—and to be shot in standing sets? (Sets which were never 'struck,' simply re-dressed, then used over and over.) That, in most instances, the director never even met the writer or writers? That the writer or writers, halfway through other assignments by now, probably at other studios, rarely knew to what extent—if any—the director understood, or agreed, with the concept they had so painstakingly committed to paper? I remember writing in my foreword to the original hardbound edition of *All About Eve* [Random House, 1951]: 'Inasmuch as his filmscript may be on the stage many months after he has written it, and inasmuch as he may be not only mentally but geographically remote from it, the writer's voluminous technical exhortations act sometimes within his filmscript as a sort of last testament—as a plea, by remote control, for a voice in what goes on the screen, and how it gets there.'

"I think it's important that I define, getting back to my concept of *film author*, what I meant by screenwriter. I did *not* mean just any member in good standing of the Writers Guild. Nor, by screenwriting, did I mean only the particular talent to fit the proper word to the dramatic point, mood, or emotion. I cannot think of a topflight director—from Griffith through Lubitsch up to and including Fellini—who was not also, in a very true sense, a topflight screenwriter. That they by themselves could not actually commit the words to paper was, and is, relatively unimportant. What is important is that the shooting script must faithfully represent the one concept of whatever individual talent guides and controls the making of the film. True, the professional writers with whom they would work in close collaboration throughout the building of the script undoubtedly contributed a great deal of their own—but always within the concept of the dominative creator. Similarly, the professional cinematographer and other creative talents would thereafter also contribute much of their own—this time, to the second half of the *film author*'s work.

"Still, there are always those craftsmen, varying in both talent and basic approach to film-making, writer or director, who—for reasons of personal temperament or simple disinterest—remain seemingly content to perform only their designated half of the *film author*'s function. There are good writers who are satisfied with the contributive participation I've just described. Also hack writers who 'knock out' the screenplays, hack directors who carry out the directing. These two categories make most of the movies 'turned out' in the world. That dichotomy works, perhaps, for television. Television, after all, demands nothing

more than precisely timed driblets of distraction between advertisements.
Film can't survive such dichotomy. A screenplay just might happen to
be good. If it is, then implicitly a pattern of direction, a condition of
having-already-been-directed is one of its major assets. For a director
simply to 'shoot the script' is, in effect, to superimpose a second direction upon an already existent one. That's obviously destructive. Writing
film and directing film are not, and should not be, separate and mutually exclusive functions."

There is no such superimposition in the direction of the script of *All
About Eve*. While the shooting script is not a blueprint of camera move-
ments nor detailed editing instructions for the cutting room ("The
privilege of directing my own scripts," Mankiewicz has written, "has
enabled me to use far less technical terminology than is usual."), it is
most explicit as to directorial business and ambience, all of which are
realized in the completed film. After I had seen the film for the
umpteenth time, I mentioned several bits that I hadn't remembered
from a recent reading of the screenplay. Mankiewicz answered:

"I think you'll find those in the script. Certainly, many details and
nuances of characterization emerge from discussion and rehearsal with
talented actors. But by and large, major deviations are rarely improve-
ments when arrived at under pressure, off-the-cuff. One of the many
advantages of being able to write your own shooting script is the happy
fact that it provides not only an opportunity to work out interpretative
problems leisurely and away from that pressure of being on the stage,
under the gun—but also the luxury of committing most of the solu-
tions to paper, within the script itself."

I double-checked Mankiewicz's screenplay to see whether the bits I
hadn't remembered were there or not. *Mea culpa.*

III

After finishing the script, Mankiewicz began his "assignment as director"
at the beginning of April 1950. His first concern was the pre-production
planning of the film: conferences concerning costumes, sets, final
casting, budgeting, and the preparation of a shooting schedule. *All About
Eve* was given a forty-day shooting period; as soon as actual production
began, this was to prove unrealistically optimistic. Though it finished

over schedule, the film was still made in an astonishingly short length of time. Mankiewicz's first rough cut was delivered on June 24 (the date on which his 'assignment as director" terminated). According to Fox records, the film cost $1,400,000 ($500,000 of which went to cover cast salaries); this sounds exceedingly modest in the light of today's production costs, but at that time, was by no means inexpensive.

All About Eve may seem tame today, but in 1950 much of its dialogue and some of its situations for the time were very daring indeed. At that time it was obligatory to have scripts approved by the production code office. Like most companies, Twentieth Century-Fox employed their own experts to forewarn them of any trouble areas that might develop when the script was submitted. In a memo dated April 5, Colonel Jason Joy, Fox's liaison officer to Joseph Breen, who was chief administrator of the production code, warned Darryl F. Zanuck of the problems that might lie ahead. Among them were the following, gleaned from Col. Joy's memorandum to both Zanuck and Mankiewicz:

1. Re Margo's speech in the first dressing room scene, "Ah don' understand about all these plays about sex-stahved Suth'n women—sex is one thing we was nevah stahved for in the South!" Col. Joy felt that it might be expedient to change "sex-stahved" to "love-stahved." Mankiewicz, answering this memo on April 6, stoically agreed to this change.

2. Re Margo's comment later on in the same scene, "You know, I can remember plays about women—even from the South—where it never even occurred to them whether they wanted to marry their fathers more than their brothers," Colonel Joy thought a happier turn of phrase might be "whether they had a fixation for their fathers or their brothers." Mankiewicz answered, "I do not like Jason's substitution of 'fixation' for 'marry' in Margo's teasing line about Lloyd's plays. I cannot imagine even censors objecting to the line as it is now written—delivered in a light, ribbing tone. The proper word, in any case, would be 'screw.'"

3. Re a stage direction which asks Birdie to run the water in Margo's bathroom, Col. Joy remarks enigmatically, "The bathroom, will, of course, be all right." Mankiewicz enlightens us to the meaning of this delicate reference by commenting, "By my Oscars, I promise to show no indication of a toilet. Has it ever occurred to Joe Breen that the rest of the world must be convinced by now that Americans never relieve themselves?"

4. Re Birdie's line, "Everything but the bloodhounds snappin' at her rear end," Joy remarks encouragingly, "Insomuch as Birdie's line is at the end of the shot, perhaps you can let it go the way it is and clip off 'rear end' if we have to, although I don't think we will." Mankiewicz is obviously beginning to lose his temper: "The word *should* be 'arse.' What do you suggest we substitute for 'rear end?' 'Backside?' 'Butt?' What would you think of 'snappin' at her transmission?' "

5. Re the line "Meet me in the ladies' room," Col. Joy wondered, "If you think that changing 'ladies' room' to 'powder room' would not hurt the following speech of Bill Sampson (referring to Eve, he says, 'I understand she is now the understudy in there.'), I think you would like to do it." Mankiewicz, however, didn't like: "Changing 'ladies' room' to 'powder room' is not only childish but will most certainly hurt Bill's comment. 'Understudy' refers to ladies and not to 'powder.'"

There was, however, a positive side even to Hollywood's abject capitulation to any and all censorship demands. Says Mankiewicz:

"The bluenosed restrictions of the time were not just crackbrained (for many years I treasured a memorandum, issued in all seriousness by the Will Hays Office, banning the udders from the cows in the Mickey Mouse cartoons); they were iniquitous, of course, and suppressive. Still, there they were. And you worked according to them—or you didn't work. Those same 'industry' leaders who had been quick to remove Jewish names from the credits of movies they kept selling Nazi Germany until Hitler threw them out, were not about to do battle with the censorship boards and Catholic Church here at home.

"The challenge facing the creative craftsman was to come up with ways in which he could 'intimate' 'suggestions' of 'implications' of 'allusions' to subject matter and/or human behavior he was forbidden either to describe or to show. For both the screenwriter and director, this put a premium on, above all, ingenuity. Thus the techniques of 'indirection,' the nuances within both dialogue and performance, obliqueness of narrative structure and intent flourished during those years of Procrustean censorship, in my opinion, as never before or since in the American film. Lubitsch, for example, could induce more enjoyable and provocative sexual excitement by his direction of a fully dressed young woman deciding whether or not to open a bedroom door—than any one of, or combination of, the most explicit hand-held full-screen close-ups of intertwined genitals presently before the public eye."

Mankiewicz's greatest problems during the pre-production period were caused by casting. Darryl F. Zanuck, head of the Twentieth Century-Fox Studio at the time, had decided personally to produce *All About Eve* after reading Mankiewicz's first-draft screenplay. His first choices for the roles of Margo, Eve, and Addison DeWitt were: Marlene Dietrich, Jeanne Crain, and José Ferrer. Mankiewicz objected strenuously to two of those choices. He remembers, "I was, and am, a great admirer of Marlene. But from what I knew of her work and equipment as an actress, I simply could not visualize—or 'hear'—her as a possible Margo." Claudette Colbert was Mankiewicz's first choice for the role and she was signed for it in February 1950.

Jeanne Crain was a favorite of Zanuck and the exhibitors of the period. Mankiewicz, however, had not been happy with her performance in A *Letter to Three Wives*. (He was to use her again, his objections overruled, in *People Will Talk*.) "It was probably my falut," he emphasizes, "but I could only rarely escape the feeling that Jeanne was, somehow, a visitor to the set. She worked hard. Too hard at times, I think, in response to my demands, as if trying to compensate by sheet exertion for what I believe must have been an absence of emotional involvement with acting. I wouldn't think she took the role home with her at night; she would assume it, rather, every morning with her wardrobe change for the day. I remember Jeanne Crain as a very pleasant, very shy, and very devout young woman, mother, and wife whose husband was doing very well in some business. She was one of the few whose presence among the theatre-folk I have never fully understood."

Zanuck yielded this time to his plea that he could not elicit from Jeanne Crain the degree of "bitch virtuosity" needed for the proper playing of Eve—and approved Mankiewicz's suggestion of Anne Baxter, also under contract to the studio at the time. Celeste Holm, still another contract player, was approved for Karen, a part for which the actress was ideally suited. Mankiewicz does not now remember how José Ferrer was replaced in the role of Addison by George Sanders.

There had never been any doubt as to the casting of Birdie Coonan, Margo's dresser/companion (and another of Mankiewicz's *alter ego* commentators). "Birdie was written for only Thelma Ritter," Mankiewicz confirms. "I adored her. Thelma was that rare performing talent which the writer and/or director must treasure as a fiddler would a Stradivarius. Prior to *A Letter to Three Wives* she had appeared on the screen only in a 'bit'—a memorable 'bit,' to be sure—for George Seaton in *Miracle on 34th Street*. I shall always be proud of my share in creating her image for the film audience—and in providing that audience for her. Thelma Ritter was one of the last of, by now, an almost extinct species in our theatrical ecology: the great character comedienne."

Shortly before the picture was to begin production, Claudette Colbert had an accident in which she severely wrenched her back and as a result was forced to withdraw from the film. The hurried search began for another leading lady. Mankiewicz's second choice had always been Gertrude Lawrence. She had read his screenplay treatment and liked it enormously.

"However," says Mankiewicz, "'submitting the actual screenplay to her suddenly became a highly complicated procedure. To this day, I don't know whether Gertie ever did read it; I'm quite sure that if she had, she would have crawled to California to play it. Somehow, a protocol of approach to Miss Lawrence had come into being. All scripts were first to be submitted to, and approved by, her lawyer, the re-doubtable Fanny Holtzman (celebrated for having represented the Yussoupov family in its eminently successful libel suit against MGM over *Rasputin and the Empress*). Miss (Mrs.?) Holtzman read the screenplay and called me at home to say she found it very good. There were only two changes she would insist upon: 1) The drunk scenes would have to be eliminated. It would be preferable, in fact, if Miss Lawrence neither drank nor smoked at all on the screen. 2) During the party sequence, the pianist was not to play 'Liebestraum.' Instead, he would accompany Miss Lawrence as she sang a torch song about Bill. (Something I thought Helen Morgan had already done, rather successfully.) Since my own lawyer had always admonished me to respond to other lawyers with either 'yes' or 'no' and urged me to 'keep the witty ripostes for when you're shaving'—I said nothing but 'no'. And that's how Gertrude Lawrence did not play Margo Channing."

There was one very good reason why Bette Davis had never been offered the part: throughout that period she was filming *Payment on Demand* and was therefore considered hopelessly unavailable. But now that Miss Colbert's illness had delayed the start of *Eve*, Darryl Zanuck submitted the script to Miss Davis on the off chance that the two schedules might fit. *Payment* actually finished shooting no more than two weeks prior to the new "must" starting date of *All About Eve*. Miss Davis read the screenplay, liked it so much that she agreed to forgo any vacation between films, and launched forthwith into wardrobe tests.

The casting of Davis had a memorable effect on the film. It also raised, and still raises, the question of whether Mankiewicz had, as has often been maintained, Tallulah Bankhead in mind when he created Margo—or whether the similarity emerged only from Bette Davis's performance of the role. Mankiewicz smiled when I put the question to him:

"I've always told the truth about that, and nobody has ever quite believed me. I remember being asked the same question, by somebody in the audience, at the time I received the New York Film Critics Award for directing. I answered truthfully then, too. I said that I was happy to have the opportunity of revealing, at long last, who the archetype for Margo Channing had been. That it had been none other than Peg Woffington.[7] Late, very late, of Old Drury Lane . . .

"Peg Woffington. I think I've read everything written about her, fact and gossip. Woffington was/is Margo Channing. From her talent and triumphs on stage to her personal and private torments off. She was also Bette Davis. Also Mrs. Bellamy, Maggie Smith and Isabella Andreini, Mrs. Siddons and Joan Crawford, Modjeska, both Molière's wife and his mistress, Jessica Tandy, Laurette Taylor and Rachel, Zoe Caldwell, Sybil Thorndike and, yes, Tallulah. Every woman for whom acting was identical with existence. Glorious broads, all of them, baffling and sad and exciting, and they've made living in this world a richer experience ever since (in Italy, of all places) they first liberated

---

7. Peg Woffington was one of the great actresses and beauties of the eighteenth-century English theatre. Offstage, she was notorious for her amours (a particularly tempestuous one with David Garrick); on stage, for her brilliant performance and feuds with her arch-rival, Mrs. Bellamy.

woman's right to play a woman. Don't hold me to that list; I've left out hundreds. Woffington, to me, was their prototype, all of them. And all of them in part are Margo Channing, I hope. Performing women. I won't stop being fascinated and terrified by them; I won't stop thinking and learning and writing about them until I die."

According to Mankiewicz, it never occurred to either Bette Davis or him that there was any particular "Bankhead quality" about Margo. The surface resemblances came about through happenstance. On the night before Davis arrived on the set in San Francisco, "in the course of a pointed discussion about domestic problems," she had burst a tiny blood vessel in her throat. Throat specialists were consulted and they advised that the actress could work without danger to her health. But the accident had provided an added huskiness to her voice, which recorded surprisingly like Bankhead's very individual bourbon contralto. And as Mankiewicz warned Miss Davis: once she spoke the first words in her new register, the die was cast. She would have to maintain it throughout the film. And so she did. As for the shoulder-length mop of hair, Mankiewicz remembers that it was simply an expedient choice: Miss Davis had worn it before; it was attractive and "Margo-like," easy to keep in place without undue fuss.

Mankiewicz recalls that some time after the film was released, he was approached by a mutual friend of his and Claudette Colbert's who asked the director, "What the hell made you ever think that Claudette could have played Margo Channing?" I interrupted to say that I thought a lot of people wondered the same thing. Mankiewicz's reply:

"When *All About Eve* was released there was quite a hullabaloo concerning it as a *film à clef* about Tallulah Bankhead. Tallulah, understandably enough, did little to dispel the assumption; on the contrary, she exploited it to the hilt with great skill and gusto. (Even to the extent of asserting that I had visited the set of *A Royal Scandal*, back in 1945, to study her mannerisms. I visited the set, true. But I was studying Lubitsch, not Bankhead.) At any rate, what with all the public brouhaha, Tallulah's star re-achieved a certain amount of ascendancy. She wound up with a popular ninety-minute radio program called *The Big Show*, of which the basic joke was an imaginary Davis–Bankhead feud. (Imaginary show biz 'feuds,' à la Jack Benny–Fred Allen, were in vogue at the time.) No, she

did all right for herself, did Talloo. The performance of Bette Davis provided Miss Bankhead with quite a run.

"And therein lay my answer to Claudette's and my friend—and to
you: 'If Claudette had played Margo Channing,' I told him, 'either Ina
Claire or Lynn Fontanne, if so inclined, might well have had a ninety-
minute radio program.' I'm not sure he understood my analogy—he
was a 'private person'—but it should be perfectly clear to anyone who
has ever written, acted, or directed professionally. Both Bette and
Claudette are greatly talented and resourceful actresses, equally profi-
cient in the art of utilizing their superb equipment—yet not at all alike,
necessarily, in either the nature of that equipment or their approach to
the same role.

"Of course Claudette could have played the part. Beautifully. If she
had, Margo would simply have emerged on a different plateau of performance. Possibly no more effective, but certainly no less. The same
dramatic points would have been made; their sum total the same. The
difference would lie in the orchestration, if you will—the utilization, as
I've said, of different equipment, different instrumentation, different
emotional components within each actress. One would use ice instead
of heat; the foil could replace the karate chop; an increasingly bitchy,
ever more piss-elegant drunk would equate with the boozy slugger-from-
the-toe; unhappiness is no whit happier if examined from the intellect
rather than the gut—and here I go, belaboring the obvious again. In just
one season we've had three very exciting, very different Hedda Gablers
(Maggie Smith, Claire Bloom, Irene Worth) with one thing in common—*Hedda Gabler*. There is no one way to play a properly written role,
any more than there is only one actress for that role. Otherwise, the art
of interpretation would require little talent indeed—and the director's
contribution would be minimal. Traffic cops would suffice."

For the minor role of Miss Caswell, Mankiewicz's choice was Marilyn
Monroe. She had previously been under contract to Fox for two or three
years, as a member of the studio "stock company." (As Mankiewicz
describes the services she was required to perform, they had little to do
with acting. "For the most part she auditioned a great deal, late afternoons, in executive offices. She also functioned agreeably as a compan-
ion for corporative elder statesmen visiting from the east, and on
hostess committees for sales conventions. Occasionally, she was

squeezed into old Betty Grable costumes and used as a dress extra or for unimportant bits in some films.") Marilyn Monroe was dropped by Fox, as a contract player, about two years before the casting of *All About Eve* took place. Some of what Mankiewicz had to relate about her return to the studio:

"One of the most irritating aspects of the vast amount of crap that has been thrown up into print about Marilyn, apart from its sickening mawkishness, is its inaccuracy. Particularly as it relates to her second start at Fox, and her subsequent trip to the Hollywood moon. Let me testify at once that while I was instrumental in getting her the part of Miss Caswell, I did not make a star of Marilyn Monroe. No individual, to the best of my pretty extensive knowledge, ever made a star. That is a power and privilege restricted only to the unfathomable, improbable, and altogether unworthy authority known as the Mass Audience. The so-called Hollywood 'Star-Makers' have invariably been crap-shooters with other men's money; to mix my metaphors, after betting every horse in the race they would hold up only the winning ticket. Louis B. Mayer, for one, did exactly that.

"To get back to Marilyn and *Eve* and Fox. Let me state one fact quite simply: the only person importantly associated with *All About Eve* with no supportable claim whatsoever to having brought her back to Twentieth Century-Fox (except, of course, his ultimate reluctant approval, which was legally necessary) was Darryl F. Zanuck. Upon my proposal of her name his opposition was instantaneous, vehement and—based upon her earlier 'career' at the studio—possibly justifiable. Nor, I must add, was my championship of her equally vehement and adamant. True, I thought she'd be good for the role. I'd interviewed some eight or ten young actresses for the part, all of them of equal physical endowment and professional prowess—I believe Sheree North was one—and I felt Marilyn had the edge. There was a breathlessness and sort of glued-on innocence about her that I found appealing—and she had done a good job for John Huston in *The Asphalt Jungle*. Still, I wasn't about to tear up my contract and stomp out if she didn't get the part.

"As it turned out, I didn't have to. Standing my ground was made easier for me because my endorsement of Marilyn was merely support-ive to the major force that desperately wanted her in my film. That major force was a very important agent named Johnny Hyde—at the time certainly no less than the #2 or #3 power at William Morris. Like most great agents, he was a tiny man. (There's a book there, too; or maybe just a minor address at some psychoanalytic congress.) Johnny Hyde was also a very honest and a very gentle man. He was also deeply in love with Marilyn. And more than anyone in her life, I think, provided for her something akin to an honest *ego* of her own; he respected her. Permitting her, in turn, to acquire a certain amount of self-respect. After Johnny died—suddenly, not too long afterwards—it has always seemed to me that Marilyn, despite all of the intellectual and cultural and personality flurries, gave up on herself. The biographers of Monroe, when they mention him at all, are seemingly overinfluenced by the unhappy fact that he never hit a ball out of Yankee Stadium, never even wrote a play.

"It was Johnny Hyde who brought Marilyn to me for Miss Caswell. It had been six months or more since *Asphalt Jungle*; he knew the importance of momentum to any career. He knew especially the importance to Marilyn, for herself, to work in an important film. He haunted my office. And once I'd said 'yes'—more than anyone, it was Johnny Hyde who fought the good fight to break down the considerable resistance to her return to Twentieth Century-Fox. On March 27, 1950, Marilyn Monroe was signed for five hundred dollars a week—on a one-week guarantee. I imagine there was appended to it the usual very long-term contract, at the option of the studio. It was an enormously profitable one for Fox, and lasted until she took her life."

When Mankiewicz speaks about Marilyn Monroe, there is tenderness and a protective quality in his voice: "There is one particular remembrance I have of Marilyn which I think tells a great deal about her at the time. One day on the set—we were shooting the party sequence—she walked by me, carrying a thin book. Had she been carrying a thin snake, I would have thought nothing of it. But a book. I called her over and asked what she was reading. She didn't say; she just handed it to me. It was Rainer Maria Rilke's *Letters to a Young Poet*. I'd have been less taken aback to come upon Herr Rilke studying a Marilyn Monroe nude calendar.

"I asked Marilyn if she knew who he was. She shook her head. 'No. Who is he?' I told her that Rilke had been a German poet, that he was dead, that I myself had read less of him and knew less about him than I should—and asked her how the hell she came to be reading him at all, much less that particular work of his. Had somebody recommended it to her? Again, a shake of her head: 'No. Nobody. You see, in my whole life I haven't read hardly anything at all. I don't know how to catch up. I don't know where to begin. So what I do is, every now and then I go into the Pickwick (a bookshop on Hollywood Boulevard, one of the very few in the entire City of the Angels which exists independent of being a required adjunct to an institution of learning) and just look around. I leaf through some books, and when I read something that interests me—I buy the book. So last night I bought this one. Is that wrong?' No, I told her, that was far from wrong. That, in fact, it was the best possible way for anyone to choose what to read. She was not accustomed to being told she was doing anything right. She smiled proudly and moved on. The next day Marilyn sent me a copy of *Letters to a Young Poet*. I have yet to read it.

"I thought of her, then, as the loneliest person I had ever known. Throughout our location period in San Francisco, perhaps two or three weeks, Marilyn would be spotted at one restaurant or another dining alone. Or drinking alone. We'd always ask her to join us, and she would, and seemed pleased, but somehow she never understood or accepted our unspoken assumption that she was one of us. She remained alone. She was not a loner. She was just plain *alone*."

IV

Production began at the Curran Theatre in San Francisco on April 15, 1950. It soon became evident that the time allotted for the sequences to be shot in the theatre had been over-optimistically estimated; Mankiewicz fell behind schedule. The usual "catch-up" harassment from the studio production office ensued.

"Nothing more accurately reflects the assembly-line approach to moviemaking which then prevailed," says Mankiewicz, "than the process by which shooting schedules were arrived at. And which still prevails, in general. A film script, to a studio production office, is a mathematical something. It consists of a specific number of pages which are to be committed to film in a specified number of days. The daily production reports, handed in every evening by the script girl, never refer to the difficulty or sensitivity of the day's work; she is required to stick to the factory facts, ma'am. How many pages has the director knocked off; how much estimated (her estimate) assembled film time has been completed. The former determines the amount of pressure to be put on the director to catch up. The latter (estimated film time), if running long, will usually lead to suggested—and sometimes enforced—eliminations from the script. (John Ford was once being harangued, while shooting, by a Fox production manager—one of the Wurtzels, probably. It seems that Jack was three or four days behind—and did he really need such-and-such a sequence—and how was he gonna catch up—and Mr. Zanuck was personally getting upset—and so forth. Jack just sat behind his dark glasses and listened, sucking at his pipe. Finally he reached for the script, yanked out a random handful of pages, and tossed them at the Wurtzel. 'I am now back on schedule,' said Jack. 'Get the hell off my set.')

"Directors, at the time, were rated—and the ratings confidentially interchanged by studio production departments—as 'fast' or 'slow,' based upon their past performances. One would be 'good for five or six pages a day'; another, 'two and a half, if you're lucky.' Woody (W. S.) Van Dyke was MGM's pride and joy; no matter what the schedule, he'd invariably wind up a week under. A lot of it couldn't be cut together, or wouldn't match, or Joan Crawford's right eye would be offscreen—and just as invariably, there'd be a week of retakes for every week he'd finished ahead. He shot *San Francisco* in forty-six days, and there were fifty-four days of retakes.

"Lloyd Bacon was another favorite of the production offices. If Lloyd had his camera set up in the corner of a living room, say, he'd shoot everything that could conceivably be played in that corner throughout the entire script—in that same set-up. First, everything that called for day lighting; then everything lit for night. He figured it was quicker to change wardrobe than camera set-ups. He demanded very little from his actors; as soon as he'd yelled 'Cut!' he'd turn to his script girl and ask 'Did they get the titles right?' If she answered in the affirmative, he'd say 'Print it. What else happens here?' Lloyd Bacon never referred to dialogue as anything other than 'titles.'

"They were the golden boys of the major studios. Variants of Woody and Lloyd constitued a majority of the directors under term contract;

they made most of the films of the thirties and forties. No, the enormous amount of retakes didn't bother the studio bosses. You see, there were no overhead charges applied to retakes. Which made for cheaper overall production cost. Which is just what the fake cockamaimy 'industry' wanted: 'product' short enough to be run seven or eight times a day, 'turned out' as inexpensively as possible and fed, at the rate of one a week or better, to the *real* Minotaur of the American film (*and* the British, *and* the Italian, *and* the French, and so forth), the retail 'outlet.' The exhibitor.

"The exhibitor—the movie-theatre owner—has always pocketed the lion's share of what the public pays to see a film. Regularly, in *Variety*— that highly inaccurate 'bible of show biz'—you will read figures purporting to be the box-office 'grosses' of films. The work 'gross' is a deliberate (not *Variety*'s, but they go along with it) misdefinition. *Nobody* except the exhibitor has ever had a share of the box-office gross of any film ever made. Quite a statement? I'll compound the heresy. I'll wager that nobody has ever *known* the box-office gross of any film ever made. How much has, let's say, *Gone with the Wind* been reputed to have 'grossed'? Seventy or eighty million dollars, roughtly? That figure, or whatever the stipulated figure is, represents about one-third of what the public paid at the box office to see the film. The other two-thirds has stuck to the sticky fingers of the real-estate operators who owned the theatres attached to those box offices—and who call themselves 'showmen.' The approximate one-third is what they've reluctantly passed on to the distributors of the film. That one-third is blithely called the 'gross.' But it is not a gross. It is very much a 'net.'

"How the distributor in turn then lops off a basic 30–50 percent of that so-called 'gross,' which is really a net—in addition to a variety of charges, interests, fees, and other larcenies which would embarrass Ebenezer Scrooge—before he, yelping with pain, hands over a reluctant buck to the actual film maker—that's a whole different book.

"Still not clear? Let's assume that you have never produced a play on Broadway. That your grandmother has never written a play—and your grandfather has never starred in one. But suddenly your grandmother does write a play. And you decide to produce it, starring your grandfather. You've raised the money. You don't want to put it on in a cellar; for some reason you want a Broadway theatre. So you go to the

Shuberts; you've heard they control a lot of them. Now let's say the Shuberts read your grandmother's play and think it stinks. They've never heard of you as a producer—and are not impressed by the box-office appeal of your grandfather. Still, you have got the money—and they have an empty theatre or two. Remember, you're dealing with the Shuberts—reputedly, the toughest of the tough. They lay it on the line. You can have a theatre, they say—but on their most stringent terms. Take it or leave it. Of what the public pays at the box office to see your play—the only honest definition of gross—they get 35 percent and you get 65 percent. You gulp—and take it. That worst deal the Shuberts can hand out is better than the best any film exhibitor is prepared to offer for nine-tenths of the movies he runs through his out-of-focus projection machines. And don't forget, the Shubert theatres—a lot of them—are dark for many months in the year. Yet it is written—on some Tablet, on some Mount—that the projection machines of America, for twelve hours (or more) a day and for seven days of the week, must never stop running.

"Remember the great Hollywood labor scandals of the mid-forties? Willie Bioff and George Browne? The total capitulation of the studio heads, their frantic payoffs, anything to avoid that threatened strike? It wasn't the carpenters or electricians the moguls wanted to keep from striking. Disconcerting as it is to contemplate, they plus the Screen Actors Guild plus the Writers Guild of America plus the Directors Guild of America could walk out together, arm in arm—and the 'product' would still 'somehow' be fabricated. No, there is only one union—and one union alone—of which the 'film industry' lives in terror. If the Projectionists of America were to strike—if the Projection Machines of America were to stop for so much as a week or a month—that monolithic 'industry'-exhibitor superstructure which has controlled and stifled the American film for as long as I can remember, would collapse like a stabbed soufflé.

"Odd, isn't it? Of all the troubled unions that come to mind, and considering the widespread dissatisfaction and unrest within labor ranks generally—the projectionists, to my knowledge, have never struck. It's good to know they're being kept happy in their work. There's no boss like a terrified boss.

"Anyhow. Where was I—with *Eve*? In San Francisco, two or three days behind schedule after a couple of weeks of shooting. The memos

and calls from the studio were getting less and less understanding—
and more and more pointed about what the hell was I up to. You must
understand also about studio production offices, their unshakable conviction that whenever a director left the actual studio confines with his
company—it became his avowed purpose to squander recklessly the
studio's resources.

"Also, my own production office 'rating' was neither 'fast' nor 'slow';
I belonged to a third classification which irritated the shit out of
production managers. The 'can't-figure-him' type of director. This
meant, usually, that the director was either unpredictable in his
shooting methodry or that he was (in their opinion) over-meticulous in
certain aspects of his work. It might be the number of takes, the super-
fluity (in their opinion) of camera angels, a propensity for mid-rehearsal
setup changes, and so on. That type had to be 'handled,' 'pressured,'
whatever his idiosyncrasy. In my case, it was the actor's performance.
That has always been, and remains, the one component of film-making
with which I find myself least able to compromise. In many a production office I've been, and remain, snarlingly categorized as a
'perfectionist.' I'm not. If I were, I'd still be rehearsing the first scene of
the first film I ever made.

"And so, in San Francisco, the pressure was on. Lubitsch once said to
me, concerning the director's general approach to his film, that by and
large he should make it for himself, as a film *he* would buy a ticket to
see—and then pray for millions of people to agree with him. That
seems pretty self-evident. But it wasn't all that easy to accomplish back
then, when the studio–director relationship was too often one of
continual petty harassment. It could result too often in continuing
small compromises which would turn out, in the end, to have been
very damaging, indeed. 'Perfectionist' or not, I've made my share of
them. More than my share.

"A touch of clairvoyance would have come in handy. Thus, when
that memo or phone call came in asking whether you couldn't shoot
the reverse back in the studio—or why must the scene be played so that
the whole auditorium has to be lit—or whatever—you could yell: 'Get
off my back! This film is going to win fourteen Academy Award nominations; five of the actors will be nominated; it will win every frigging
Best of the Year Award from the American and British Academies to the

New York Critics; from Cannes to Japan, Cuba, points East and West—
so shove the three days I'm behind schedule!' But you're never clairvoy-
ant, you don't yell those things—you have no way of knowing,
actually, that the film won't wind up on its ass. So you go right on,
functioning as you always have. You've done your best on the hits;
you've done your best on the flops, too. In the end, the outcome seems
to depend upon a magical intangible that no one has ever been able to
define—much less control. I wouldn't have it any other way. That
intangible is what the theatre is all about."

Throughout the entire shooting period, Mankiewicz must have
succeeded in keeping the behind-the-scene production pressures from
affecting his company of players on the set. As witness the oft-repeated
testimony of all concerned to the effect that the making of the film
was, for each, a memorably gratifying professional experience. Even
though Mankiewicz is noted for his firm hand with so-called 'star
temperament,' it should be pointed out that, in addition to the
inevitable tensions that can arise among important actors playing
essentially competitive roles, three of his leading ladies had already
won Academy Awards[8] and the fourth was an accomplished scene-
stealer whose role had been hand-tailored to her talents.

Actually, according to Mankiewicz, the only moment he experienced
of even apprehension occurred before the filming of *All About Eve*
began. No sooner was it announced in the trade press that Bette Davis
was to play Margo Channing, than Mankiewicz received phone
calls from two or three directors who were his friends and who had
worked with the actress in the past. To a man, they predicted a
Davis–Mankiewicz head-on clash that could end only in disaster. The
director grinned as he recalled the incident:

"I remember most vividly Eddie Goulding's[9] prophecy of doom and
destruction. 'Dear boy,' moaned Eddie. 'Have you gone mad? This

---

8. Bette Davis: 1935 and 1938; Anne Baxter: 1946; Celeste Holm: 1947.
9. Edmund Goulding directed Miss Davis in four films: *That Certain Woman* (1937), *Dark Victory* (1939), *The Old Maid* (1939), and *The Great Lie* (1941). On the last film, it is a Hollywood legend that Miss Davis and her co-star, Mary Astor, rewrote the script daily.

woman will destroy you, she will grind you down to a fine powder and blow you away. You are a writer, dear boy. She will come to the stage with a thick pad of long yellow paper. And pencils. She will write. And then she, not you, will direct. Mark my words.' The others weren't as vehement as Eddie (I assumed they'd merely been scratched whereas he might still have an open wound or two)—but I did mark his words and prepared for the worst. Always a good thing to prepare for, among the-atre-folk.

"Instead of the worst, of course, what eventuated was the very best—another turn of events not uncommon to theatrical experience. Working with Bette was, it goes without saying, from the first day to regrettably our last, an experience as happy and rewarding as any I have ever known. Barring grand opera, I can think of nothing beyond her range. She's intelligent, instinctive, vital, sensitive—and, above all, a superbly equipped professional actress who does her job responsibly and honestly. To this day I regret deeply that I hadn't worked with her before *Eve*—and that I haven't since.

"Still, that first day of shooting, I was marking Eddie Goulding's words. I had my antennae deployed to pick up possible storm warnings. Miss Davis arrived on the set, fully dressed and made up, at least a quarter of an hour before she'd been called. She carried nothing but her copy of my script. A pleasant 'good morning,' and she sat in her chair. I watched for her to 'case' my provisional camera placement and the rough lighting of the set. (Not at all uncommon, then. Norma Shearer knew her 'key' light as Dr. De Bakey knows the human heart. Rex Harrison—jokingly, of course—would occasionally say 'Good morning, old cock' to the lens. 'If you cahn't see the lens, the lens cahn't see you' was his credo.) Bette didn't even glance at the set; she lit a cigarette and opened the script—not, I noticed at once, to the scene we were doing that first morning.

"I called rehearsal. I know I can't generate any suspense in describing the day, so why try? Bette was letter-perfect. She was syllable-perfect. There was no fumbling for my words; they'd become hers—as Margo Channing. The director's dream: the prepared actress. It shouldn't be, really; it's a prerequisite, after all. Unless the actor is prepared, the director cannot truly function—nor, for that matter, can the actor. Acting otherwise becomes simply a struggle to articulate basic content.

Directing becomes a tense concentration on progress, at the expense of performance.

("Let me interpose quickly, here, that Bette's professional attributes were not unique within the *Eve* company. Without exception, the entire cast was no less conscientious. It was a rare treat, believe me, even then—a time when the inarticulate had not yet, as now, replaced the coherent. I suppose over the years I've been luckier than most directors in having had responsible acting talent to work with—but never more fortunate than in *All About Eve*.)

"To return to those first few shooting days. The gloomy predictions of Goulding and the others hung on a bit, like the leftover of a head cold—but it soon became evident that either they had been wrong about Bette Davis or I was working with an imposter. So one afternoon, sitting around between set-ups and without identifying any of the Cassandras by name (although Eddie, I must say, had maintained bravely, 'and you may quote me, dear boy'), I told Bette about the forewarnings I'd received, about my first-day apprehensions. And that where I'd been led to expect Lady Macbeth—in her place had arrived Portia. Was it a rib? A put-on of some kind? Or what? Bette snorted. That inimitable Davis snort. Then she laughed. Her snort and her laugh should both be protected by copyright. I can't quote her reply exactly, of course, but in content it was roughly as follows:

"Said Bette: 'I am neither Lady Macbeth nor Portia; I'll play either at the drop of a hat anywhere. But yes, I suppose my reputation, based upon some experiences I've had, is pretty much as advertised.' (I said something to the effect that I'd certainly seen no sign of it; very much the opposite, in fact. Another snort:) 'Look, you're a writer, you're a director, you function behind the camera. You do not appear upon the screen, forty feet high and thirty feet wide or whatever the proportions are. Me, I'm an actress, and I do appear upon that screen, that big. What I say and do, and how I look, is what millions of people see and listen to. The fact that my performance is the end result of many other contributions as well, matters to them not at all. If I make a horse's ass of myself on that screen, it is I—me—Bette Davis—who is the forty-feet-by-thirty-feet horse's ass as far as they're concerned. Not the writer, not the director, the producer or the studio gateman—nobody but me. I am up there as the representative horse's ass for all concerned.

"'Now you know as well as I' (she went on) 'that there is nothing more important to an actress, nothing she wants more, than a well-written part—and a director who knows what he wants, knows how to ask for it, who can help her provide it. *This* is heaven, for instance.' (She said some nice things about my script, and about how well we worked together.) '*But*, as often as not, the script has been at best a compromise of some sort; the writer's guarantee ran out, or the producer's patience, or just plain time. So, you've turned to the director as the source of salvation; with his help, you think, it'll turn out fine. Or, at least, hold together.

"'Then, one morning, the director drops by your dressing room, casual-like, for a cup of coffee—and in a very strange voice asks what you think of the scene you're about to do that day, and do you really like it. That *does* it, for me. Right now. When you've been through it as often as I have, that does it. Bells and sirens go off inside me. I know at once that *he* doesn't like the scene—that *he* doesn't know what to think about it. Invariably, rehearsal proves me right. The director can't make up his mind whether we're to stand, sit, run, enter, or exit; he hasn't the foggiest notion of what the scene is all about or whether, in fact, it's a scene at all. He may suddenly bawl the hell out of some member of the crew for no reason—just to *do* something. The producer's been sent for—God knows where the writer is by now—and the producer's assistant—maybe an executive or two—and pretty soon there's quite a gathering of overhead on the set, throwing worn-out clichés at each other.

"'By this time, I am back in my stage dressing room. Fully aware—as you would be, as any of the many, many actors who have gone through that time after time would be—that the result of it all, nine times out of ten, will be a botched-up abortive scene which will wind up with me as a thirty-by-forty-foot horse's ass on the silver screen. So. It seems I made up my mind, a long time ago, that if anybody is to make a horse's ass out of me, it's going to be *me*. So, yes, I'm afraid there have been times—and probably will be again—when the responsibility for what I say and do on the screen is one I feel I must meet by myself.'

"I haven't phrased Bette's position nearly as well as she told it to me. I've made it sound too much like just another bit of *Once in a Lifetime* foolery; it wasn't, really. It was a vivid and precise statement of the two sources of support upon which the good actor must rely, and without

which he cannot fully function. First of all, that part. Soundly constructed, and so properly phrased that the actor can absorb the 'alias'
comfortably and confidently. And number two, the director. The leader,
if you will, of the theatrical conspiracy (and I'll defend that as properly
defining either a play or film). The director is not only 'in' on all the
'aliases' (or parts—and there is no word in theatrical terminology which
should be more literally interpreted); he must control their interplay
and interrelation, from the broadest sweep of action to the least percep-
tible nuance of mood; his is the responsibility for the eventual coales-
cence of all the separate parts into the one dramatic whole. So—the
sound script, the equipped actor, the prepared director—the three basic
components of the theatrical conspiracy. Only rarely will it successfully
overcome the weakest of the three.

"There were, of course, actors (make that Stars) who were indulged in
childishly excessive demands that in no way improved the quality of
their work; they served merely to sustain whatever offstage ego-
fantasies they were enjoying at the time. Overelaborate dressing-room
suites, stereo equipment on the set (complete with recordings to accompany their daydreamings, and a retainer—on the company payroll—
who did nothing but change the discs), a stand-by limousine whose
sole function was to take them to the toilet (I'm not kidding), and too
many other infantile indulgences. The major studios started that nonsense, too. (It was, after all, cheaper to give so-and-so a black onyx bidet
than a raise in salary. The bidet stayed on the lot, as inventory. It was
charged to capital improvement, not picture cost.)

"Nor have directors been innocent of such self-indulgent absurdities.
C. B. DeMille *did* have His (with a capital H) 'chair boy'—a staff member who followed Him around, chair in hand, ready to shove it under
His ass at the precise instant He chose to sit. There were directors, too,
who had music especially piped in to accompany their cogitations. At
one time, if you wanted to speak to Joe von Sternberg on his set, you
wrote your name on a huge blackboard set up for that purpose—and
waited for the Imperial Nod. Directors, by the dozen, wear 'uniforms'
which can serve only to establish immediately for the visitor's eye
just which one is the director. They sure as hell don't help him direct.
There's that darling of the *Cahiers du Cinema* who starts—or used
to start—every scene by firing a .45 caliber revolver; there's the

yeller-louder-than-anybody-else type; there's the coat-over-the-shoulders school—one wonders how Fellini manages to get his work done in an ordinary pair of pants, white shirt, jacket, and sometimes even a necktie.

"I have found, though, in my own experience, that zany behavior while at work (and I stress 'at work') can be equated, usually, in inverse ratio to the talent at hand. (Ask a precocious child to spell a word or do a sum she should be able to but can't—i.e., own up to even temporary inadequacy—and watch her act the clown as a reactive cover-up.) Bette Davis's discourse was not applicable to such. Nor to those actors and directors who 'play' big-time actor and who 'play' big-shot director for self-assurances of whatever nature. Bette had reference to the serious artist of indisputable talent, whose demands on the set were in the cause of optimum working conditions, but who was nevertheless bruited about as being 'difficult.' Quite a different cup of tea from the limousine-to-the-toilet brew. I know whereof I speak. I've drunk a-plenty from both cups.

"A word or two might be in order here on behalf of the so-called 'difficult' actor. As a theatrical epithet, it's applied much too readily—and much too often as an easy cop-out for shoddy dramatic material and/or irresolute direction. I've worked, as I say, with many of the most notoriously 'difficult.' Not always without sizable script weaknesses to overcome; nor, as director, have I always been omnisciently ready with that exactly right answer to the problem at hand. But with one Notable Exception—after more than forty years of writing, directing, and producing for and with actors, with some of whom it's been pretty rough going, indeed—there isn't one whose behavior I can honestly describe as having been motivated by any purpose other than giving the best damn performance possible. And with whom, at the end of our engagement, I didn't wind up on the best of terms. 'Engagement.' The word has the connotation of love, an emotion not necessarily involved in the theatrical experience.

"The Notable Exception? No, it was not Marlon Brando. Not even close. But he's a good example of what I mean by the too-easy application of the epithet 'difficult.' I've worked twice with Brando. Each venture was something new for both of us. I'd never directed Shakespeare professionally; Marlon had never played it at all. You may recall the snickering reaction when it was announced that he was to play Mark Antony; to the TV and other comics of the day, that bit of casting was a richer source of material than Spiro Agnew as Vice-President of the United States. We worked hard and long together, just the two of us; he worked his ass off, preparing by himself. After the film was released, the jokes stopped. The British Film Academy (Shakespeare, remember, is all that's left of the Empire) gave Marlon its award for best performance by a foreign actor (Gielgud's Cassius was judged best by an Englishman). We had every right to be happy about our collaboration on *Julius Caesar*, and we were. I can't recall a moment of 'difficulty' from Marlon; there was neither time nor occasion for it, we were both too occupied with working hard at something we wanted to do well.

"The same was true even of *Guys and Dolls*. Here again we were try-ing a dramatic style and form strange to both of us: musical comedy. I had staged an opera for the Met;[10] dubious preparation for a stylized fairy tale set in Damon Runyon's Never-Never Land. Marlon, as far as I knew, had never sung or danced. Actually, he turned down the role of Sky Masterson when Sam Goldwyn first offered it to him. I was in Europe at the time, finishing up *The Barefoot Contessa*; Sam phoned and asked me to intercede. I sent Marlon a cable: UNDERSTAND YOU'RE APPRE-HENSIVE BECAUSE YOU'VE NEVER DONE MUSICAL COMEDY. YOU HAVE NOTHING REPEAT NOTHING TO WORRY ABOUT. BECAUSE NEITHER HAVE I. LOVE, JOE. Marlon promptly signed to do the part.

"Whether or not we succeeded in carrying it off to everybody's satisfaction—the differences of opinion were varied and vehement—is beside the point I'm talking to at the moment. The point being Marlon Brando, the 'difficult' actor. There was no more evidence of it on *Guys and Dolls* than there had been on *Julius Caesar*; we worked together equally hard and well on both films. Directing Marlon was an exciting and rewarding experience at all times; I found him quick, sensitive, and of course enormously talented. Naturally, if I'd ask him

---

10. In 1952 Mankiewicz directed Puccini's La Bohème for the Metropolitan Opera. His original staging, altered according to the whims of changing prima donnas over the years, was eventually billed, at his request, as Mankiewicz's "production of." The most success-ful production of *La Bohème* in the history of the "Met," it was the last regular opera presented when the old "Met" closed on April 16, 1966.

to do or think or feel something contrary to his instincts or intuition, we'd have to work that out. But, hell, that, too, is what directing is about. And acting.

"The Notable Exception, surprisingly enough, wasn't any of the male actors I've directed. Yes, that narrows it down by half. No, it was not Elizabeth Taylor. Talk about bum raps. I think I'm as knowledgeable about Elizabeth—or was throughout the time of the Great Brouhaha—as any of the Public Scolds who were, and remain, in pursuit of her like a pack of self-righteous beagles after a strangely unwily vixen. Believe me, I have been privy, and sometimes closer, to much of the offscreen, offstage delinquency of theatre-folk; it is indistinguishable in every way from that of the extended-lunch-hour, 'just shopping, dear . . .' private people. Except, perhaps, for the attractiveness of the participants.

"There's more of it, to be sure, among theatre-folk; their behavior, after all, is motivated more by emotion than calculation. But among those theatre-folk, Elizabeth Taylor is one of the least promiscuous, one of the least profligate beautiful women I have ever known. Perhaps if she had been more calculating and conniving—techniques more palatable to the morality mores she's reputed to have outraged—she'd have saved a great deal of wear and tear on herself. But she took it. Head on. It's the only way she knew; hardly that of a schemer. Elizabeth is a good and generous and honest human being. I'm her friend.

"As an actress, I thought she might have become a brilliant one. And still might. For a while, her personal tribulations seemed to have become interwoven with her work; how could they not have? When all at once her public image ceased being that of an actress—and became, instead, a sitting-duck target with unlimited free shots for all comers? We worked together twice; I'm quite sure Elizabeth recalls the second with no more joy than I do—although she would up with a more valued memento than I did.

"But *Suddenly, Last Summer* was in every way a gratifying experience for both of us. It wasn't my screenplay; it was by Tennessee Williams and Gore Vidal. Their locutions were characteristically elaborate and stylized, not easy to commit to memory and demanding a great variety of approach in the playing. The last-act 'aria' of the girl, Catherine (Elizabeth), was as long and difficult a speech, I venture, as any ever attempted on the screen. It was also the dramatic climax of the film. There was no compromise possible: either it came off, or you could drop everything that had gone before into the out-take bin.

"Well, after four or five takes I called a break; we'd been close, but no cigar. Maybe a short rest would do it. Then somebody, one of the gaffers I think, waved at me—and took me around behind the set. There, slumped on the floor beside a flat, was Elizabeth. Physically and emotionally exhausted. Sobbing in great dry gulps. Convinced she'd let herself and everybody else down. This was no 'showboat' for the benefit of agent, lover/husband, or just attention-getting; I'd seen too many of those, by masters of malingering, to be taken in. Elizabeth had quite simply been brought to her kness by her own demands upon herself. Her talent is primitive in its best meaning: she hadn't the techniques for rationing herself; her emotional commitment was total each time.

"So I squatted beside her and made a very calculated suggestion, knowing damned well what the reaction would be. I proposed wrapping it for that day—and starting again, fresh, in the morning. I got the answer I expected. 'Tomorrow, my ass' (in effect), said Elizabeth, 'I'll do it now.' She got up, fixed her make-up, Jack Hildyard hit the lights— and the next take was the print. Elizabeth's performance in *Suddenly, Last Summer*, particularly that last, long Williams 'aria,' was quite remarkable, I think. Run it again some time, and study it—objectively. If that's presently possible about anything Elizabeth does, or did.

"Of course, it might not reflect the aesthetic implications of Antonioni's wall—and it might not reveal those transcendental nuances with which entranced cinema buffs endow the stoic stare of almost any continental actress through a rain-swept windshield—surely the film directors of the Common Market countries can do no less than establish a memorial to the inventor of the windshield wiper—but you'll rarely come across a more honestly realized performance by an actress.

"No, the least of my problems have been with so-called 'difficult' good actors and actresses. The Notable Exception? I've told you she was female, and very Notable—and we've eliminated the most obvious guess. No, not Ava Gardner, either. She was a joy. No more guesses. I never talk about, or identify, Notable Exceptions."

V

Mankiewicz delivered his rough cut of *All About Eye* by the end of June; the next two months were given over to final editing and scoring. It was during this time that the film was shorn of the footage which clearly established and maintained the three interrelated points of view which formed the narrative structure and—in particular—the replaying of Eve's scene about the meaning of applause as first Margo and then Karen recall it. Mankiewicz strongly opposed the deletion. (Although he prefers not to discuss his creative tanglings with Zanuck, it seemed obvious to me that the eliminations still rankled.)

At any rate, when the time approached for the scoring of the film, Mankiewicz apparently thought it politic to present his thoughts about the music in the form of a lengthy detailed memo to both Darryl Zanuck and Alfred Newman, who had been assigned to compose the score. Essentially he stressed the importance of having the music thematically identify each of the narrators and their subject, Eve. The entire memorandum reflects clearly Mankiewicz's concern about retaining, as far as possible, the original interwoven structure of his film. Near the beginning of it, he writes:

"Three characters tell the story of Eve: Addison, Karen, and Margo. In other words, the musical entity of our film consists of a basic theme, *Eve*—and three very different variations on that theme, coloured by the three very distinct characterizations of Addison, Karen, and Margo. These, of course, are supportive to the basic *Eve* theme—to which we give full play particularly at the film's end when Eve, too, is fully revealed and when the audience sees her not through any one else's eyes but her own." Again, in the last paragraph of his memorandum:

"The very finish would be the *Eve* theme—out in the open for the first time. Emphasizing the emptiness and bitterness of what she is. The final music cue should start after the last line of dialogue in the film. It should build constantly, underscoring and underlining the cumulative steps by which the little girl from Brooklyn (Phoebe) assumes Eve's character—first her mantle, then her manner—indicating clearly that she will become another Eve—and finally the full realization, dramatically and musically, that the world is filled with Eves and that they will be with us always. (The mirror SHOT.)"

All About Eve had its premiere at the Roxy Theatre in New York on October 13, 1950. Critically, it received unanimously glowing reviews from all eight (at the time) daily newspapers. As the release of the film widened, accompanied by the enthusiastic word-of-mouth endorsement of its audiences, so did the flow of critical acclaim.

(There were a few exceptions, most notable for their scarcity. *Life* magazine dismissed the film as an inept attempt to denigrate aging actresses. Leo Rosten in *Look*, on the other hand, acclaimed it as "by all odds, the most literate film of the year" and as "an incisive piece of anthropology—a field trip into that curious and specialized society known as the Theatre" while asserting that "Mankiewicz has put the seal of personal monopoly on an entire area of dramatic material—the field of social commentary.")

Abroad, the reception of *All About Eve*, was, if anything, even more enthusiastic—and the negative appraisals even fewer. The English critics, ever chary with superlatives, were unstinting in their approval; their glowing reviews were prophetic of its ultimate designation by the British Film Academy "as the best film from any source released in Great Britain during the year 1950." Dubbed into as many foreign languages as the countries of its world-wide release, the film continued to gather critical acclaim and awards—ranging from First Prize at the Cannes Film Festival (of which, oddly, Mankiewicz has never received any official notification) to "Best Picture" citations and trophies from sources so geographically far-flung as Cuba and Japan.

(Commenting on the fact that more often than not, his work has been reviewed more thoughtfully and appreciatively abroad than here in America, Mankiewicz observed drily: "My films—particularly those I write as well as direct—seem to lose something in the original English.")

Even had he been so inclined, Mankiewicz could not have enumerated for me all of the awards accumulated by *All About Eve*. Unhappily, in 1951, while he was in the process of abandoning Los Angeles as his habitat to become once more a resident of New York, one of the moving vans carrying his effects crashed and was consumed by fire en route. As a result almost all of his files, manuscripts, correspondence, and professional mementos dating back to 1929 were destroyed. It was a tragic, irreplaceable loss for Mankiewicz—and obviously for film historians as well. Understandably enough, as he puts it:

"Forgive me, but I can't attach much importance to the fact that somewhere in those melted filing cabinets was the dust of a few more back-patting certificates or statuettes. I don't mean to sound ungrateful. It's just that I miss so terribly all of my project notebooks, my manuscripts, my letters and diaries—the private documentation of my twenty-year stretch out there."

Whatever the intrinsic merits or significance of awards may be, qualitative or quantitative, *All About Eve* must surely be the most honored screenplay ever written. In addition to the host of scrolls and citations from regional literary and/or film groups, and "Book and Author" societies, there were widely publicized medallions and trophies from *Look, Holiday,* the Foreign Correspondents Association, and other organizations. It was chosen Best of the Year by both the Writers Guild of America (screenplay) and the Directors Guild of America (direction). *All About Eve* was also the first individual screenplay to have been published in hard-bound format. Much in demand over the years by aficionados of the screenplay, copies of the original printing (Random House, 1951)—when available in second-hand bookshops—now sell for upwards of twenty-five dollars.

At the twenty-third annual award ceremonies of the Academy of Motion Picture Arts and Sciences, in March 1951, *All About Eve* established two records which more than twenty years later have yet to be equaled. For one, Mankiewicz, by winning two Oscars—one for screenplay and another for direction—became the first, and remains thus far the only, film maker to have been awarded four Oscars in two consecutive years for both writing and directing. (In 1950 he had won the same two Oscars for *A Letter to Three Wives*: one for his screenplay, and one for his direction.) The other record was set by the film itself. *All About Eve* received no less than fourteen nominations for Academy Awards, a figure which has also not yet been equaled.

Unfortunately affecting the number of ultimate Oscar winners—but nevertheless clearly indicating the high regard by the Academy members for their accomplishments—all four of the leading actresses were nominated. Bette Davis and Anne Baxter received two of the five nominations for "Best Actress"; Thelma Ritter and Celeste Holm were two of the five nominated for "Best Supporting Actress." Miss Baxter and Miss Davis were therefore competing for the "Eve vote," as were Miss Ritter and Miss Holm in their category.

The outcome was foreseeable, and not uncommon when two or more candidates from the same film are among the five nominees: the split in the voting resulted in none of the four winning the coveted Oscar. George Sanders, however, the lone male nominee of the cast, was awarded an Oscar as "Best Supporting Actor." Additional Oscars were won for best costume design and best sound recording. *All About Eve* was chosen "Best Picture of the Year." Darryl Zanuck, accepting the award as its producer, simply held up his Oscar and said, "Thank you, Joe."

Earlier that year, on January 28, it had been the intention of the New York Film Critics to present their annual awards from the stage of the Radio City Music Hall. However, 1951 was also the year of Cardinal Spellman's public condemnation, as blasphemous, of *The Miracle*, which had been chosen (as part of the trilogy, *Ways of Love*) Best Foreign-Language Film.[11] Mounting threats of picketing and a Roman Catholic boycott against the Music Hall necessitated withdrawing the ceremonies to the Rainbow Room of the RCA building where they were held privately, entrance "by invitation" only. As Mankiewicz described it: "The first public award, I should think, ever to be presented furtively."

The New York Film Critics had chosen *All About Eve* for the "Best English Language Film" of 1950, Bette Davis for "Best Performance," and Mankiewicz for "Best Director." Darryl Zanuck was not in attendance; Spyros Skouras appeared on his behalf. Both Miss Davis and Mankiewicz were very much present. (As if corroborating Mankiewicz's earlier reminiscences to me about the Davis–Bankhead identification crisis, *The New York Times*, in reporting the occasion, wrote: "Speculation concerning the real-life identity of the stage star portrayed by Miss Davis had been lively, with the name of Tallulah Bankhead mentioned

---

11. Joseph Burstyn, the distributor of the film, who had fought for and won the landmark decision against the hitherto unchallenged censorship power of the New York Catholic Diocese, was to receive the citation on behalf of the film's three directors: Pagnol, Renoir, and Rosselini.

most frequently. In his receptance remarks, Mr. Mankiewicz sought to settle the matter by saying:

'It might be fitting here to disclose that the woman who was in my thoughts, who always has fascinated me, was none other than Peg Woffington of the old Drury Lane.'

"Both the Old Drury Lane Theatre," continued *The Times*, "and Miss Woffington have been dead for at least a century.")

Bette Davis, after receiving her citation, said of Mankiewicz (again, as reported by *The Times*): "We all followed him blindly, and this is Joe's night." It was Leonard Lyons, however, in the *New York Post*, who recounted the particular actress–director exchange in the course of the ceremony which has since become an oft-repeated theatrical anecdote. As Lyons reported it:

"When Bette Davis received her Film Critics Circle prize for *All About Eve*, she paid glowing tribute to Joe Mankiewicz, insisting that he alone was responsible for her performance; he'd written her lines, directed her every move and inflection, etc. Then she pulled Mankiewicz—who had already accepted his own award—to the platform for another bow. 'Bette forgot to tell you,' said Mankiewicz, 'that on the seventh day I rested.'"

Twenty years later, almost to the day—on January 19, 1971—Miss Davis and Mankiewicz were once more on hand, at the invitation of the New York Film Critics, this time to present the "Best Actress" and "Best Director" awards for the year (Glenda Jackson for *Women in Love*; Robert Rafelson for *Five Easy Pieces*). From the ovation which greeted Miss Davis—and in particular, the appreciative response to an abundance of "inside" quips which presupposed an intimate knowledge of the film's content[12]—it was evident that the film, and her performance in it, had not only emerged during the intervening two decades as film classics, but that her personal identification with it had become so marked as to suggest that *All About Eve* might more fittingly have been entitled *"All About Margo."*

Indeed, the part of the actress is written with such unrelenting larger-than-life bravura and is so enhanced by the memorable *tour de force*

---

12. Among the so-called cult films, *All About Eve* has long been one of the all-time favorites. As in Mart Crowley's play, *The Boys in the Band*, the true *Eve* cultist will have committed to memory large segments of Mankiewicz's screenplay.

of Miss Davis that it becomes difficult to accept the role of Margo as nevertheless a supportive one within the structure of Mankiewicz's screenplay. As he pointed out more than once (even stressed in his memorandum concerning the scoring), Margo is but one of three narrators of an entity which is, after all, all about Eve. One recalls almost with disbelief the fact that Margo (and thus Bette Davis) appears practically not at all in the last third of the film.

This dramaturgical reality apparently either escaped the attention of, or was ignored by, the talents who converted *All About Eve* into a Broadway musical comedy entitled *Applause* (March 1970). It was designed as essentially a vehicle for the actress playing Margo (Lauren Bacall). Therefore, the roles of Eve and Karen being reduced to virtual nonentities (and that of Addison DeWitt incomprehensibly eliminated, his plot functions fused to a witless version of the producer Max Fabian), the librettists were inevitably faced with the dilemma of having no second act. As a result, their only recourse was to have Margo, after Bill walks out on her, repeat endlessly her need for him in both song and dialogue (drained of Mankiewicz's wit) until enough time has elapsed for the final curtain.

(At Mankiewicz's request, I must point out that any appraisal of *Applause* contained herein is my own. The musical version of *All About Eve* was another topic he preferred not to discuss, especially qualitatively, except to make it crystal clear that he was in no way involved with the production—and that he has received no compensation of any kind for the utilization of his screenplay and direction. However, some of what he had to say is illuminative, I think, of major studio control over creative talent, particularly at the time *All About Eve* was made.)

"I wrote and directed *All About Eve*," said Mankiewicz, "as a salaried employee, a 'gun for hire,' as it were. As studio contracts were then written, whether you were Bill Faulkner, Bob Sherwood, Joe Blow, or Joe Mankiewicz, every conceivable right to what you created—in every conceivable medium, past, present, or yet to be invented (my Paramount writing contracts as far back as 1932 refer by name to the television rights!)—was, in every conceivable aspect, turned over to the studio. As if the studio were, in fact, the creator. Apparently, under the laws of equity, a craftsman who is paid to create a specific article for a specific medium—i.e., a photoplay to be projected upon a screen in a movie theatre—can be utterly deprived of any future relation to, or compensation for, his creation, even if it is utilized in a quite different medium for a quite different purpose. I know of no instance in which such incredible contractual usurpations have even been challenged.

"Twentieth Century-Fox, for instance, in regard to *All About Eve*, I assume, receives an 'author's' royalty from the *Applause* production. If so, it has by now undoubtedly taken in infinitely more than it paid me for writing and directing the film. Fox was also, I've been told, legally within its rights to permit the stage producers, adaptors, and director to utilize my writing and direction—and to append their names as authors of what I had created. Fox, I'm told, was not even obligated to notify me of the contemplated production. Nor, in fact, did it do so.

"No, the legality of the position of all concerned with *Applause* is apparently unassailable. As to the morality of the position—professional or otherwise—I keep remembering Bill Fields once telling me (talking of his carnival and circus days) the true purpose of the sign on the box office which reads: 'No mistakes rectified after leaving the window.' It was to keep the short-changed rube from yelling 'copper.'"

VI

What, I asked Mankiewicz, would he regard, in retrospect, as personally the most gratifying aspect of *All About Eve*'s enduring high repute as a film? Could he point to any one particular accomplishment within the film—or tribute from without—which had afforded him the greatest amount of personal gratification? He grinned at the question, seemed to welcome it, and answered without hesitation:

"Whatever else *All About Eve* may have been, or is, or will be as a film—it has already provided for me, as a writer, a reward bestowed upon only the very few. Certainly very few such as I, within the craftsman category. Please note that I said reward, not award. Actually, it was a particular award that culminated in the reward—both uniquely attributable to *Eve*:

"Every good satirist—and I am, or have been, or have tried to be, a good one—directs the probe of his satire at what he believes to be a truth: a fact of manners or mores or morality which society either evades, disguises, or denies. And, thus probing, hopes to penetrate the sham and expose said truth or fact. The goal of every satirist would be to have his satiric point proved valid; his dream would be to have its validity established by the very object of his satire, itself. Just as there can be no greater gratification for the author than to have his fantasy become reality. To have nature, however restricted in scope, mirror his art—however small the *a*.

"As I told you, way back—somewhere in that mountain of cassettes— my original concept of *All About Eve* was, and remained, to tell a satiric tale of theatre-folk, utilizing the flashback techniques within a satirical framework of the presentation and acceptance of that theatrical totem known as The Award. Creating a physical setting for the ceremony was no problem: it became a vague amalgam of the New York Players Club, of which I had been a member for many years, and the Garrick Club in London. But dreaming up a name for the theatrical society itself was less easy; it had to serve, after all, also as the inspiration for the physical appearance of the award. Then one day while I was rummaging through some old theatrical portraits to choose some to be reproduced and used as set dressing—Sir Joshua Reynolds's famous portrait of Sarah Siddons as *The Tragic Muse* popped up at me. And that was it.

"So, sometime early in 1950, I created both 'The Sarah Siddons Society' and that award which is presented annually for 'Distinguished Achievement in the Theatre': 'The Sarah Siddons Award.' Working from an enlarged print of the Reynolds portrait, the Twentieth Century-Fox prop shop started making up statuettes according to my specifications. The first approved model of 'The Sarah Siddons Award' is right over there, on my mantelpiece. Walter Scott (the set dresser) even put my name on it. So actually I was the first recipient of the 'Sarah Siddons Award.' So much for the fictional materialization of my fantasy, in 1950.

"*All About Eve* had its widest general release throughout 1951. Then sometime early in 1952—as far as I have been able to determine—those charged with such responsibilities at the Ambassador East Hotel in Chicago bethought themselves of an inspired publicity gimmick for their Pump Room Restaurant and its eighteenth-century English ambience. The inspiration, I have been informed, struck both James Hart and Ernest Byfield, Jr., of the Ambassador East's administration; whether or not it was a simultaneous revelation, I do not know.

"But, *mirabile dictu*, in 1952, in Chicago, a 'Sarah Siddons Society' came into being. It had as its avowed purpose the furthering and flowering of the Theatrical Arts in that meat-orientated metropolis—and established, as symbolic of its lofty undertaking, 'The Sarah Siddons Award.' It was to be bestowed annually upon an actress chosen by the society for 'Distinguished Achievement' in the Theatre of Chicago—a feat not easy of accomplishment out where the winds of culture blow cold. The presentation ceremony, one may assume, would be destined to become a traditional rite at the—surprise, surprise—Ambassador East Hotel. So much for reality plagiarizing my fantasy, in 1952.

'Could anyone conceivably have been taken in by such an 'Award'? With *All About Eve* and its satiric connotations about 'Awards' still playing the movie theatres of Chicago? With the ads, magazines, Sunday supplements, and lobby displays still filled with exploitation layouts for the film, always featuring the 'Sarah Siddons Award' which I had dreamed up as an object of satire? An award of which the Chicago gimmick version was, what's more, an *exact replica*? You can bet your ass it was taken seriously.

"And not only by those culture-hungry matrons of Chicago who to this day attend meetings faithfully and deliberate the winner with all the solemnity of the Nobel Prize Committee. Their 'Award,' from its very inception, became a much sought-after accolade by many of our most distinguished actresses. It has endured for twenty years now, this bit of my intended satiric fantasy which has become unintended satiric reality. Yes, I'm quite prepared to accept your estimate that, next to the Tony Award, the 'Sarah Siddons Award' is the most treasured trophy for an actress in the American Theatre.

"Its first recipient, in 1953, was none other than Helen Hayes. Since then, among others similarly honored by this reproduction of my movie prop have been such actresses as: Beatrice Lillie, Deborah Kerr, Nancy Kelly, Geraldine Page, Shirley Booth, Gertrude Berg, Carol Channing—and of late, of all people, Celeste Holm. I can't help wondering whether Celeste had a feeling of *déjà vu*. Or whether she placed it alongside the 'Sarah Siddons Award' I gave her when we finished the film (the one her playwright-husband passed on to her). She probably threw out that old original fake. I hope she keeps the new fake fake. I wish long life both to the 'Sarah Siddons Society' and to its 'Award,' believe me. They will provide for me an annual and infinitely gratifying reaffirmation of what *All About Eve* was really all about."

As he envisaged all those Sarah Siddons Awards multiplying into infinity, a gleam came into Mankiewicz's eyes. He seemed to be recalling the film's final prismatic image: that in which Eves and Awards and the hunger for applause are projected endlessly into the future. With as much chagrin as relish, Mankiewicz added a final word on the subject:

"It would seem that the idiocies of theatre-folk within their world share with the idiocies of the outsiders, 'the private people,' within their world, one common characteristic. They are continuing, self-perpetuating idiocies."

An Interview with Joseph L. Mankiewicz

MICHEL CIMENT/1973

KNOWN FOR SPEAKING HIS MIND and for his individual-
ism, Joseph L. Mankiewicz makes his home away from it all at Willow
Pond, his farm near Bedford, New York, some eighty miles from New
York City. It is here that he greets me in an old grange converted into a
library, the realization of a dream Mankiewicz had entertained since he
was seventeen. The rustic yet fancy décor is right out of one of his films
with thousands of books surrounding windows opening onto a coun-
tryside that seems both domesticated and wild at the same time in the
true English style. In this immense room, reality flirts with fiction in a
game of echoes that must please the author of *The Honey Pot*. Above a
large portrait of his father, who was once a university professor but has
now passed on, there on the chimney's mantle sit the four Oscars he
won for *All About Eve* and *A Letter to Three Wives* and next to them sits
the Sarah Siddons Award, the fake gold trophy that Walter Hampden
presented to Anne Baxter in *All About Eve*. Nearby there is the small
bust of Edgar Allan Poe that adorned Andrew Wyke's home in *Sleuth*.
Among the chairs one sees a brown leather director's chair on which fittingly appears the name of my host.

This man, who spent part of his life as a publicity agent but who
nevertheless doesn't make television appearances and has never partici-
pated in a festival, is more secretive than Stanley Kubrick and is even
more parsimonious in his granting of interviews than is Billy Wilder,
that other great disciple of Lubitsch. The only substantial interview

From *Positif*, September 1973. Reprinted by permission of Michel Ciment. Translated by
Robert Vallier.

with him was published in French by *Cahiers de Cinema #178,* and while it is very insightful, Mankiewicz later complained about it because when the American edition of the revue was published, the French translation of the interview was retranslated back into English rather than using the original English transcript of it, thus yielding bizarrely deformed versions of his original statements. He also conversed with Gary Carey, and the two of them then took this discussion, edited and polished it, and presented it as an introduction to a new edition of the screenplay of *All About Eve,* which Jean-Loup Bourget talks about in this issue [of *Positif,* in which this interview also appeared in September, 1973—ed.].

Like most filmmakers of his generation, Mankiewicz disdains and avoids being interviewed about his work. "I will write my memoirs after my death," he tells me, "like a posthumous work. To write one's memoirs is to have the impression that one is on one's deathbed." His disdain for critics is proverbial, but when it comes to expressing himself, it is better, he says, to take the time to do so with the most precision possible. When he does agree to a rendezvous, Mankiewicz becomes a playful interviewee and is not one to take pleasure in anecdotes or in some sophisticated and sibylline declarations. With Andrew Sarris (in *Show,* March 1970), he revealed his hostility towards the pompous character of the Antonioni school of obfuscation [*obscursissement*]: "There's nothing new about the director with the jacket draped over his shoulders and the pseudo-philosophical cop-outs: 'What do you mean, where are the tennis balls? Life is a tennis game without tennis balls. . . .' Back in 1928, a Romanian director named Buchowetski came to Hollywood on the Chief, and the newspapermen were there, and they cornered him as he stepped off the train, and there he was with the jacket draped over his shoulders and the hired lackeys, and somebody asked him about his philosophy or point of view or something, and he drew himself up and declared, 'Life is like a camera,' after which cryptic comment he swept into the Paramount limousine with the Paramount press agent, who was a little desperate, because he knew that the press would want some amplification on a remark like 'Life is like a camera.' So the press agent asked the Romanian director to explain what the remark meant, and the director gave him a withering glance and said: 'How should I know what it means? I'm a director, not a philosopher.' He, too, couldn't be bothered to explain the invisible tennis balls."

For Mankiewicz, on the contrary, speech must come to terms. The interviewer finds himself submitted to his own question or transformed into an attentive listener of a sinuous discourse. He becomes an actor in one of Mankiewicz's scenes, directed by the master who has imperiously taken charge of the dialogue. Outside, a storm is rumbling, and Mankiewicz, smoking his pipe with a malicious eye, lays out his insightful rationale mixed with flashes of wit. He appears to me—I guard against the trendy ideas of the "death of the author"—as the alter ego of one of his characters. Along with Rosi, Kubrick, and Lang, Mankiewicz is one of those directors fascinated by rigorous reason and implacable logic which these directors develop in a tight, dry dialectic. Aside from their obvious differences, their films are reflections on the will to power, films which both emerge from and lead into an analysis of power. But the study of the political mechanisms which are used to control society, i.e., hyper-rationality, often leads their work to revel in madness—and to give us a glimpse of a darkly fantastic version of an ordered world. Mabuse, Mattei, Folamour, Cicero are beings who aspire to domination, observed by a totalitarian director who diabolically demonstrates the workings of their power over things.

I give myself over to these types of reflections at the end of the night, after Mankiewicz, with a pointed and commanding intelligence, had let me record his infinite, labyrinthine, and Borghesian discourse in which passion debates with reason, revealing the old *lion* (Joseph *Leo* Mankiewicz, producer, screenwriter, and director) savoring his renewed success and his influence over the world of cinema.

MICHEL CIMENT: Sleuth *is a play by Anthony Shaffer, but the film strangely resembles an original screenplay by Mankiewicz!*
JOSEPH MANKIEWICZ: The screenplay is very different from the play. I have to say that Anthony Shaffer could not have been more cooperative or understanding. I wanted once again to treat one of my favorite themes which has always fascinated me—and that *The Barefoot Contessa* probably expressed most clearly—which is that life ruins screenplays. Each one of us, whether it be Nixon giving a speech to Congress or you shaving in the morning, writes a screenplay for the day. You, for example,

imagine how the afternoon will pass, what this grange will look like, how I will be, etc. But life is not a screenplay and the dialogue isn't real. Realist dialogue doesn't exist. We are all actors and we all play roles [*jeux*: games].

I'm quick to read French critics to know if I hit the mark because for as long as I can remember the French critics are the only ones who really listen to a film and are not content simply to watch it. They alone are not fooled by the showy tricks and the fireworks of the young man working with camera in hand.

Thus, I opened this film with a proscenium and with cardboard figures—which anticipates a scene later in the cave in which Wyke shows the tableaux with these figures as if they were recreations of his books—and then I closed the film with a freeze-frame in which the characters become cardboard silhouettes as the camera pulls back.

Andrew Wyke and Milo Tindle, as well as the events they live, become part of the oeuvre of Wyke: the game they play is transformed into one of his novels which almost gives a metaphysical dimension to the story. Yet to my knowledge, no one in this country has ever taken note of that, no one has noticed that they become silhouettes, that the camera, which is to say the director, withdraws while laughing and declaring: "What you've just seen was my game. It was one of the works of Andrew Wyke." The life of this man has become his work. The American critic is not ready to watch an American film of this type. The American critic carries a cilice, the habit of penitents. Because so many of his compatriots are noisy and vulgar, he has to be hyper-modest. Because so many of his compatriots are disinterested in culture, he has to be hyper-cultural. But only with respect to foreign works! When he watches American films, he says "This is American and so must have its limits," limits that he refuses to impose on works like those by someone as grotesquely dishonest as Antonioni. To a great extent, Antonioni has been created by the American critic who says "I see things that nobody else sees in his films." At the end of the day, the perfect film will be one that no spectator will understand, but for which the critic provides the key to understanding. But here I am once again digressing and losing sight of your question.

Let's get back to *Sleuth* and to the game. I wanted to accentuate in this adaptation the contrast between the classes and to show that the intellectual, precisely because he is an intellectual, believes himself to

be mentally superior to the non-intellectual. This is the case with
Andrew Wyke, who obviously is not the most intellectual of intellectuals: he is pompous, but he has read a lot and is the author of successful
1930s-style crime novels (and this is another fascinating thing for me:
people who are stuck in one epoch and no longer evolve)! In the middle of the 1930s, I myself played at all these games: charades, treasure
hunt, murder. And so when some powerful member of high society like
Wyke humiliates the poor and the weak, he can create in his adversary
a frightening talent for revenge, a talent that would have had no reason
to exist were it not for him. And this is what Andrew Wyke is not prepared for.

In the original play, Milo Tindle wasn't a Cockney, but instead
directed a travel agency and was half-Jewish and half-Italian. I preferred
to make him a hairstylist, someone who had climbed the social ladder
by fornicating, and the hairstylist is good at this. One of the most brilliant aspects of Michael Caine's portrayal is his accent. I tried to get him
to use his accent like a violinist uses his violin. He puts on the accent
of a proper gentleman and then drops it. Michael, who enters the
labyrinth at the beginning with a proper accent, is, at the moment of
his alleged murder, nothing more than a hysterical Cockney who cries
and sobs, and who has abandoned every pretense of being a proper
gentleman and of trying to sound like one. Throughout the film,
depending on the situation and the tension, I tried to get him to control his accent. It was very funny.

I make films for different reasons and I think that I've left my mark.
In *The Honey Pot*, I unfortunately threw away the good script. There had
been two stories in one: an imaginary part and a modern version of
Volpone. In the original story, the film is stopped and the cinema owner
comes on the scene to protest that it had become too vulgar, insisting
that the film clean up its act. The characters who had not yet appeared
on screen talk to him and ask him to leave so that the film can continue, even telling him that he has no right to be there. I wanted the
censors to prohibit certain characters from appearing on screen. Every
once in a while, there are overlays of memos from the Hays Office con-
demning certain scenes. One of them announces to parents that in two
minutes there would be a scene inappropriate for children and that
they should send their children to the bathroom.

Unfortunately the film's backers refused these scenes because they made fun of directors and censors, and as Kazan says, I let myself be persuaded too easily, so I agreed to cut all the imaginary scenes. This is why the end of the film is so mysterious. They seem to speak from heaven and say "Oh, if only once the story could be played as it had been written."

MC: *But you had already filmed some of the imaginary scenes?*
JM: Yes, but not those that were commentaries on the film. The others I cut from the final montage. You have to understand that my experience with Zanuck had been traumatic and had destroyed me for three or four years. I lacked confidence in what I should or should not do, despite my age and experience. After having tossed out the right screenplay, some of the imaginary sequences no longer seemed to me truly to belong in the film and so I tried to make a sophisticated comedy. It seemed to me that the film lacks a flavor even if it contains some very good scenes. One of the best scenes that I had written in a long time is between Rex Harrison and Maggie Smith, where he talks to her about the weather.

MC: *What was it like to collaborate with Shaffer on* Sleuth*?*
JM: He worked in this small room where we often met. We spoke before and if I had any suggestions to make, I inserted them in the text and he either accepted them or didn't. I worked in the same fashion with Benton and Newman on *There Was a Crooked Man*. Being a writer myself, it is difficult for me not to write the film that I'm going to direct. But it was Shaffer's screenplay, even if I added a few lines. At the beginning of my career, after *Dragonwyck*, I deliberately directed screenplays written by others because I wanted to learn the technique and to work in particular with actors, to get to know them, to gauge them, and to get their best work out of them. But even during this time, I collaborated on screenplays. What I prefer above all, however, is to write and direct my own screenplays. Even today I don't quite understand how, in the space of two years, I was able to write and direct *A Letter to Three Wives, No Way Out, All About Eve*, and *People Will Talk!* It's true that at the time I bounded up and down stairs quickly and ran faster. But writing takes time and I like to work alone knowing that writing is a solitary job.

I don't see how one can really collaborate with someone on a screen-play, and so I've never sat down next to someone and written with them. As a director, I can discuss the screenplay with someone else and tell him what I think, but I can't collaborate with him as a writer.

MC: *Your experience is the opposite of Wilder's, who always had a co-writer.*
JM: I think that Billy's method is due to a feeling of insecurity with respect to the language. And imagine that Lubitsch wrote dialogue word for word in his office with Wilder, Reisch, Rafelson, etc. You know how much I love and admire Lubitsch—I had been his protégé and it is because of him that I became a director—but I've never been able to understand how this collective work was possible.

MC: *Who came up with the idea of the labyrinth for* Sleuth*?*
JM: It came from me, as did the idea for the mirror. The marionettes were likewise not part of the screenplay and they almost began to direct me.

For each film I need to spend at least one day completely alone on a perfectly decorated set. This is how I spent one afternoon, arranging the marionettes here and there. As filming continued, I began to have the feeling that each of these dolls had its own unique personality. And one night when I was trying to get to sleep, I thought that the little balle-rina was in love with Michael Caine, and then I began to think about what I hadn't filmed yet, about how she would wait for him to come down the stairs, or how he would turn his back when he got hit by a bullet, or how she would look at him when he called the police. And about this severe, dominating woman at the piano who really con-trolled Andrew Wyke and didn't want another female presence in the house, or anyone else for that matter. And about the sailor. I began to think more about the dolls than about the real actors! The game was "playing" the people, and the things were directing me! This is what fascinated me in *Sleuth*, so I began to play these pointless games. I did a zoom on one car: why would this car be found here? I wanted to have fun. Can anyone understand the presence of Marguerite's red coat? In all my films, there's something like this, but this film was in every respect the most satisfying because I was pushed constantly to invent because of the very limits of the subject: two actors in one room. After all, this is the first time in the history of cinema that the entire cast was nominated for Academy Awards.

MC: *Since you argue that no one really listens to films anymore, it must have been quite a challenge for you to make a film in which two actors do little more than talk for two hours and twenty minutes.*
JM: Up until the film came out, I had to wage a terrible battle against the producers of the film so that they didn't cut out entire scenes or impose an intermission. If the film hadn't been a commercial success, I can assure you that it would now be truncated, and I can't even be sure that someone is not in the midst of editing it as we speak. I was anxious, of course. It was definitely a challenge to force the public to listen to films once again. Shaffer wrote a brilliant screenplay and I had two equally brilliant actors who created a peculiar chemistry between them, as one finds when the cast is adequate. Nobody has ever created a star and nobody ever knows if something is going to be a success or not. Nobody ever knows if the public will like a film or not. Only the public has the power to create stars. Marilyn Monroe would not be distinct from eighteen others just like her except in the eyes of somebody who isn't one of them—the public, which sensed in her something that nobody else had noticed. This is marvelous because the uncertainty of it all allows for creativity. In the 1930s, they hoped to be able to get rid of actors, directors, and screenwriters; they hoped to be able to find a way to fabricate fifty-minute movies that people would be happy to watch with their mouths agape, just as they do with television. I thought that the public would listen to *Sleuth* because they would be afraid.

MC: *In the powerful conflicts that you always show in your films, what value do you put on the conflict between men and women?*
JM: We neglect women because they are simultaneously the most complicated human beings and yet offer the most in return to screenwriters and to directors. The American male is the least interesting in the world. He is the only man on earth who, as soon as he is twelve or thirteen years old, is taught that his primary responsibility, his function in life, is to have more value dead than alive. As soon as a young American boy hits puberty, we begin talking to him about life insurance

and telling him that when he dies, he has to leave enough money to his wife and kids so that they can be better off than they were when he was alive. His function in life is to be a rich and powerful cadaver. The worst thing that can happen to an American male is to be physically handicapped. He can no longer work. He's been educated exclusively to acquire things, but he hasn't developed any interior resources. If he is deprived of his ability to acquire and has to stay in a chair reading or thinking, he's completely lost. The American male, just like the French or English males, is so much easier to understand than is the woman.

The woman can say "yes" and "no" at the same time. She can want and not want at the same time. The woman lies and dissimulates infinitely better than the male does because she has been obliged to do so by society. But I hate that she is losing these marvelous qualities. They are also natural qualities. Woman is physically weaker. I have a seven-year-old daughter whom I love dearly, and believe me, we've never taught her to mind her place. The boys at school may push her around a bit, but she can dish it out just as well as they can. She must be viewed by them as a weaker boy. When I see her maneuvering, playing me, flirting with me, she manipulates me very differently than did her brothers when they were seven.

I agree entirely with women when they speak about how society has made life impossible for them, but I am jealous of their superior equipment for dealing with life. All the social injustices perpetrated against them have bolstered their defenses. Over centuries, just as the laws of evolution predict, they have developed certain instincts, certain talents that they are not ready to give up, and I don't want them to. I find women infinitely more fascinating than men. In *Sleuth*, the absent woman is much more present than in the play. I would have preferred to have two women rather than two men on the screen. One of the reasons why I made so much use of the dolls is probably that the two main characters were men. With two women, I probably would not have felt the need for the dolls because I would have found in them a sufficient number of complications and contradictions.

MC: *Isn't this the subject of* The Barefoot Contessa?
JM: I wish I could write *The Barefoot Contessa* today. I conceived it in the era when it was not allowed to write about these things in the way

they demanded. It was the history of a Hollywood Cinderella who marries a prince only to discover that he's homosexual. But you couldn't
put that on the screen back then. I couldn't even say that he was impotent unless I also made up some sad story about war injuries. You had
to be careful about which words you used. We forget today how quickly
a more permissive society came about. When I wrote *All About Eve*, I
was not allowed to use the word "tart" and we couldn't even show the
toilet in a bathroom. I watched *Notorious* recently; it's a bad film, but
through no fault of Hitchcock. It's because of Selznick and his ideas
about high society: during their honeymoon, the couple sleeps in twin
beds. In Great Britain the rules were even stricter: there had to be six-
teen inches between the beds, and if a man and a woman were both
seated on a bed, one of them had to have at least one foot on the
ground. You couldn't say "God" on screen, etc.

MC: *In films about Hollywood, it's remarkable that the director in the film
is not very involved in doing his job.*
JM: Harry Dawes, the character in *The Barefoot Contessa*, is in my view
a very well-written character. A lot of details about him were cut during
the editing of the film, in particular when he talks about his profession.
I was inspired by several directors whom I had known, real Hollywood-
types like Gregory LaCava, Howard Hawks, Eddy Sutherland, William
Wellman—they all had an American eye, a cynical eye. Like Dawes said,
"I began to make films well before there were three dimensions.
Sometimes there were no dimensions at all." The film about Hollywood
was usually either a burlesque comedy or a sumptuous film because the
producer was at the center and making all the important decisions. All
films that try to show a director at work seem to ring false to me, to miss
reality. Every filmmaker works in a different manner. If I had to write a
novel about Hollywood—and I have a lot of notes on this subject—it
would be about a director like Harry Dawes who, from the point of view
of truth, may well be my favorite character.

MC: *Your absence-presence, your apparent effacement on the set, approximates your attitude about the* mise en scène *of cinema.*
JM: For me, it's an essential aspect of direction. I know that the vast
majority of the next generation of filmmakers are violently opposed to

me in this respect. They want to insert themselves between the public
and the screen and say, "Look at me, I'm a filmmaker." If during the
film there's an effect, or a shot, or a camera angle, or an editing montage that makes the spectator poke his neighbor and ask, "Wow, how
did they do that?" or exclaim, "That's a great shot," then for me the
whole film is destroyed. I'm sorry, but for me the raison d'etre of a film
is to transport the public either outside of reality or somewhere else
inside reality, it doesn't matter. What it has to do is absorb the spectator's attention entirely, because remember, there's a difference between
theater-goers and movie patrons. As soon as theatre-goers buy their
ticket, they make a pact with you and agree to abandon reality. "I enter
the Comedie Francaise," says the theater-goer, "and I'm ready to
believe that there is a fourth wall, and that these walls and doors are
true, that this piece of crumpled fabric is the Mediterranean, that this
man in a wig that doesn't quite fit is King Lear. I am on your side; I join
with you in accepting the pretense." Movie patrons, on the other hand,
say, "You have an interest in making me believe what you want to
show." It's strange that these two audiences demand exactly the opposite. This is why we can no longer pull it off with the set: the audience
will make fun of it. We can no longer pull it off with makeup. One of
the most difficult problems during the production of *Sleuth* was
makeup. I said to my cinematographer Oswald Morris: "We are going to
film the eyes in a close-up. We are going film the pores of the skin," and
the makeup people had to work with this, but in the theater, the spectator is only twenty feet away from the stage. If the director got in the
way he'd destroy the effect of reality.

MC: *But in* Sleuth *you played with fire by showing the theater curtain,
while insisting on the pretense in order to make the spectator accept the
reality of the events.*
JM: That was a provocation because I said to them that it was a joke
on my part only at the end of the film. *Suddenly, Last Summer*, which
was made in 1959, used subliminal montage. When Elizabeth Taylor
was trying to remember, brief shots appeared on the screen and just as
quickly disappeared: her memory escapes her. It wasn't very common at
the time. Andrew Sarris noted that Truffaut had used freeze-frames in
Jules and Jim. But I had used the technique in *All About Eve* in 1949. I did

what was necessary with technique and I think that its possibilities must be maximized, but only to aid the subject of the film.

MC: *What's your attitude concerning set decoration?*
JM: I try to use the talents of each of my collaborators. The worst thing that a filmmaker can do is to take the view-finder and to go around with the cinematographer telling him which lens to use, at which spot, where his marks should be, etc., because you might be in the midst of castrating a great cameraman. I first prepare the scene and then ask him how he sees it. He might propose something I hadn't thought of. As the director, I have the privilege of saying, "That's exactly what I was thinking" or of proposing my own solution if his suggestion doesn't satisfy me. Another stupid thing is to take a piece of paper and draw a plan on it while telling the set decorator that this is what you want. The set decorator has to read the screenplay. I tell him what I envisage and he comes back to me with his ideas. For the beginning of *Sleuth*, we used an astonishing new procedure, a round bowl in which the camera is placed and that one directs from afar. I could follow Michael Caine and do a close-up of him in the deepest parts of the labyrinth then dig deeper still, which I didn't want to do with a crane or a zoom.

MC: *How are your screenplays written from the point of view of the* mise en scène?
JM: There's only a general plan. Whoever writes with technical cuts in mind is wasting their time. If the director is writing his own screenplay, he doesn't need to indicate the camera position, and if it's the screenwriter who writes the screenplay, then it's pointless because the director will do whatever he wants. What is necessary is to visualize the film, to have a general conception. As Olivier said on *The Dick Cavett Show*, the director has to know exactly how every detail will relate to the whole. For *Sleuth*, I had to begin very calmly and even conventionally because I knew that I had a lot of ground to cover. I could not get too near too quickly or become too bizarre too soon. I had to conserve things for later. On the whole, the use of the camera is dictated by the dramatic content of the scene and by the effect that it will have on the audience.

MC: *Does psychoanalysis interest you?*
JM: I have shelves full of books about psychoanalysis and I've studied it. The emotions, mental mechanisms, and motivations for human behavior have always interested me as long as I can remember. The shocking abuse of the absence of dialogue in films today, the guttural groanings that the majority of the young emit in trendy films frighten and worry me. They talk a lot about communication with others, but occupy themselves with nothing other than learning the most basic form of communication which is language. There are other ways of communicating like passing a joint around or fucking, and I hope that they are doing more of the latter than the former. And I don't think that they're fucking all that much, not as much as we used to fuck, and probably not as much as I still do. From precisely the emphasis that this generation puts on the extravagance of their dress and their behavior, I think that we can detect an inner void. They have to show gaudily-colored plumage in order to hide the absence of body as in Dennis Hopper's films. There is a total lack of reflection. This generation has had a unique opportunity: in two or three years the world of cinema has been handed over to it on a silver platter, and nothing comparable has taken place since Israel was carved out of the Sinai Desert. Suddenly only people younger than thirty were able to make films, and they've totally wasted this unexpected opportunity. Curiously the young think that there were no actors before James Dean, no actresses before Jane Fonda. When I go to universities, I speak to them about Moliere's wife and his mistress, about the Italian actress Flaminia, and about actresses in English restoration comedy, and I say that we can hardly tell them apart from actresses today, that they were the same women facing the same problems, that they are called Armande Béjart and Tallulah Bankhead. I tell them that they are part of a historical continuum which they have to study and where they have to look for their roots. It's like telling young directors not to direct the lenses, but rather to direct the actors, which requires preparation and time. But time is exactly what this generation is missing the most. For the first time, man has the power to destroy the universe. I grew up in a world where the future was just as permanent as the past. There was going to be a future. We held on to letters, to objects. Today we don't hold on to anything.

MC: *In your films, there is a desire for clarity and rationality which masks a fantastical element.*

JM: I don't believe in conclusions. I think that human idiocy perpetuates itself. I am essentially an iconoclast and I take pleasure in observing the way in which humanity constantly abuses itself.

At the moment, I'd like to direct a horror story revolving around mechanical spouses, robots. I wouldn't want to direct a true horror film because horror as a subject doesn't interest me all that much, but the horror that's present just beneath the surface of everyday behavior does. I don't believe that man is born good; he's born angry. Look at the fetus safe and secure in a comfortable sac of amniotic fluid for nine months living totally in a self-sustained state, nourishing itself, doing what seems good for it, without any need for anybody. And then it is suddenly pushed out into this world, greeted by a slap on the ass, and is now totally dependent. Its first cry is a cry of rage against the destruction of it autarchy. This subtends everything man does. In everybody, from Nixon to Danny Kaye to the circus clown (I don't see a lot of difference between Nixon and the clown), there is a pent-up anger which, if it isn't sublimated into work or love, will find a multitude of outlets. This fascinates me. The horror of the opening coffin is masturbatory; what interests me is the uncontrollable, the emotions that suddenly take possession of a man who was previously unaware that they were in him. What interests me, once again, are the screenplays that people write everyday, the lies that they constantly tell themselves, the games they play at every moment, and how they find themselves prisoners of their own lies. And women, more so than men, have had to perfect a great variety of lies, tricks, substitutions, crutches, etc.

MC: *Does your interest in flashbacks come from the fact that one cannot truly know the past?*

JM: The past exists in the present. Your way of listening to me right now impregnates this room, but at the same time it is Kazan that you hear along with all the other people you have interviewed. Unconsciously, you have already thought of three or four filmmakers, of questions identical to those that you asked them. You wondered why you will speak to me today. You cannot deny that past and maybe future interviews have crossed your mind. While we have been playing out this scene—I am playing the interviewee and you the interviewer—I imagined myself in the nearby house, I glanced at the mail. I had thoughts about my daughter because the thunder rolled, and you thought about other interviews. We went to a lot of different places. And if you had not gone to these other places, you would not be here today in your current mental state. If the scene had been one in which I follow my wife with a camera from the house to the grange as she walks in to surprise us in conversation, this would have been very different from fixing the camera on the two of us.

MC: *You wanted to adapt* Twelfth Night, A Midsummer's Night Dream, *and* Macbeth *to the screen?*
JM: For me, Shakespeare is by far the greatest and most creative of all writers. There is an incredible chasm between him and the rest. I wanted to treat him like a living author. For *Macbeth* I wanted Brando and Maggie Smith. I am very attracted by theater, but I couldn't make my debut there as an anonymous director. I am very aware of the fact that I would be a famous director and that it would be in my interest to prepare for serious examination. I love the theater, I would love to write for the theater, and I have notes for a half-dozen plays, but once again, there's a strange blockage. I suppose that I am afraid of being rejected, but I will work in theater. I already am afraid, and I've already put it behind me. I have never been more terrified than when I was making *Julius Caesar* for the screen while thinking of the reaction of the English, who in fact loved the film.

MC: *Did you leave Los Angeles in 1952 because of the loyalty oath and the witch hunts?*
JM: No, that was in 1950. Cecil B. DeMille wanted to call into question my leadership as the President of the Screen Directors Guild because I had attacked the loyalty oath that had been imposed while I was away on vacation in France. Louella Parsons accused me of being a communist, and this all ended with a big meeting of the Directors Guild. If DeMille had obtained a majority, I would have packed my bags for Europe just as the people on the black list had done. In fact, it was thanks to John Ford, a totally unpredictable Irishman, that DeMille was thwarted. It was a victory for me, and so if I left Los Angeles two years

later, it was simply because I hate that town. It's a town where it is illegal to talk about the United Nations in public schools. It is a reactionary town, Goldwater's town. It terrified me, and I didn't want my two sons to grow up there.

MC: *In your choice of subjects, you have often treated independence. In* No Way Out *you treat racism and in* People Will Talk *the witch hunts.*
JM: I have never known great financial success. When you look at *Variety's* list of the one hundred biggest grossing films in the history of cinema, you'll look in vain to find one of mine with the exception of one film that I never talk about [*Cleopatra*]. On the other hand, I've had only two films that failed to make some return on the investment: *The Quiet American* and *The Honey Pot*. *There Was a Crooked Man* is a separate case because there was an act of sabotage during the change in leadership at Warner Brothers. The man whose taste coincided the most with worldwide audiences' was probably Cecil B. DeMille. He made biblical films with his talent and based on his beliefs. He really believed that Moses acted like that and, to everyone's astonishment, the rest of the world agreed with him! He had his finger on the pulse of the global public. Take Zanuck's musical comedies. Daryl never compromised as a producer; he never decided to produce a film that he didn't like. He simply let his taste follow his natural inclinations which allowed him to achieve the lowest levels that the public could tolerate.

MC: *Even the Zanuck of* The Grapes of Wrath?
JM: In an interview given to a French journalist, he said that the best film he had ever produced was *The Oxbow Incident* directed by John Ford. But *The Oxbow Incident* was directed by William Wellman and produced by Lamar Trotti! Moreover, at a preview Zanuck said, "I don't want to put Fox's name on such a piece of shit." Zanuck didn't produce *The Grapes of Wrath*! Please! Don't say that! Fox made forty films per year, *The Grapes of Wrath* was on the list, and it was a little bit like roulette. Zanuck once wanted to raise himself to the level of the greats by producing *Wilson*, but after the failure of this film he gave up. He had been just as stupefied by the success of *The Grapes of Wrath* as anyone else. He became the producer of *All About Eve* after reading the first draft of my screenplay.

MC: *How did you approach the problem of Southeast Asia while making*
The Quiet American?
JM: It was very personal. If you read the novel, you read a book without
humor; it is bitter, and dominated by an absurd anti-Americanism. You
get the impression that some idiotic bureaucrat from the State
Department had refused a visa to Graham Greene who then out of anger
decides to write a novel about an absolutely imbecilic American who
graduated from Harvard when he was twenty-seven (that's very late!),
a virgin who drinks Coke all day while shipping plastic materials to
Indochina to make bombs. What interested me while reading this novel
was to see how the emotions of a man can affect his political convictions.
I went to Saigon in 1954 and I discovered that Greene, whose French was
far from perfect, had translated the French explosive *"plastique"* as the
English "plastics," which in French means plastic materials. Throughout
the whole book he spoke of exploding plastic materials! I wanted to give
a different angle in the film and to show exactly how a man's emotions
can affect his political convictions! Greene hated the film, but it was well-
liked in France. Godard rated it as the best film of the year. I doubt that
he would have the same opinion today, but he thought so at the time.
The film spoke of a third force which was a reflection on the problem.
And the character of Claude Dauphin spoke for me, particularly at the
end. In the majority of the films I've written, I usually have a spokesman.

MC: *If you had written* Sleuth *yourself, would you make Laurence Olivier's
character die, or would you rather show that in our society, it's always the
Michael Caines who die?*
JM: I've never thought about it. I think that it was necessary that he die
in order to convince Olivier. This represents an important aspect of our
society. It cannot allow someone to know his own weakness. But at the
end, he had to seem ridiculous in every way since the little friends he had
created turn on him and mock him. His only refuge is to return to his
boyhood, to become a child again, a child who cries because all of his
toys are broken. But I too played. Now I'm happy simply to watch others.

MC: *How do you choose your actors?*
JM: If I had to choose between an actor who "feels" his role and an
actor who "understands" it, I would always choose the latter. It doesn't

matter what an actor "feels" provided that he makes me think that he's feeling something. The ideal of course is to combine the two. The actor who thinks and who can control his emotions is a great actor, but the actor who plays with his emotions and doesn't think is far too common today. All these actors who tell you, "Let me say it in my own way," and who ignore the dialogue in favor of some pretentious improvisation— this is not only an absurdity, it's an obscenity. How can an actor come on the set and claim to be able to deliver his lines better than the experienced writer who has spent six months or maybe a year writing the text? I have no patience for those who mistake the spoken language.

MC: *You seem to demand of the critic the same effacement as of the director.*
JM: The best magazine for literary criticism is the *Times Literary Supplement* because there is not one single signed criticism in it. There are some brilliant bits, sometimes even cruel, but always anonymous. That for me is the essence of criticism. Look at television in America: even the weather report has its own sponsors and publicity. For five minutes the weatherman talks to you about low pressure over Greenland, in Ecuador, in the North of Alaska, even though all you really want to know is what the weather will be like tomorrow. Then a man whose qualifications are dubious comes on and has anywhere from forty-five seconds to a minute and a half to deliver criticism about something that another man has spent a year or two creating. He must have run from the cinema to the studio and developed his critique in the taxi! On one channel there is a man with a ridiculous moustache who had a favorable review of *Sleuth*, but whose only purpose seems to be to make fun of the films he has seen, and, if possible, to make other people on the set laugh at his jokes. To use the work of a filmmaker in order to crack a few jokes so that one can become a television personality is an extremely cruel exercise.

MC: *What do you think of the evolution of production conditions in America?*
JM: They have never been worse. I was criticized recently by the Academy of Motion Picture Arts and Sciences because I said that it would be good if we had a Motion Picture Academy in America. They try to maintain this idiotic concept of "the industry" even though there

is no industry. The carpetbaggers and the looters who direct it now, or who squeeze it like a lemon in order then to sell it as real estate, or who, while representing the grand firms, concern themselves with their leisure time, completely mock what cinema is. At least those horrible men like Mayer and Warner and Cohn liked what they did and thought that the duchies they created would exist forever. It is always the film distributors and the cinema-house owner who make money on a film.

This profession will not be viable if the filmmaker is not in direct contact with the audience who goes to see his work in the same way that the theatre-going public goes to the theatre. Meanwhile, the creator will always be fucked and will never see the revenues of his film unless the profits are so fantastic that they can't be hidden. Until then, be sure that those who invest money in a film don't lose it because it is all a question of credit and debt, interest calculations and bank charges. And I don't think that Mayer, Cohn, or Warner would have understood very much of this. It has become an accountant's business. The artist has never been in a worse jam.

A Conversation with Joseph L. Mankiewicz

DAVID SHIPMAN/1982

IN AUGUST, JOSEPH L. MANKIEWICZ came to the National Film Theatre for a Guardian Lecture, answering questions put by me and by the audience. He seldom gives interviews, and what follows is, with his permission, a transcript of his conversation on stage at the NFT and during some preliminary meetings.

I said in introducing him that the evening was a celebration of the time when Hollywood movies were literate, erudite, and witty—meaning, anyway, that his movies were. As he himself is. My generation first knew him as the writer-director of two films rich in those qualities, *A Letter to Three Wives* (1949) and *All About Eve* (1950), but we were to learn that his career in movies began long before. His elder brother, Herman J. Mankiewicz, then a leading writer with Paramount, got Joe a job there writing intertitles for silents. He began writing dialogue and/or scenarios with the coming of talkies—and, as far as I am concerned, would rate immortality for *Million Dollar Legs* alone, the 1932 comedy with W. C. Fields and Jack Oakie which makes the antics of the Marx Brothers seem logical in comparison. He also wrote the dialogue for *Our Daily Bread* (1934) and joined MGM to work on the screenplay of *Manhattan Melodrama* (also 1934). In 1936 he became a producer at Metro, responsible for a number of Joan Crawford vehicles, as well as such films as *Fury* (1936), *Three Comrades* (1937), *The Adventures of Huckleberry Finn* (1939), *The Philadelphia Story* (1940), and *Woman of the Year* (1942). He turned down Louis B. Mayer's offer to make him Thalberg's successor, and Mayer turned down all his requests to direct.

From *Films and Filming* (November 1982).

In 1943 he moved over to 20th Century-Fox on a contract specifying that he might produce, write, and direct any film on which he was engaged. He was anxious to begin directing, but agreed to work only as writer and producer on *The Keys of the Kingdom* (1945). He made his directorial bow on *Dragonwyck* (1946), since it gave him a chance to work with Lubitsch, whom he regarded as friend and mentor since their days together at Paramount. Fox had bought the property for Lubitsch, who didn't feel up to the task of directing after a heart attack; Lubitsch produced, and Mankiewicz directed, if not with much enthusiasm for the novel on which the film was based. He regarded his next films as a means of learning his new craft—*Somewhere in the Night* (1946), *The Late George Apley* (1947), *The Ghost and Mrs. Muir* (1947), and *Escape* (1948).

In 1949 he won two Oscars for *A Letter to Three Wives*, for writing and directing, an unprecedented feat in the history of the Motion Picture Academy; he did so again the following year for *All About Eve*, which was also voted the Best Picture. He directed some other stylish entertainments before leaving Fox—*No Way Out* (1950), *People Will Talk* (1951), and *Five Fingers* (1952)—and then returned to MGM on a three picture contract: but after *Julius Caesar* (1953) there was no agreement on properties and he decided to set up his own independent company. For this company, he wrote and directed *The Barefoot Contessa* (1954) and *The Quiet American* (1958); he wrote and directed *Guys and Dolls* (1955) for Goldwyn and directed *Suddenly, Last Summer* (1959) for Sam Spiegel. Then came *Cleopatra* (1963), about which he declines to speak publicly—not because of the publicity during its making, but because he was removed from it (if only temporarily) during the editing stage; he dislikes the version Fox released and feels that the four hour version—which he envisaged as being released in two parts—was much superior. He is no happier over *The Honey Pot* (1967), after the distributor (United Artists) altered his concept and cut both the script and the finished film. He resolved never again to direct one of his own screenplays, and worked with other people's material on his last two films to date, *There Was a Crooked Man . . .* (1970) and *Sleuth* (1972).

Of himself today he says:

JM: I've painted myself into an arrogant or an honourable corner, I don't know which. I turned down *The Front Page* and the golden opportunity to direct Farrah Fawcett Major's first film. I thought *The Front Page* dated too much . . . Billy [Wilder] called me to make sure I didn't want it before taking it on; and who goes to see television stars? I aborted a screenplay which could have been the best I ever wrote, based on a novel by Dee Wells, *Jane,* because huge overheads were being run up unknown to me.

DS: *Let's start with* All About Eye, *because it's many people's favourite movie. Was Bette Davis your choice or Zanuck's?*
JM: Zanuck's choice was Marlene Dietrich. He wanted Jeanne Crain as Eve and José Ferrer to play the critic, Addison de Witt. I wanted Bette but she was unavailable. The part was offered to Gertrude Lawrence by me. She had a lady lawyer by the name of Fanny Holtzman, who decided what Gertie would play. She wrote me a letter, followed by a lengthy telephone call, saying that she didn't want Miss Lawrence to play in anything that would even intimate that Miss Lawrence drank. I was thinking to myself that perhaps I knew the wrong Gertrude Lawrence. Then Fanny said that in the party scene there should be a song for Gertie to sing, something like "My Bill." I said that I thought that that had already been done in *Show Boat.*

   Claudette Colbert was my next choice: and I'm always being asked how I thought Claudette could have played Margo Channing. Well, Claudette is a good actress, but nothing like Bette drunk, Bette emotional, Bette going through all the trials and tribulations of the ageing actress and more particularly the actress-woman dichotomy. I don't think Claudette could have identified with it as completely as Bette did, but Claudette solved the entire problem by slipping on a step and dislocating her back. And it seemed to me a doomed movie until Bette read the screenplay and made herself available by quickly finishing *Payment on Demand* and going straight into costume fittings.

DS: *You have said somewhere Tallulah Bankhead made a new career out of what she said was Davis's impersonation of her.*
JM: Tallulah had a husky voice and behaved rather flamboyantly. Well, we shot the interiors of the theatre at the Curran in San Francisco, which is the closest thing to legitimate to be found in the state of California, and Bette showed up on the first morning talking like this: she had ruptured

several blood vessels in her throat screaming at her then husband the night before. I said, "Kid, that's your voice and you go and get yourself hoarse every day because we're stuck with it. And it's good voice for the part." And Tallulah was not doing too well at the time, but she had a marvellous publicity man who got a radio show for her, *The Show of Shows*, and she manufactured a sort of feud for herself on the air between herself and Bette Davis—like the Jack Benny–Fred Allen feud. So when someone asks me how Claudette Colbert could have played Margo I say that, if she had, Ina Claire would have had a very successful radio show!

DS: *You actually wrote the film in the first place because you were interested in the problems of actresses.*
JM: I'm besotted by women and the problems of women. They offer so much more to a writer, to a director: they're more complicated, more exciting than men.

DS: *You directed one of the very special ladies, and she is in that film, Marilyn Monroe.*
JM: Marilyn had an agent by the name of Johnny Hyde, and he was madly in love with her and wanted a career for her. Now we're deluged with books about Hollywood and the poor little thing that Hollywood destroyed. Marilyn was destroyed long before she reached Hollywood. Nothing I did in *All About Eve* suddenly made her into an attractive star. The audiences wanted to know about her.

She had been at Fox for two years, one of the stock company. The stock company girls were called upon to entertain out-of-town buyers and to acts as "hostesses" at conventions—to be charming and consoling to ageing executives in the late afternoon. Every few years there would be an economy drive and the stock company would go and four secretaries and three waitresses. (At MGM the matzo balls and chicken soup would go.) Marilyn was fired.

Johnny wanted the part in *Eve* for her and Zanuck didn't want her on the lot. I told Johnny, "I think she could do it." Sheree North was up for it: any number of big-bosomed young ladies could have played it. I found Marilyn a very strange person in some ways. She was alone. I don't mean a loner, which has its own meaning. After a day's work a group of us would be having drinks and Marilyn would come in by herself. She'd come in and sit across the room. We'd invite her over, and she'd be pleased to come, but the next night the same thing would happen. She was never *with* anyone. Forgive me, but her reputation was not a savoury one—too many of the grips, the electricians had been, er, intimate with her. The hairdressers weren't mad about doing her hair. And lo and behold, these letters started coming in: it is always the audience that makes a star. All the billing in the world and the billboards can't do it. It's the people who pay their hard-earned money across the ticket window who make stars.

Look, I liked Marilyn. She walked by me one day carrying a book—like it was an adder. I asked her what she was reading, and it was *Letters to a Young Poet* by Rainer Maria Rilke. I asked her how come she had chosen that, and she said, "You see, I haven't read many books and what I do is walk into the Hollywood Bookstore at night and sort of pick books at random, and if it catches my attention I read it. Is that wrong?" I said, "Marilyn, I can't think of a better way in the whole world to buy a book." And she was so pleased, sent me a copy of the book the next day.

Well, jump ahead to when she killed herself: she was not wanted. Nobody wanted to make movies with Marilyn Monroe. Fox had put an enormous amount of money into *Something's Got to Give* and it was never going to be finished. And nobody else was going to hire her. She was drinking a lot and, when I think now of Rita Hayworth, I think that Marilyn would be fifty-six. The most dreadful things that happen out there are what happens to the Hayworths, the Hedy Lamarrs—I can rattle the names off. They sit with the wrinkles, the sags, and no one wants them any more. I think that Marilyn died at the time she should have died. I think Marilyn would have loved becoming, fake or no fake, a symbol of unrequited ambition. I think it's wonderful that people think of her in glowing, glorious terms, but then she was a young lady who was very busy—busy paying back the hatred she felt towards the man who had made her do some dreadful things when she was scrambling to get a foothold.

DS: *The columnist Joe Hyams once insisted that the role Ava Gardner played in* The Barefoot Contessa *was based on Rita Hayworth.*
JM: Well, vaguely.

DS: *You were disappointed in the film?*

JM: I made *The Barefoot Contessa* at a time I couldn't make *The Barefoot Contessa*. Let me remove the mythological definitions and say that it wasn't the major studios which refused to let us do certain things but the censors—the Hays Office, and even worse, the Catholic Legion of Decency. My Hollywood Cinderella of *The Barefoot Contessa* married her prince and found that he was either homosexual or impotent. I couldn't do either, so I manufactured some tale about his having been wounded somewhere below the belt in the War.

And then again with the language: Mr. Lubitsch was my master—he could say so much without words, let alone today's easy expletives. He could put Jeanette MacDonald into an unrevealing gown, and just show her having her hand reach out for a door knob, and then look around and go in: and the camera would remain on the door knob. And he could generate more truly enjoyable sex out of that instant of indecision and suggest more going on behind that door than any forty square feet of intertwining genitals. The rules of the Code were idiotic, but they called for that much more ingenuity from the writer and director.

Today merely provides a field-day for all the hot-buck pornographers who have put light bulbs in front of their stores. But then you're always hoist on your own petard: the moment you say you don't want censorship, the pornographers move in. I wish I could have made a better film out of *The Barefoot Contessa*. I wish I could have got Thelma Ritter [in *All About Eve*] to say, "God, what a story, everything but the bloodhounds snapping at her arse." They wouldn't even let her say "bottom." I had to go through all the synonyms and ended up with "rear end." On the set there used to be a man who used to examine Lana Turner's cleavage, and with him was a wardrobe woman with a roll of lace: he would put his finger in, and so—the lace would go in. It drove the designers crazy. But that's what they did. That's the type of idiotic thing that happened.

DS: *Did you challenge the Hays Office with* People Will Talk? *After all, Jeanne Crain is pregnant and unmarried. And it's a film with as much good music as good talk: in those days movies seldom suggested that good music was an adjunct to civilised life.*

JM: As far as the pregnant heroine was concerned, that was a boo-boo. She was not punished. *Back Street* had to wind up unhappily.[1]
As far as the music was concerned, my point is that civilised, articulate people have problems worth dramatising. The underworld is interesting—the poor, too, ethnic groups, gangsters: but there are a tremendous number of well-spoken, well-dressed people who have problems worth putting on the screen.

DS: *In* Five Fingers *you dealt with the sort of people, the diplomatic set, which movies usually fight shy of.*
JM: God knows I hated the Germans. I fought against them. All the Nazis didn't say, "Ve haf vays of making you speak." But von Pappen, for instance, was an educated man. Granted the upper classes are worthy of extinction, they're still worth dramatising. Royalty: there are good movies to be made about Princess Margaret and her marital problems and Anne and her horses. Suppose these bright young Princes turn out an embarrassment to the Queen Mum: that could make a marvellous high comedy—except that high comedy has become an endangered species. Where are the Carole Lombards? You have Maggie Smith . . . Bette could have done it, but Bette's getting on. Where are the young Rex Harrisons?

DS: Five Fingers *was your last film under your Fox contract. Henry Hathaway was to have directed, but Zanuck reassigned it to you because you liked the subject and wanted to fill your last commitment.*
JM: What I did was not to take a writing credit. Because I had a letter from Mr. Zanuck saying that he couldn't take it any more. If Kazan directed a film, Zanuck was still the producer. If Moss Hart wrote a film, Zanuck was still the producer. But if I wrote and directed, he got lost in the shuffle—and, I quote from the letter, "I just can't play second fiddle to anyone, Joe."

DS: *Can you tell us some more about Zanuck?*
JM: Darryl had an instinct for things which would go on the screen. He thought his film about Woodrow Wilson was the greatest film ever and was livid with the Academy because they wouldn't choose it.

1. Mankiewicz was probably referring to the fact that the public rejected *People Will Talk*.

Darryl was small, with many of the drawbacks of small men—
Napoleon, Junior Laemmle, Senior Laemmle . . . When you're little and
you're put in a position of power, you overcome it by giving orders.

DS: *Was he a creative producer? Did he contribute to any of your films?*
JM: Surprisingly, he did. When I finished a screenplay, the first person
I wanted to read it was Darryl. But after that, look out. The more often
he saw it the more damage he did. His first instincts were fine, but he
hated motivation. He loved only the peaks and he'd leap from battle to
battle and omit the reasons they were fighting. Let's get to the shoot-
out, let's head 'em off at the pass. That's what he wanted. Outside of
that, I had very little to do with Darryl till he tried to destroy what I
thought was going to be a big effort of mine.

DS: *How does he compare with the other moguls—say, David O. Selznick?*
JM: Selznick was the result of the most successful publicity campaign
in the history of movies. He's probably up there now still chuckling at
the successful job Russell Birdwell did on him. Above all else he wanted
it to be known that the producer made the film. If you examine his
record you'll find that there were always at least two directors. He
didn't, couldn't do it with Hitchcock, but he fired Cukor, he fired
Johnny Huston. When I wrote *Manhattan Melodrama* for him he broke
two directors, Woody van Dyke and Jack Conway. It didn't matter as far
as costs went. Van Dyke was known as "One-Take Woody": he worked
fast. So did Richard Thorpe. It didn't matter that they lost half of Joan
Crawford's face, and most of the film had to be reshot. At MGM they
had a budget for the film, but none for re-takes. The latter might cost
the earth, but meanwhile the Van Dykes and Thorpes were golden boys.

DS: *You chose not to work with Selznick?*
JM: Yes. He wanted me to do *Tender is the Night.* I couldn't see myself
slaving over the dialogue. Some novelists cannot write dialogue and
Scott Fitzgerald was one of them.

DS: *You enjoyed making* Guys and Dolls *with Sam Goldwyn?*
JM: Sam was tough, semi-literate. He read my screenplay and said, "You
have such charmth and warmth." Charmth? But he goes right on. He sits

by you and gives you the best to work with. One day Frank Loesser and I tried to hide from him, in a broom closet. He found us. And he looked at us with great dignity, this poor ex-glove salesman, and he said, "Say, listen, I'm not the kind of producer who slips money under the door."

You had to love that boy. And look at the films he made. Willy loved working for him. You went first class with Sam all the way. However, if there could be one person in the world more miscast as Nathan Detroit than Frank Sinatra that would be Laurence Olivier—and I am one of Larry's greatest fans. Anyway, Frank wanted to play it, and the role had been written for Sam Levene who was divine in it. Poor Marlon. He did his best. There he was trying to sing "Luck Be a Lady" and kneeling among the chorus boys is Frank Sinatra. And Marlon knew that Frank was there and Frank comes out with a single of that same song which sells two million copies. So there was no love lost there. I thought Frank was terribly miscast in the part.

DS: *You worked with Brando twice.*

JM: I gave him *Julius Caesar* to read: he never thought anyone would call on him to play in it. I myself was terrified—a Yankee swine taking on what was left of the British Empire. Really, Shakespeare and how dare I? Marlon offered to make some tapes. We were in New York and everyone out there in Hollywood was waiting to see what would happen. Marlon called me; he had a terrible pad on 57th Street—oh, it was filthy—and there were tape recordings all over the place. He locked the door and started playing these tapes. What he'd done, he'd gone out and bought discs of Oliver, Gielgud . . . I mean, he went back to Gerald du Maurier. So he imitated them, and I said, "Marlon, you sound like June Allyson." Anyway, we decided we'd take a crack at it, and for the next six months the idea of Brando, old mumbles, playing Mark Antony was material for every stand-up comic in the world. As you know, it turned out well. When the time came for it to open in London I was here, but too afraid to stay. So I ran. To Paris. One of the most treasured memories of my life is reading the British notices of *Julius Caesar*. To get back to Marlon, he didn't want to do *Guys and Dolls* because he'd never done a musical. I sent him a cable, "Understand you don't want to do *Guys and Dolls* as you've never done a musical. You have nothing to worry about as I haven't done one either. Love, Joe."

Marlon is or was one of the great acting talents of our time. What happened, I really don't know. No one really knows. He could have gone on from *Caesar* to do almost anything he wanted.

We are not as fortunate as you. In the United States we have lost four generations of writers, directors, actors. The New York theatre is *drained* annually of anyone who's any good. The agents, the flesh-peddlers send them three thousand miles from the theatre and there they sit, their work not maturing. TV is made three thousand miles from the theatre. Young actors in London make a film at Pinewood, then do TV or a play. We don't have that. That is a tremendous loss.

Marlon could have attempted Shakespeare or anything else. I ran into him on the street once, and he was getting chubby. I said, "Champ, have you one more good fight left in you?" and he said, "What are you talking about?" I replied that if we could work as we'd worked on *Caesar*—six weeks' rehearsal—we would do *Macbeth*, with Maggie Smith. He gave me a strange look and shook his head. "See ya, Joe," he said.

But you can't live anybody's life for them. For example, I think Larry Olivier has made tremendous sacrifices—especially for the theatre. He deserves his position as the leading actor of the English-speaking theatre: there is no second. But he lived with a discipline: he commuted from Brighton for years, lived on the pittance the National paid him, supported by all those cameo roles in movies. When I took the script of *Sleuth* to him, I said, "You have to start playing full-length parts again." As it's turned out he's now working very hard, for the first time in his life to make as much money as he can.

But Marlon never had that sort of discipline. He had a wild talent that could be harnessed, but you couldn't control the man. I don't think he had the *love* for theatre that Larry has. It's as simple as that. Young actors can bloom in England, whereas in the States they're put in an ivory ghetto, and they stay at the level they were when they entered it.

DS: *John Houseman produced* Julius Caesar . . . *I've just been reading his second volume of autobiography, and he says of your brother Herman that he had ambivalent feelings about you to the last, "his successful younger brother."*
JM: There's a line in *Victoria Regina*. Robert Browning is asked the meaning of a line and he says, "When I wrote it, the meaning was

known only to me and God. But now only God knows." I don't know what Houseman means.

DS: *On your brother, very briefly: who wrote* Citizen Kane?
JM: That's very easy to answer. Poor Pauline Kael didn't have to suffer through her own idiom and so many pages. Orson [Welles] had complete say on *Citizen Kane*, that was true. Here was a newcomer given complete charge of everything. So let's work by what we used to call internal criticism in the faculty room: if Orson Welles had written the screenplay, do you think he would have taken *second* billing as the writer? To a professional, this was clearly a case of the boss sticking his name on the screenplay. No, my brother wrote *Citizen Kane*. My brother was a *brilliant* man: he would have made the best political commentator or columnist that ever lived. Knew more about American and British politics of the early nineteenth century than any other man I've ever known. And very witty.

DS: *Neither of you had much respect for the tycoons. Were you luckier than he was, or more tactful? You didn't like Louis B. Mayer.*
JM: An evil man. Did me one good favour: he let me produce *Fury.* He didn't like the subject, wasn't interested in films with a social purpose. But Thalberg was producing *Romeo and Juliet*, and Mayer wanted to have an "intellectual" baby of his own to throw against that. So that was *Fury*.
    My blazing row with him was about Judy Garland. Judy was then about eighteen and we were very good friends. She was beginning to show those signs—not showing up on time and taking too much benzedrine, that sort of thing. She was incredibly beautiful, enchanting. I was concerned about her. Her mother was a dreadful bitch—I mean, she pushed this child out on a stage at the age of three to sing *Jingle Bells*, and she used to scream at her, in my presence, "You know you're ugly, you little hunchback. The only thing people want from you is to hear you sing." She used to lock her in cupboards.
    At any rate, Carl Menninger of the Menninger Clinic in Topeka was a good friend of mine, and he was in Beverly Hills. I persuaded Judy to go and see him and he said, "Miss Garland, you have some problems, and we might be able to work them out if you'll give us a year. If not with us, some other psychoanalyst."

Judy wanted to start, but unfortunately told her mother. And the next thing I knew I was summoned to Mayer's office, and he was *choleric* as I walked in. Obviously the word "psychiatrist" was enough to set him off. And Mrs. Gumm [*Garland's mother*] was there screaming, and Eddie Mannix, the wonderful Irish manager, sitting in a corner. And Mayer yelled, how dare I interfere in the life of Judy—a mother's love was all she needed. And I said, "A mother's love, my ass." The mother said, "I know what to do with my daughter"—and it got into one of those screaming fights. I was so aghast that I finally said, "Look, Mr. Mayer, the studio is obviously not big enough for both of us. One of us has to go." At that Eddie Mannix fell off his chair and I was at Fox within a week.

DS: *But that was a good thing for you, since you had wanted to direct and he wouldn't let you.*

JM: I call my six years producing my black years. I was pretty good with screenplays so I was supposed to take the ones they couldn't lick off the shelf: there was always a couple of million dollars worth of them. Not a pleasant job, I may add. I begged for a chance to direct what I had written because the two disciplines are interwoven. I don't think there's a good screenwriter who doesn't "see" his scene as he writes it, sees certain images, is aware of certain tempi, maybe even hears music. A good screenplay has already been directed. But in those days the screenplay was taken away from the writer, who might not even know the director—and the director could go off in another direction altogether.

DS: *You went to Fox with a splendid record as a producer, and got a contract on your own terms.*

JM: Well, there was Joe Schenck, who didn't like Louis Mayer, and I was fortunate to get to Fox while Darryl Zanuck was liberating Africa. Joe Schenck was running the studio and he gave me the contract I wanted. Mayer had always said direction was out of the question.

DS: *Didn't Mayer ask you to work for him after he was sacked from MGM?*

JM: Yes. I never thought I'd hear from him again, but after he was thrown out by his boss, Nick Schenck, and I went into independent production he sent for me to ask if I would become his partner. I didn't think it would work.

DS: *That was just after the McCarthy period. Your career was in peril for a while.*
JM: I had been involved in a bewildering, fascinating battle with Cecil DeMille about a compulsory loyalty oath for directors. I was president of the Directors Guild. I am completely apolitical, belong to no political party, and that was what confounded DeMille when he tried to look me up. I was away in Europe when DeMille and the board of the Guild had passed this compulsory loyalty oath, which meant that in order to direct a film in the United States of America you have to state that you were not, and had never been, a member of the Communist Party. I came back to find that this had been passed in my absence and that the members had been asked to sign open ballots, yes or no, which was a violation of our constitution, the right to a secret ballot. Mr. DeMille said that this was the time to stand up and be counted, and I simply said, "Who gave you the right to do the counting?"

As president, all I could do was call a meeting: it was the only opposition I could manage. I wanted to keep the debate going, and I kept working on a man called John Ford, who was supposed to be extremely conservative. Clearly, there was going to be a blacklist of directors who refused to sign the oath, and I thought I could swing Ford because he was Irish, hated the idea of blacklists. So, I called a meeting. DeMille countered that by sending out men on motorcycles to have me impeached before the meeting so that it would be cancelled. It was unbelievable to me that 99.3 per cent of the Guild's six hundred members were in favour of this oath.

The meeting took place, the most dramatic meeting I was ever at. Willy Wyler was there, Fritz Lang, Mamoulian, Huston, Zinnemann, and one woman director, Ida Lupino. George Stevens led my group. All the old timers were with DeMille—Leo McCarey, Clarence, Brown, Raoul Walsh . . . Frank Capra agreed with DeMille as far as the worth of the oath was concerned, but he did not show at the meeting because of those motorcycle riders. Frank said, "I want no part of that."

It got to be two-thirty in the morning, and my eyes were fixed on one man, wearing a cap, sneakers, puffing his pipe. That was Jack Ford, and I knew that the way he went the Guild would go. If he went with DeMille and the Guild, I would be out of work. Forget my four Oscars. Ford eventually introduced himself and said, "My name is Ford. I direct westerns." That was his famous introductory line and he looked at DeMille in the friendliest way. He said, "Cecil, you and I go back to 1916, maybe even earlier, right? Let me tell you something, when it comes to providing the people of the world with the kind of movie they want to see there isn't anyone in this room who can touch you, and I respect you for that." I was sick to my stomach. He went on and on. I once said that DeMille had his finger *up* the pulse of the public, and here was old Jack Ford saying, in effect, I gotta hand it to you.

Then he paused, as only Ford could pause, and he said "But, Cecil, I don't like you. And I don't like a goddam thing you stand for. I move that we go home and start making *movies* because that's our job." And John Huston jumped up and said, "I second that motion," and there was acclamation and that was it. Except, however, that Willy Wyler demanded that each member of the board resign individually, which they had to do.

DS: *You were once asked at a function like this whether you didn't miss Montgomery Clift, and you gave what I thought was a perfect answer, "Yes, and I miss Jean Arthur and all the other marvellous talented people."*
JM: Clift was difficult. Have you read Johnny Huston's book? He went through it, too. The man was impossible. But I never got any thanks for the trouble I took.

DS: *He wasn't Clark Gable.*
JM: I worked a lot with Gable. I was all of twenty-five when I wrote *Manhattan Melodrama.* Clark was a marvelous character. The movie stars of his generation were a different breed. He did four films a year. Joan Crawford did four films a year. Divide fifty-two weeks into four. Now they do one film every four years, and they get more for that one picture than Clark made in his entire career at MGM. If Clark was late, they'd all be down on the set wanting to know why. It was a whole different attitude. The major studios in those days were individual duchies. In the early days we worked six days a week. So you had to know each other pretty well. There was an *esprit de corps* and an *esprit de*

studio. If you left MGM to go to Fox, your loyalties went with you. Mayer created a duchy at Culver City. The prop-makers brought their sons in to be prop-makers, and so on. They had their bungalows around the studio, within the walls of the castle, as it were.

One of the great pities to me in the collapse of the studios is that there is no longer any continuity: the master prop-man's son isn't going to inherit his prop-wagon, and pass his expertise on to young directors. Fred Zinnemann got his chance at MGM: he went from a two-reeler to a B-movie to an A-movie. That's the way the studio system worked. And the word star has become utterly meaningless.

In all my years in Hollywood—I left there in 1952 or 1953, because I didn't want my children to grow up there—I never ever heard the word "superstar." That's a TV invention. I guess they had to have something, because everybody's starred. Also starring, co-starring, starring with, and if they are not starred they get their name in a box. It's absurd. I remember Hume Cronyn coming into my office one day so excited— and this was a man who'd grown up in the theatre—and he said, "I've made it! I've got first featured billing!" That meant something then. But acting meant something then. Writing meant something then. Directing something meant something. Just poking at audiences in the eyeballs wasn't the purpose of films.

DS: *Looking back, don't you wish now that you'd been directing comedies with, say, Carole Lombard, Margaret Sullavan, and Jean Arthur, instead of producing melodramas for Joan Crawford?*
JM: I wish they were all alive today. I loved Margaret Sullavan. She was a darling, wonderful, unhappy woman. Her unhappiness, I think, crept upon her as the years went by. Because Maggie lived to act and it was rough [*i.e. Sullavan's growing deafness*]. I don't know that my life would have been *happier*, though. I adored Jean as a person, but I can't say that she was the easiest person to work with.

But I wish there was material around of the type they had. I wish there were more players with their skill. Maggie Smith and Carol Burnett: that's it for the women. I wish . . . Hollywood would collapse and move to New York. I wish they hadn't closed the cinemas and changed them into garages. I wish film-makers had some of our discipline.

DS: *You are not in sympathy with recent trends?*

JM: No. [Elia] Kazan used that word to me just two weeks ago—
sympathy. He said, "I'm not in sympathy with the movies, with the
people making them, nor with what they're doing." I agree: if I go back
to work, it will be to make movies about human beings. With rate
exceptions, today's Hollywood movies are cartoons, rich, yes, and beautifully illustrated, but with no particular depth. There are a few human
beings scattered among the robots, but their dialogue could be written
in balloons, like comic strips. I enjoyed *E.T.* It was charming, enjoyable
to look at. But it didn't tax my mind at all. On an emotional level it was
like watching one of the old Lassie films. I don't mean to put it down:
you felt for the kid and that was nice. Spielberg has an incredible talent
for that sort of thing. But . . . I'd like to be working. I'd like to do more
Shakespeare. *Coriolanus.* Love to do that.

Joseph Mankiewicz, Master of the Movies

PAUL ATTANASIO / 1986

HERE, IN THE DEN of his big brick house, at the end of a hard dirt road, in the midst of a leafy, puncture-proof country quiet that he has perhaps never known in his soul, and that he certainly never put on the screen, Joseph Mankiewicz, the extraordinary man of movies, fishes in his pocket for a biscuit he offers his black Labrador, Cassius, who beseeches him with an appropriately lean and hungry look.

"You know you're getting old when you start buying affection from your dog," he says. "He's a whore, and I'm a pimp," he says, half to Cassius, half to his visitor. "Yes, that's right, sure."

At seventy-seven, he is still handsome, a face etched by intellect, a broad forehead and square jaw. And those marvelous eyes! Pale and pearly blue as the sky over Hollywood, eyes that make the frames of his glasses a proscenium arch, behind which passes a drama of winces, winks, and bull's-eye stares.

"Man of movies" is the best you can do. The usual vocabulary—producer, director, screen writer—fails to encompass him, for at various times he has been one, the other, or three at once; and among the best at all of them.

"I have a lot to be sad about," he says. "Not bitter in any way. But I think it can be said fairly that I've been in on the beginning, the rise, peak, collapse, and end of the talking picture."

On the mantelpiece preside four Oscars from 1949 and 1950, the miracle years when he won back-to-back writing and directing awards

---

From the *Washington Post* (June 1, 1986). © 1986, *The Washington Post*. Reprinted with permission.

for *A Letter to Three Wives* and *All About Eves*; around the room, shelves full of books on English drama. Twin poles of a life, of a career rich with achievement, and a career that was lost.

In the coming weeks, as part of its celebration of the fiftieth anniversary of the Directors Guild, the American Film Institute will honor Mankiewicz with a series of screenings of his films, culminating in his appearance here June 25 at a presentation of *All About Eve*.

The AFI tribute may augur a renewed, and long overdue, appreciation of Mankiewicz's work, which began at the end of the silent era at Berlin's famous UFA studio, where he translated titles into English, and ended in 1972 with *Sleuth*, for which he was nominated for the Best Director Oscar.

The general neglect of Mankiewicz stems from an emphasis that has developed over the last twenty-five years on the visual, or cinematic, element in films, a light in which Mankiewicz's films suffer. For the most part, his movies were visually routine, the filmmaker's tools—the camera, lights, sound, and editing—merely functional. Or as he says now, "I'm a guy who doesn't know anything about a camera."

What he knew, and cared passionately about, was words. "Since the beginning of western theater," he says, "the conflicts of the human being have been best dramatized, and best understood, and best enjoyed, and best wept at, by *conversation*, by conflict of *talk*. Not by wars, not by being blown up or sunk. It started with the Greeks and their complaints against the gods, man against God, and later man against society, man against himself."

When Mankiewicz refers to the "talking picture," the emphasis is on talking. In the specialized world of the old studio system, Mankiewicz started as an expert in dialogue, sitting across the desk from another writer who wrote the scenario on one side of the page, then passed it across for him to fill in the words, and the craft stayed with him. You knew his characters by how they talked, and he was a virtuoso of sarcasm, brittle, brutal, astringent, and ultimately exhilarating sarcasm—his movies were always best when he had actors like Cary Grant or Bette Davis or George Sanders or Katharine Hepburn, who knew their way around a line.

Today, it's simply accepted that a film belongs to its director. But Mankiewicz was a screen writer *auteur*—his films were his because he *wrote* them—and as a screen writer *auteur*, his only equal, perhaps, was

Billy Wilder. He came to Hollywood at a time when—despite the dictum of Irving Thalberg, the boy wonder of MGM, that writers were just jerks with Underwoods—writing *mattered*. His colleagues were men and women who grew up in the disciplines of the theater and the short story, who knew the essentials of storytelling; and more than his flair for dialogue, what made Mankiewicz a truly great screen writer was his sense of structure, his intimacy with an audience's expectations.

Listening to Joe Mankiewicz talk about a story is like listening to Ted Williams talk about hitting a baseball. Consider *Woman of the Year*, the classic '40s comedy starring Katharine Hepburn and Spencer Tracy, which he produced for director George Stevens. The highlight of the film is a sequence at the end where Hepburn, a high-powered newspaper columnist, tries to make breakfast for Tracy, her husband, and spectacularly, hilariously fails—a sequence that, as Mankiewicz remembers, was not in the original movie.

"We took *Woman of the Year* out and previewed it, and it laid the biggest egg," he says. "So back we went to the studio and I sat there with George and we called in John Lee Mahin, who was a very good writer. Visualize the effect on a woman sitting there in the audience, a plain, ordinary woman from Glendale or Riverdale or anywhere. And Kate Hepburn—God she's beautiful, God she plays golf well, God she can get anyone in the world on the phone, God she knows what to do all the time, God she wears clothes well. And the woman says to herself, 'What can I do that she can't do?'

"So I said, 'George, I think that's the key.' He said, 'You're damn right it is. We gotta put her on her rear end.' So I sat down with John Mahin and I wrote the kitchen scene, where she tries to make breakfast. At that moment this woman in the audience can say, 'She can talk to Batista but she can't make a goddam waffle! *I* can make a cup of coffee!' And then she loved Kate. She felt sorry for her—she can't keep a man! And that was as simple as that."

Mankiewicz didn't just know screenplays—he knew actors, and the chemistry between actors. The pairing he created in *Woman of the Year* became a noun, and an adjective, in the Hollywood lexicon: Tracy-and-Hepburn.

"I introduced them," Mankiewicz remembers. "Spence and I were walking over to the Thalberg Building one day on our way to lunch, as

Kate was coming up. She looked at him and you could tell there was gonna be a conflagration there. Big fire. And I said, 'I think you two should meet.' He said, 'How do you do?' And she said, 'I think I may be a little tall for you, Mr. Tracy.'

"I said, 'Look, Kate, don't worry about that. He'll cut you down to size.' "

What Mankiewicz saw in an instant, of course, became the essence of a series of classic films—Tracy cutting Hepburn down to size was what the Tracy-Hepburn films were all about.

He saw possibilities in actors that other directors didn't always see. Elizabeth Taylor was as good in *Suddenly, Last Summer* as she ever was. And Mankiewicz was the man who took the T-shirt away from Marlon Brando by casting him as Marc Antony in *Julius Caesar*.

"Marlon and I were both scared, oh boy," Mankiewicz remembers. "When I cast him as Marc Antony, he was material for every stand-up comic in the English-speaking world. They couldn't wait to do thier Marlon Brando bit, doing this 'Friends, Romans, countrymen' speech.

"We were both living in New York. He said, 'Just let me study this for a couple of weeks.' And what he did was wonderful, disarming and wonderful. He had a pad on 57th Street across from Carnegie Hall, and he called me in a couple of weeks. Oh God, what a place! He kept *possums* in there. He had wildlife . . . filthy place. He sat me down, and he played some tapes that he had made. Apparently he had gone out and gotten all the recordings that had ever been made, starting with Forbes-Robertson and Gerald du Maurier, Beerbohm Tree, right up to Michael Redgrave and Gielgud. And I listened to these tapes.

"And at the end of it, he said, 'Well?' I said, 'Marlon, it sounded exactly like June Allyson.' All I could think of was June Allyson reciting Shakespeare. I said, 'Boy we got work to do.' He said, 'That's what I thought, too.' And we worked."

The result was a performance that captured Marc Antony's caginess, but, more than that, found the animal anger at a warrior's center, something Mankiewicz and Brando discovered in rehearsal.

"We were in rehearsal clothes, I'm sitting on a ladder right behind Marlon, and I'm looking past James Mason, who played Brutus, at these faces, the Roman citizens, three hundred bits of Los Angeles riffraff, and they're all listening to Mason, and they're very intent. And suddenly, at the proper moment, I squeezed a button and the light comes on and out comes Marlon carrying Louis Calhern—it was like carrying the Frigidaire. He weighed 250 pounds, enormous actor. Good actor.

"And Brutus says, 'Now here comes Marc Antony, and I beseech you to listen to him.' And Brutus starts off, and they're mumbling to each other. They're obviously upset at the sight of Caesar, but they bought what Brutus has told them. And as they get done there's Marlon. 'What does he have to say, that SOB—they're talking that way. And suddenly, Marlon speaks up, and he says, 'Friends, Romans, countrymen, lend me . . . , And they can't hear him. 'Bury the bastard!' And he starts again.

"And suddenly it occurs to me, and I say, 'Marlon, get mad.' And he said, 'Friends, Romans, countrymen, *LEND* me your ears.' And I swear to you, the only time in my life that I felt a chill go up my spine, that's the only moment I ever felt in my entire career. 'Oh my God, I know why this man, this greatest of all writing or thinking men, used the word "lend."' For a *minute*, lend me your ears, not give me your ears. *Lend* me your ears, and that had the effect of quieting them down, that word "lend." I'd never heard it read that way before.

"But that moment of revelation that you get, when you understand why he picked a particular word, that joy comes out of direction. It happened, that's all. It's one of those pleasures."

Once upon a time, Joe Mankiewicz swore he would never go to Hollywood.

He delivered that oath to his father, a professor at New York's City College and elsewhere, and to John Erskine, a playwright who had been his mentor at Columbia University, saw some talent in him and had groomed him for a career in academia. But when he found himself in Paris a year later, washing dishes for food, fresh out of Columbia and fresh out of cash, he cabled his brother Herman, already established as one of Hollywood's best screen writers (he would later write *Citizen Kane*), who told him to head West.

He arrived in Hollywood in 1929, nineteen years old and nineteen hours late. "Herman met me at the train, and he said to me, 'Did you bring a dinner jacket?' I said, 'A *what*?' He said, 'A tuxedo, tuxedo.' I said, 'What, are you out of your mind?' I had one pair of underwear! Brown shoes! So he said, 'I'll lend you one of mine.' He said, 'I'm taking you to a party tonight, that's why I asked. A party at Jesse Lasky's beachhouse [Lasky was then head of production at Paramount].' Just picture: Nineteen years old. I had just come across the country on this train. I spent the afternoon, I remember, putting black polish on my brown shoes, to go with my brother's tuxedo. I had a straw hat which I gave to Lasky's butler and I never saw it again, and I've never worn a hat since.

"I went to Lasky's beach house, first night in Hollywood. I gave my hat to the butler, he vanished with part of my trousseau, and I stood there like a kid who had been locked into a candy store, or F.A.O. Schwarz. My God, there was Clara Bow! Olga Baclanova, Kay Francis, Gary Cooper, George Bancroft . . . these women, stars, they all were there.

"I couldn't take it, and I saw a familiar back. A familiar back, broad, tall. And it turned around.

"And it was Professor John Erskine.

"Who else in the world could have shown up and made me feel guiltier? Horror. I had given my oath to this man. And he looked at me and he said, '*Joe?*' And I said, kind of sickly, 'Hello, Professor Erskine.' He said, 'Joe, what are you doing here?' I said, 'Well, what are you doing, Professor Erskine?' He said, 'I'm writing at Warner Brothers, where are you?'"

At twenty-two Mankiewicz was nominated for an Oscar for writing *Skippy* and would have won if David Selznick hadn't shown up at the eleventh hour with a fistful of votes for *Cimarron*. ("The votes in those days there was none of that nonsense about Price Waterhouse," he recalls. "The votes were counted like a floating crap game on the floor of a bedroom in the Hollywood Roosevelt Hotel.") He wrote gags for W. C. Fields. He rewrote F. Scott Fitzgerald's dialogue ("Maggie Sullavan took me aside and said, 'I can't read this, it's unplayable,' and I did what I could"), dined with William Faulkner, drank with Sinclair Lewis. At thirty-one he produced *The Philadelphia Story* for Louis B. Mayer's MGM.

Mankiewicz worked for six years as a producer for Mayer, who referred to him, for reasons that remain obscure, as "Harvard College."

"Have you ever been present when you yourself have said something very witty, you know it's witty, but you've said it in the wrong place, with the wrong people?" Mankiewicz begins. And suddenly, though you sit in a den in Bedford, New York, you're transported to a bygone, magical Hollywood.

"Mervyn LeRoy was the producer of *Wizard of Oz*. And they ran way over budget. Nick Schenck himself [the head of MGM's parent company Loew's], we used to call him the General, has come out from New York, and he says, 'Why is *The Wizard of Oz* costing so much, Louie?'

"So Louie called this executive meeting, and everybody's there, the production manager, other producers, and so on. All of them, 'Yessir, yessir General, yessir.' I'm sitting down, a little too much lunch, kind of dozing. Wasn't paying attention to it. 'LeRoy's doing this, for God's sake, where's Mervyn?'

"At any rate, nobody knew why the picture was going over budget. And Schenck would say, 'Louie, you don't seem to be in control here.' It was getting very dicey for L.B. And L.B. says, 'Look, why are we talking back and forth? General, I've got a man here: Harvard College. He knows production, he knows screenplays, he knows acting, he knows everything. Believe me, he'll tell ya.' And he looks at me. And Nick turns to me, I'm sitting right next to him, and he said, 'Well?'

I looked up and down the table, and the General said, 'Yes, tell me.' I said, 'I'm sorry, I didn't hear the question.' And Nick Schenck, president of Loew's Incorporated, said to me, 'Why is *The Wizard of Oz* running to over two million dollars? You're supposed to know these things.'

"And I said, 'Well . . . LeRoy *s'amuse*.'

"He said, 'What?'

"I said, 'Nothing.'

"He said, 'Yes, you did, you said something in French! Louie, he's talking French to me!'

"If I had said this at the writer's table, boy, they would have all broken up. It was the worst gaffe I ever made in my life."

"This is the first time they've shown any interest in me at all," Mankiewicz says of the AFI tribute. "I've been on their public mailing list: 'Dear Friend of Films.' For example, when they had the best fifty films ever made, remember that occasion? It was about seven or eight years back and the membership was going to vote, and they got down to the top fifty. I had one, maybe two in the top fifty. And they sent me an inviation this thick, again, 'Dear Friend of Films. You are invited to pay 350 bucks a ticket and come and mingle with the people who've made these films.' So I said, 'How the hell do I go mingle with myself at 350 bucks a ticket?' At the start of the year I receive these religiously: Come and mingle with people like me."

After *Sleuth*, which earned Oscar nominations for both Mankiewicz and his stars, Laurence Olivier and Michael Caine, Joseph Mankiewicz left the movie business, exiled in part by the times, in part by his refusal to bend to the times, in part by a sort of Hellenic desire to retire from the field with his reputation intact.

Aside from his long friendship with director Robert Benton and an occasional party, he has almost no connection with the Hollywood he helped build.

He remembers ruefully how Darryl Zanuck, the czar of 20th Century Fox, brought in his cutter and butchered Richard Burton's performance in *Cleopatra*, a performance that Burton, shortly before his death, said was the best work he ever did. "These are all the things you sit and contemplate if you're me," he says, "and you say, 'Who needed it?' "

And he looks at the books of English drama, and the Oscars on the mantelpiece, and he weighs them in his mind. And he looks at the portrait of his father, a stern-looking man staring out from above the Oscars, and he muses on the plans Dad and John Erskine had for young Joe, plans that he be a professor and a playwright, an eighteen-year-old kid who had whipped through Columbia and might have had a little talent as a writer.

"I wish now that I had done that," Mankiewicz says. "Because by now I'd be sitting here, I hope, I'd have been a professor emeritus, I think. The thing I love is in those books. I would have written two or three very good plays, I think. Maybe even a good book or two. I would have had something I did that stood for something. Instead of which I did a lot of movies that I'm sorry my name is on, but who doesn't? That's not the point.

"You won't believe this, it'll sound like crap, but I finally figured out that I'm so in love with the theater that I'm in awe of the theater. One thing I did not want ever to fail in was the theater. And I think if I had followed my father's and Erskine's advice, I'd have a standing. These goddam things," he says, waving at the Oscars, "these don't give what I call a standing. I won a hatful of awards, but the award is a pretty defenseless thing when you think of it. What they're supposed to reflect on me I don't know."

Maybe he's right about the Oscars, but the movies that won the Oscars? No.

What Mankiewicz proved, in *The Philadelphia Story* and *Woman of the Year* and *People will Talk* and *A Letter to Three Wives* and *All About Eve* and all the rest, was that movies could transcend the vulgarity that they have so often since slipped into, that they could be in every way the theater's equal, in mesmerizing us, enthralling us, provoking us, seizing our experience and capturing our hearts.

And as you walk out to the driveway with him and his dog, in Bedford's green serenity, you wish that Cassius were truly Cassius and could, without the resentment of Cassius, tell Joe Mankiewicz that he doth bestride the narrow world like a Colossus.

All About Joe

PETER STONE/1989

JOSEPH L. MANKIEWICZ, the versatile writer-director of *All About Eve*, *The Barefoot Contessa*, *Five Fingers*, and many other screen classics, was born in Wilkes-Barre, Pennsylvania, in 1909 and grew up in New York City. The son of a German-immigrant intellectual and the younger brother of Herman Mankiewicz, the co-author of *Citizen Kane*, he began his film career after graduating from Columbia University at nineteen, writing English intertitles for German silent films in Berlin. He soon joined his brother in Hollywood, where he worked as a screenwriter at Paramount before moving on to become a successful producer and director, primarily at MGM and Twentieth Century Fox.

Mankiewicz's literate style and scathing wit put the emphasis on *talking* in talking pictures. (Richard Burton referred to him affectionately as "an Oxford don *manqué*"; Richard Schickel called him "one of the tiny handful of epigrammists that have written for the screen.") As a screenwriter he contributed to such diverse films as *Alice in Wonderland, Our Daily Bread, Forsaking All Others*, and W. C. Fields's *Million Dollar Legs*. As a producer he was responsible for *The Philadelphia Story, Three Comrades, Woman of the Year*, and Fritz Lang's first American film, *Fury*. He directed his own first film, *Dragonwyck*, in 1946.

Mankiewicz consistently worked with the best actors of his time and shaped some of their finest performances. He reached what many consider to be the pinnacle of his career when he wrote and directed four films in 1949–50, including the double-Academy Award-winning *A Letter to Three Wives* and *All About Eve*. He went on to direct

From *Interview* (August 1989). Reprinted by permission.

Julius Caesar (with Marlon Brando and John Gielgud), *Guys and Dolls*, Tennessee Williams and Gore Vidal's *Suddenly, Last Summer*, the notorious Burton-Taylor *Cleopatra*, and *Sleuth*, his last film, with Laurence Olivier and Michael Caine. He is the subject of *Pictures Will Talk* (1978), a biography by Kenneth Geist.

Peter Stone, himself a screenwriter in the Mankiewicz tradition, found the filmmaker, never one to mince words, in the library of his house in Bedford, New York, just before this year's Oscars.

PETER STONE: *It's auspicious that, tonight being Oscar night, I'm sitting here with my back to four statuettes on the mantelpiece; and while there have been occasions when someone has won awards for writing and directing the same picture, you did it not just once but twice, and in back-to-back years— with* A Letter to Three Wives *and* All About Eve—*a feat which I'm sure is never going to be equaled. Are you still astonished by that?*
JOSEPH MANKIEWICZ: Yes, but probably not by the same things as you. I'm astonished by the fact that *All About Eve*—which was the result of a memo I received from a fellow named James Fisher, who used to be head of the story department at Fox—was actually about winning such awards. I myself had been trying to do a film about the awards—what you go through to win and what the award means in the end. There's a kind of post-award withdrawal; depression can set in immediately after winning. It happened to me.

PS: *Now, to put this in context, you* won the Academy Award for writing and directing A Letter to Three Wives *in April 1950, and* All About Eve *was completed that same year. The project hadn't even been written when you won the awards for* A Letter. *Today it takes three or four years to make a movie.*
JM: Actually, I did *A Letter to Three Wives, House of Strangers, No Way Out,* and *All About Eve* in two years.

PS: *That's astonishing. When the American Museum of the Moving Image in Queens honored Sidney Poitier,* No Way Out *was prominently featured. And you, in your absence, were prominently featured. Everyone thought you were out of the country.*
JM: As a matter of fact, I was sitting right here. I had received a letter from the museum a couple of months before, saying it was honoring

Sidney Poitier's achievements in the movies and asking if I would care
to join the honorary committee and buy tickets for myself and my wife
at 350 bucks apiece.

This past year has been a strange one for me. I've been presented
with honors from all over the world—I've just become the first
American ever to receive the Kurosawa Award. So when I received this
letter about the Poitier thing, I got a little angry, quite frankly. I have
never been recognized by any *American* film society—not Lincoln
Center, not the American Film Institute, not even the Museum of the
Moving Image in Queens, for Christ's sake. So I wrote back and said
that I'd just received this letter and I thought that being a museum carried with it the responsibility of exactitude. People are going to credit
you with the final word. Now, Poitier's entrance into motion pictures
was a direct result of my seeing *Pinky* and exploding with rage and having a big fight with Darryl Zanuck about it. I said, "Goddamnit, this is
the last time I want to see a white girl play a black girl."

PS: *Jeanne Crain played Pinky.*

JM: Right. Elia Kazan directed it beautifully; it was a well-written,
marvelous screenplay. But how dare they continue to do that and at the
same time bawl out people for continuing the minstrel show? Blacks
have got to play blacks. So Zanuck said, "All right, if you've got a story
we'll make it."

If I didn't have a story I wouldn't have opened my mouth in the first
place. It was about this young black intern who's sent in to give an
injection to a white hoodlum who's been brought in after a race riot.
The white man dies. It was the first time in the history of film where
you saw a white woman spit in the face of a black doctor and say,
"Take your black hands off my kid."

PS: *The confrontation between Richard Widmark and Poitier is almost
unbearable. It's the most virulent scene I've ever seen.*

JM: We did that deliberately. I wanted to shock moviegoers out of
their seats. I don't think the picture played in five theaters below the
Mason-Dixon line. It was banned in Chicago. I have a letter from the
police commissioner telling me that it would cause unrest and civil disorder. I wrote back and said, "I'm glad Chicago has a police commissioner

who is keeping the city free of disorder," and I sent a copy to Al Capone.

Getting back to Poitier . . . I went East and tested about eighteen actors. Sidney was working, I think, in a pantry, but he had done a lot of black theater. Black actors worked their asses off, but nobody wanted them for anything.

PS: *It was all right to make* Stormy Weather, *it was all right to make* Cabin in the Sky, *but Hollywood wasn't making racially mixed films.*
JM: That's right. I said, "Sidney, you're going to be awfully good in this movie—you're like a Roman candle—but you've got to find a follow-up. Because what the black actor is going to need in this country, more than anything, is continuity of appearance." I found out that Zoltan Korda was doing *Cry the Beloved Country.* I cabled Korda and said, "I understand you're looking for good actors. Would you please let me send you a piece of film on a young man who's going to knock your hat off?" I told Sidney to go to New York, and he met Zoltan himself. Zoltan said, "Oh, you're the one Mankiewicz sent. I want you." That is why, on every occasion when he's been asked, Sidney has always said, Everything I am in the movies, I owe this guy, because he did this for me. That's why I resented the shit out of the fact that I heard not a word from the museum except to invite me to pay for my tickets. I did hear from Dick Widmark, who said, "I don't see your name on the program. Aren't you going?" And I heard from Sidney, also in a rage.

Now I want to talk to you about a PBS documentary on Bogart.

PS: *The one Lauren Bacall narrated?*
JM: Yeah. Just about the only film they left out was *The Barefoot Contessa.* I thought it was a little odd. After all, it was the next-to-last movie he made, and it's getting to be a better movie all the time because of some of the things it says. I was moved to call the filmmakers— which I've never done in my life. I asked why they didn't use it, and they said it was because the film said some pretty sharp things about the film business. They didn't think it was appropriate to use it. Three nights later the same station ran *Million Dollar Legs,* which had an original screenplay by me.

PS: *With Jack Oakie and W. C. Fields.*

JM: Right. W. C. Fields is the president of a country.

PS: *I never understood the title.*

JM: Good. You're going to get some instruction now. Paramount, like all the other studios, used to sell its theaters titles. They sold them the title *Million Dollar Legs*, which had nothing to do with the picture. Man Ray said this was the first surrealist film comedy. All the girls are called Angela, and all the boys are called George.

PS: *Why?*

JM: Why not? There was Fields, so fucking outrageous, and a song by Larry Hart and Dick Rodgers, one of their first film scores. I remember one line—Bill Fields, the president, says to Andy Clyde, "Fetch me my privy counselor." Clyde says, "Where would I find him?" And Fields says, "Where would a privy counselor be?" It was that sort of joke all the way through.

When it was shown, the writing credit said, "By Joseph L. Mankiewicz and Harry Myers." When it was over, the next thing you heard was a man who said, "Ladies and gentleman, this is one of the early comedy classics, and W. C. Fields wrote every word of the dialogue." I am beginning, for the first time in my life, to be paranoid.

PS: *I understand what you're saying, but film writers have to expect this. What might make your case an exception is your eminence, Your Eminence. The rest of us have come to expect bad treatment as a matter of course.*

Now let's talk about People Will Talk. *Cary Grant is a doctor and he's got his class in the operating theater. On the table, he's got a corpse—a woman. And there's a towel around her hair. I haven't seen the picture in maybe twenty years, but it's indelible in my mind. He takes off the towel, and this raven-black hair falls from the gurney almost to the floor. It is long and shiny, and it's clear that this corpse not only was but still is a very attractive young woman.*

JM: But dead.

PS: *Dead. And during the scene, in discussing her as just a medical entity, he starts idly playing with her hair. He's fingering it and fondling it. That's one of the most shocking scenes I've ever seen. Not that it was obscene, but because—*

JM: Because he gave you the impression that the corpse was alive.

PS: *Yes. And that she was attractive and that she had been a person.*
JM: Every bit as good and as sane as they. The point I was making in that scene was that this crazy doctor—

PS: *Who was an idealist.*
JM: He understood that patients were more than just medical problems. When I wrote *People Will Talk*, I wanted to show a doctor who identifies a dead human body with the person who lived inside of it. He's not carving up horse meat; he's carving up someone who used to be one of us. I wanted to establish this doctor's humanity. Later on Cary says, I will not have my patients wakened at eleven to be given a sleeping pill. I will not have my patients' meals served to satisfy the rules of a culinary union. They eat when they get hungry. So it costs a couple of bucks more.

PS: *How old are you?*
JM: Eighty years old. I don't know why I ended up in pictures. You know, when I left Columbia—not the studio, the college—my father had a whole big plan for me. I was to go to the University of Berlin.

PS: *Your father, Frank Mankiewicz, was a classicist.*
JM: Right.

PS: *Your whole family was scholastic, pedagogical.*
JM: Pedagogical, yes. I was supposed to go to the University of Berlin and then to the Sorbonne, and I had been admitted to Oxford too. When I hit Berlin at age nineteen . . . my God, what a life. Later, when I met Christopher Isherwood at MGM, I told him I could practically sue him for plagiarizing my life. I had an incredible six months in Berlin. Within two weeks I was assistant correspondent with the *Chicago Tribune*. I also became the Berlin stringer for *Variety*. But for my main job, I walked down the Unter den Linden to the offices of UFA and asked for work. I told them I was Herman Mankiewicz's brother—they knew about Herman.

PS: *UFA was the great German motion-picture studio.*
JM: It was one of the greatest of all time. It had all of them: Stroheim, von Sternberg, Fritz Lang, *Dr. Caligari*, *Metropolis* . . . That's where *The*

Blue Angel was shot. I knew Marlene Dietrich before she made *The Blue Angel*. She was a chorus girl.

PS: *When was this?*
JM: I don't know . . . maybe 1928.

PS: *Yeah, because '29 is when you got to Hollywood.*
JM: Right. At any rate, I got into some trouble and had to leave Berlin . . .

PS: *I'm afraid to ask about it.*
JM: Yeah, well, never mind. I got into trouble and had to go to Paris. I arrived in November of 1928, I guess it was, and I was nineteen years old, an American, wearing a white crew-neck sweater with a block "C" on it, and I had to toothbrush and toothpaste in my back pocket and $1.65 in American money. The French didn't know I existed. A, I was American. B, I wanted a job. And C, I had no money. So I actually washed dishes at the Dôme, in Montparnasse. It's still there. I really hated that place.

Anyway, it didn't work out in Paris. I had no contacts. I went to the American film people, but they weren't interested.

PS: *The so-called Hemingway Paris was all coming to an end.*
JM: I used to hang around Sylvia Beach's bookstore and Harry's Bar and all those places. But it was no good, so I went back to New York to try to get jobs. Getting jobs in NewYork in 1929 was not easy.

PS: *When you were at UFA, you were basically translating intertitles of silent pictures.*
JM: That's right. Because their movies went to America.

PS: *So without stretching anything, we can say that your film-writing career started there.*
JM: I would like to think it did. Sixty years ago—and I still don't have a pension plan. I had a celebrated battle with Louis B. Mayer over that very thing, and finally I said, "Well, Mr. Mayer, obviously this studio is not big enough for the two of us." Guess who left? Six months later they announced their pension plan. By that time I was at Fox.

PS: *You stayed in Hollywood a long time.*

JM: Yeah, but it's a funny thing—from the day I left the land of the postnasal drip to come East, I was forgotten out there. My list of credits in the Writers Guild book stops when I left Hollywood. I became a nonperson.

PS: *As you know, I was born and raised there. My father was in the business, so it's a town I know intimately, and I've gone back as a screenwriter. It is the shortest-memory town, the shortest-memory industry, in the world. And the people who are remembered for an even shorter time than the others are the screenwriters.*

JM: That's true.

PS: *Screenwriters are the only living reminder to directors that they didn't create the whole picture alone. Writers are the jokers of the town. But you, on the other hand, are a director, and directors are the kings of the town.*

JM: The funny thing is that writers know how to direct, but directors don't know how to write. Most of the great directors I knew were practically illiterate. They never read anything except scripts. When a screenwriter writes a screenplay, he has to visualize what he is writing. He has to see what the camera sees. My point is that a well-written screenplay has already been directed. Now, unfortunately, we are in a situation in which the writers may be God-knows-where when a director comes along.

PS: *You're saying he directs it uninformed?*

JM: What I'm saying is that he is now the second director on that film. Ask any writer who ever wrote for Ernst Lubitsch, for instance—whether it was Sam Raphaelson or Billy Wilder—and he'll tell you that screenplay was written in Lubitsch's office. They wrote it together, word for word. Ernst would say something—in very bad English, which Billy or whoever would understand—and they'd put it into the script.

PS: *But that's because Lubitsch was a European, and that's the way movies were done—and still are done—in Europe. The French directors, the German directors, the Italians work with the writer from the beginning.*

JM: It was the same in America. George Stevens did a picture written by Ring Lardner Jr.—

PS: And Mike Kanin—*Woman of the Year.*
JM: Right, and Stevens sat down with Mike and Ring and me in a meeting, and we read the script.

PS: *This was when you were a studio executive at Metro?*
JM: Right. This is how the script conference went: George would say, "How about this? I think this would be interesting." And the writers would add it to the script.

PS: *Didn't George Stevens change the ending during production?*
JM: He didn't change any of it. After the picture was shot, we went out to a preview in Glendale, and during the last two reels we laid an egg. The preview cards said so. I don't give a shit what any of the cards say. It's the number of cards that say it.

I went back to the studio, and George went home to get pissed. He was depressed. I pondered the ending for a long time. Then I remembered what had happened when we had made *Philadelphia Story.* Kate Hepburn always plays a strong, rather arrogant woman, very sure of herself, hell on wheels. What made that picture work was Cary Grant giving Kate a kick in the ass. She got her comeuppance. Otherwise, *female* audiences would not have tolerated it.

PS: *Who wrote that wonderful opening, where as he's leaving the house Cary comes out the door, turns around, and pushes her back by the face?*
JM: I did.

PS: *Cary was very proud of that. When we did our two pictures together, he must have mentioned that two dozen times.*
JM: Cary didn't want to do it.

PS: *You're kidding.*
JM: He said it wasn't manly to push her in the face.

PS: *He told me she had a mattress inside the door and would go right back onto the mattress.*
JM: Let's get back to *Woman of the Year.* Here is this woman who could call the president of the United States, a woman who could do anything, get anything. She was the most powerful woman in the country. Then

it occurred to me—I'll bet she can't make breakfast. And that's the scene Johnny Lee Mahin and I wrote.

PS: *That scene is wonderful.*
JM: George shot it and it was like a different movie—a smash. Certainly the original writers played a major part.

PS: *They won the Academy Award for it.*
JM: And snubbed me. They walked right by me at the Oscars.

PS: *You brought Hepburn and Tracy together. And Hepburn was very unimpressed with Tracy because he was short.*
JM: Poor Spencer. In the last interview before he died, he told about how he and I were on our way to lunch—he used to stay with me in my little beach house—when along came Kate. I knew the two of them had never met. They were about to do this picture together, and she looked at him and said, "You know, Mr. Tracy, I'm afraid I might be just a bit too tall for you." And Tracy, in the interview, said that *I* said, "Don't worry, Kate, he'll cut you down to size."

PS: *You* said that.
JM: Yes. Ask Kate and she'll tell you the same thing. Even if she still hates my guts.

PS: *At that time you were not yet a film director. I seem to remember that you finished directing a picture that Lubitsch couldn't complete, because he got sick.*
JM: Not remotely.

PS: *That's the story one hears.*
JM: For some reason film historians can't understand that Lubitsch only *produced* the first film I directed.

PS: *What was the picture?*
JM: *Dragonwyck.*

PS: *Right, with Gene Tierney and Vincent Price.*
JM: Fox bought the book in 1946. In those days every major studio had its readers in every major publishing house in the world, and

properties would arrive in Russian, in German, in French, all with synopses attached. I read the synopsis of *Dragonwyck*. At that time they only wanted me to write the screenplay. I still have the memo, in which I said, "Pretty good, but not the kind of picture I want to make." But Zanuck persuaded me to write it. A couple of months later I got a phone call from Lubitsch.

PS: *Were you friends? Had you met in Berlin?*
JM: No, I met him in Hollywood. He took me right under his wing. God, he was divine to me. He told me that he wasn't up to directing; he wanted to produce, and he knew that I wanted to direct and felt that I should direct this. I had only directed tests.

PS: *But not a film.*
JM: No. Anyway, he wanted me to direct this one, so I said to myself, Jesus, what am I getting myself into? And then I thought, Schmuck, if Lubitsch is the producer, that's like having the world-champion chess player as your teacher for a few months.

I'll give you an example of Lubitsch. There's this scene with Vincent Price and Gene Tierney where she's pleading with him about firing Jessica Tandy. She walks into their bedroom and he follows her, and she throws herself on the bed, crying. That's the scene. So I got a call from Lubitsch, saying, "Impossible! How can you do this? This is the first major mistake." He was so angry. I said, "What the hell did I do?" He said, "A man is scolding his wife; she's answering him back. They're coming down the hall into their room. He must close the door so the servants don't hear!"

PS: *You're an American; you don't worry about what servants hear.*
JM: Give me a couple more pictures and I'll think of that too. But I thanked him for it.

PS: *If one were to say there are two kinds of directors, you are in the Lubitsch school, in that Lubitsch nailed his camera to the floor and let the scene play. Then there are camera directors, like Max Ophüls. Someone said Ophüls should have been paid by the mile and not by the week because of how much he moved his camera.*
JM: Rouben Mamoulian, too. Because he'd been a cameraman. You don't have to be visual. That's what cameramen are for. You must

remember that the director has the most marvelous power. He can ask every department what it thinks. You hire a great art director, a great costume designer, get their best thoughts, and they can become your thoughts when you say, "That's just what I had in mind."

PS: *What do you think of today's spectacle directors, like Lucas and Spielberg?*
JM: A series of visual explosions that hurt my ears and gave me a headache. I couldn't watch. I don't really consider that direction. Spielberg directed this duel between two trucks—he did that very well. He's good at creating tension with images. But when you say this is what direction means, my God, you're wiping out 95 percent of social intercourse. Spectacle must be *part* of the story.

PS: *But there are spectacle directors; there are directors who have made spectacle their life . . . De Mille.*
JM: Jack Ford, George Marshall, Henry Hathaway . . .

PS: *Did you see directing as an extension of writing?*
JM: I think a good screenplay can't be written without being visualized.

PS: *Right, but do you see yourself as director as an extension of the film writer?*
JM: Yes, I do.

PS: *I was hoping I'd hear that. Did you ever direct a picture you didn't write?*
JM: Oh yes, I've directed several I didn't write.

PS: *You didn't write* Julius Caesar.
JM: No. No additional dialogue.

PS: *Was it Sam Taylor who got an additional-dialogue credit: "The* Taming of the Shrew, *by William Shakespeare, with additional dialogue by Sam Taylor"?*
JM: I fell right out of my chair.

PS: *So no additional dialogue in* Julius Caesar?

JM: Not a single word. I'll tell you what my contract said: No writer's name may appear on the screen except that of William Shakespeare.

PS: *People refer to your* Julius Caesar *as the most successful American version of a Shakespeare play. I would have to agree. First of all the cast was remarkable. And it was in black-and-white.*

JM: I said I wouldn't do it if they insisted on color. Because the assassination scene to me was the essence of the entire picture. In color all you'd see is red on the screen. It would have looked like a butcher shop. The blood is unimportant—it's the pain in Brutus and the love in his eyes. Shakespeare isn't in the color. Shakespeare is in the guts of human beings.

PS: *And we know you didn't write* Cleopatra.

JM: Actually I did agree to write two screenplays for it.

PS: *You and Zanuck?*

JM: No, Spyros Skouras—he was the head of Fox. At the time I was shooting, Mr. Zanuck was off making *The Longest Day*. After years of disasters, he looked and behaved like an old fool of the sort Emil Jannings used to play. Remember the beaten-down professor?

PS: *Well, he had had a* Blue Angel-*like relationship with an actress, Bella Darvi.*

JM: Then suddenly in this miraculous coup he became head of Fox. *The Longest Day* was his chance for cinematic immortality. He had every fucking star in the world in that.

PS: *You two did not end up well after* Cleopatra, *because he recut the picture.*

JM: He re-*chopped* the picture.

PS: *But you didn't start the picture. Somebody else started it, and you took it over in an absolute mess of a condition. It had ground to some kind of halt.*

JM: I'm not sure I'm ready to talk about it even after all this time.

PS: *There was a story that Nunnally Johnson was called in by Skouras to rewrite the picture. This was before you were even involved. Skouras said, "How much do you want to rewrite* Cleopatra?*" And Nunnally said, "I'll take 10 percent of the losses." So what was it you inherited? A lot of sets—*
JM: I'll tell you what I inherited. At the time this whole thing came up I had a very close friend by the name of Hume Cronyn.

PS: *A darling man.*
JM: Who is my daughter's godfather. He and Jessica Tandy owned a little cay down in the Bahamas. I used to sit down there. I was so happy because I had taken on a very tough but wonderful assignment, *The Alexandria Quartet.*

PS: *By Lawrence Durrell.*
JM: I had six hundred pages of dialogue.

PS: *It's got a kind of* Citizen Kane *crosshatch, a terrific device.*
JM: Yeah.

PS: *Your brother, Herman, wrote* Citizen Kane. *Did he have any influence on you as a screenwriter?*
JM: None.

PS: *None. O.K., go ahead with* Cleopatra.
JM: I was sitting down there at the Cronyns', and I got a call from my agent, Charlie Feldman.

PS: *He was not yet a producer.*
JM: He was never not a producer.

PS: *Well, I know, but was he still functioning as an agent at the time?*
JM: Oh yes. Charlie was functioning as everything to everybody all the time. So I got this telephone call from Charlie, asking me to come back to New York at once and have lunch with Spyros Skouras. At the Colony, of course. That's the only place Skouras ate. And he started right in: "Mamoulian is crazy."

PS: *Mamoulian had started the picture in Rome.*
JM: No. In London. He had spent $8.7 million already.

PS: *That's like $40 million today.*

JM: I'd never made a movie that cost anything like that. At any rate, it seemed he had built Alexandria out of cardboard at Shepperton Studios.

PS: *And a wet English winter was coming.*

JM: So by November he watched it all washing down the sewers. The thing had already cost nine million bucks, and Elizabeth Taylor refused to go on unless I came in and directed it.

PS: *You had directed her in* Suddenly, Last Summer.

JM: Right. I remember saying, "Spyros, why would I want to make *Cleopatra*? I wouldn't even go *see Cleopatra*." But he said, "Joe, $9 million . . . I want you."

PS: *That's like telling you you can write your own ticket.*

JM: He said, "Joe, I know you like the Riviera. Is there a house in particular that you want?" I said, "Yes. It's on Cap d'Antibes." It was right were Garbo had this beautiful house. Feldman turned to Skouras and said, "Can you get that for $300,000?" Skouras makes a note, then says, "I hear you like yachts." This was true. At one time every penny I had in the world was floating down at San Pedro. I had a beautiful sloop that I'd bought from Jasha Heifitz, and then I wound up with an eighty-seven-foot boat that I bought for $14,000 from a well-known cowboy actor, Buck Jones.

PS: *My father used to write Buck Jones movies. So Skouras said, "I hear you like yachts."*

JM: Yeah. "What kind of yacht do you want?" I began to get very nervous. I mean, a château and a yacht are all very nice, but who's going to pay the taxes? So I called my lawyer, Abe Bienstock. He was the kind of lawyer everyone should have. He was the Rothschilds' and Doris Duke's lawyer. I never did anything without talking to him about it. I told him what Skouras was offering, and he said to me, "Are you drunk?" I said no. He said he was very fond of my taste. He said he'd love to visit my château on the Riviera. And particularly, since he loved sailing, he'd love to be a guest on my yacht. "Except," he said, "I would feel a little uncomfortable, knowing that all this time you would be in a cell in a federal prison in Atlanta."

So instead of my accepting a villa and a yacht, Abe arranged it so that Fox bought out my company, which was worth a lot of money because we'd just produced *I Want to Live*, as well as *The Barefoot Contessa*. *I Want to Live*, by the way, was the first time I ever saw a $10,000 advertisement cost in a studio budget, for an Academy Award—for Susan Hayward.

PS: *Before the picture?*
JM: The script wasn't even finished and she actually won it.
So, they paid me about three million bucks and I agreed to do *Cleopatra*.

PS: *Didn't that picture finally cost about $44 million?*
JM: It cost nowhere near that. It cost about $30 million including the $9 million loss I inherited.

PS: *And what would that $30 million be today, $150 million?*
JM: Easy. The legal fees were tremendous. Zanuck was furious. At Burton and Taylor, those two scandalous creatures. Fox was going to sue them for . . . 40 million bucks, I think.

PS: *Why sue them?*
JM: In order to take advantage of the Vatican's outrage and all of the moral outrage in the country about their carrying on. Fox thought this would be a great opportunity to sue them for misbehavior, under the morals clause that's in everybody's contract.

PS: *And they charged all that against the picture?*
JM: Astounding sums of money. They took endless depositions from everybody who was on the picture—script supervisors; Irene Sharaff, the costume designer . . . But eventually they dropped the suit. Then Ms. Taylor and Mr. Burton sued *them*. And they collected. They got a big chunk of profit from that picture. Because there *were* profits. You cannot make anybody believe that, because of what's been in print so often. But that picture ended up making money.

PS: *Now, we started talking about* All About Eve *and we got sidetracked. You said you had been interested in doing a film about the winning of awards.*
JM: I had always wanted to do it. And I got this three-page memo from the story editor at Fox, saying that he'd just bought a short story

called "The Wisdom of Eve," by Mary Orr. He thought it might be exactly what I was looking for.

PS: *Addison de Witt, the drama critic played by George Sanders, did not appear in the original story, did he?*
JM: No. Very few of the characters, really.

PS: *But it was Addison de Witt that made everything work. He was the machinery, the energy of the picture.*
JM: Years later I heard they were making a Broadway musical out of it. Orr had a royalty, and Fox also had a percentage. But I had no standing. My name wasn't even on it. I never even got two seats to *see* the damn thing. Anyway, it won a whole bunch of Tony Awards. And my wife and I were watching the Tony show on television, and everybody was accepting his award, thanking everybody in the world, but it wasn't until Comden and Green walked up that Betty Comden said, "I don't think we should forget to thank the one person who made this whole show possible. Thank you, Joe."

PS: *It's hard to avoid the irony here. You write a picture about winning awards. It wins the Academy Award for you as writer and director, a nomination for Bette Davis . . .*
JM: And it holds, to this day, the record for the largest number of nominations. I was also nominated, that same year, for *No Way Out.*

PS: All About Eve *starts in New York at "The Sarah Siddons Award" ceremony. It wins the Academy Award in Hollywood. Then it comes back to New York and they get the Tonys. Every time it appears it wins all the awards.*
JM: A funny thing happened. One day I picked up a newspaper and I read that Helen Hayes had been given the Sarah Siddons Award from the Sarah Siddons Society. But I *made up* that award. It never existed. I invented it. I saw a portrait of Sarah Siddons, the famous actress, painted by Joshua Reynolds. And the propman turned it into a statue. The next thing I knew, Helen Hayes was winning the Sarah Siddons Award. Can you imagine? This was the second-most-sought-after award in the American theater, and I first made it up for a picture—nature imitating art imitating nature. And do you know who the president of the Sarah Siddons Society in the film was? Nancy Reagan's mother.

O.K., listen to the last chapter in *All About Eve*. About three years ago they presented me with the Lion d'Or at the Venice Film Festival. And I got this telephone call from an absolutely desperate-sounding woman. She said, "Mr. Mankiewicz, this is Eve." I said, "Eve?" She said, "Yes, the Eve you wrote the movie about. I was the girl who stood outside the theater." I said, "Oh, I didn't know that."

PS: *You didn't believe her at this point.*

JM: Not a word. So she says, "I know you don't believe me, so I'm going to send you something." Sure enough, she sent me a copy of this autobiography by Elisabeth Bergner, the great German actress. She wrote about a play she had done in New York, *The Two Mrs. Carrolls*. This girl, wearing red stockings, was there outside the theater every single night of the run. Bergner tells this story to a group of people, one of whom was a shy, quiet woman who never opened her mouth. A couple of months later, Bergner picked up a magazine, and to her absolute amazement, she read the whole story. And the author of this magazine story was that woman who seemed so shy: Mary Orr.

PS: *The woman who never opened her mouth, just listened.*

JM: As Bergner told the story, which was filled with many of the incidents that were also in the picture.

PS: *So the girl on the phone really* was *Eve.*

JM: Exactly. Hollywood bought the story, it became *All About Eve*, and Mary Orr made her fortune out of this. The only people who did not make anything were Eve and Elisabeth Bergner. And me . . . except for my salary.

PS: *And two Academy Awards.*

JM: I earned them.

PS: *Joe, throughout our entire conversation, I hear one thing over and over: anger.*

JM: I am angry—very angry.

PS: *Why?*

JM: I've never been recognized by my own country for my body of work. All over the world, but not in my own country.

PS: *But this is an industry that is filled with press agents who arrange awards. What does it mean, except a night where everybody puts on a tuxedo and goes out and another guy gets an award that was paid for? You're sitting here with a mantelful of earned awards. You're an important figure in film. Mankiewicz is a name that is probably recognized by every single person in this business. If you want to be recognized by housewives in Peoria, then you've got to become an actor. But there's no one in television, film, or theater today who does not know your name. What else do you want?*

JM: I don't want my name known to everybody. I want my country to show some respect. I don't want some sonofabitch on PBS to list the best American pictures and not include any of mine.

PS: *Well, I happen to think you're very fortunate. First of all, the last picture you made,* Sleuth, *was damned good. I can't think of any one of the great film directors in Hollywood—Wilder, Wyler, George Stevens, Hitchcock, Capra, anyone—whose last picture was either a big artistic or commercial success.* Sleuth *was very successful, in every sense of the word.*

JM: How many films do you think I've been offered to direct since then? . . . Not one.

PS: *But you've got to face one thing that we all have to face. If you had stayed a writer you'd have faced it long before. They have a thing about age in this business—it's awful, Joe, and you know it. I am twenty-one years younger than you are, and I am already running into age prejudice as a screenwriter. Some of it is understandable, because it is true that dialogue writers lose their ear for contemporary speech. But they do have this thing about age. It's not about your reputation or your ability, and it's not about your résumé. They say, the guy is eighty years old and that's all there is to it.*

JM: My problem is that I've still got a lot to say. I have things that are half-written; I've got a lot of stuff I still want to write. I want to say something that may surprise you. I really think I've failed. And the reason I've failed is that I didn't really play according to the rules.

PS: *I want to ask you one more thing. Are you going to watch the Academy Awards tonight?*

JM: Yes.

PS: *Are you going to care?*

JM: No. But I'm going to watch. Who knows, a naked guy might run by, something untoward. I want something untoward to happen.

Joseph L. Mankiewicz

JEFF LAFFEL / 1991

TO PARAPHRASE Addison DeWitt in *All About Eve*, "To those of you who do not read, attend the movies, listen to unsponsored radio programs, or know anything of the world in which you live, it is perhaps necessary to introduce the man of whom I write. His name is Joseph L. Mankiewicz. His native habitat is the motion picture. He is essential to the motion picture. He is one of the greats."

Mankiewicz was born in Pennsylvania in 1909 and appeared in Hollywood twenty years later. As a writer in the early years, he worked on *Million Dollar Legs* and segments of *If I Had a Million*. At MGM he produced such films as *Three Comrades, Strange Cargo, The Philadelphia Story,* and *The Keys of the Kingdom*. As writer/director at Twentieth Century-Fox, Mankiewicz turned out some of the screen's enduring classics, such as *A Letter to Three Wives, The Ghost and Mrs. Muir, House of Strangers, People Will Talk,* and one of the great films of all time, *All About Eve*. In later years, at different studios, he was responsible for *Julius Caesar; Suddenly, Last Summer; The Barefoot Contessa; Cleopatra; Guys and Dolls;* and *Sleuth*. Since retiring from the screen in 1972, Mankiewicz has lived in a sprawling home in Westchester County, New York.

The only man ever to win back-to-back Oscars for writing and directing sits on a well-worn leather chair and holds an unlit pipe. It is a raw, rainy day and he wears a grey cardigan sweater against a possible chill. But his study, lined with hundreds and hundreds of plays and shooting

Originally published in two parts in *Films in Review* (July–August 1991, September–October 1991). Reprinted by permission of *Films in Review*.

scripts, is comfortably warm with the redolence of many years of pipe smoke noticeable in the air.

Joseph Mankiewicz doesn't grant many interviews ("They never come out saying what you said.") and he looks a bit wary of this one as he welcomes me in. When he sees the stack of index cards containing the questions, he rolls his eyes. "You're not going to ask me all of those, are you? Jesus, we'll be here forever." I assure him that we will use as few or as many as he likes and he gives a soft murmur of doubtful acceptance and settles back into his chair. I also promise him that the questions will not be artsy and he smiles. "If I think they're starting to get pretentious you'll know, because I'll break out in a rash." (Something that Bill Sampson would say. Or Birdie Coonan. Or Harry Dawes.)

"You like down-to-earth, no-nonsense people."

"Real people," Mankiewicz agrees.

"Like Thelma Ritter."

A big smile. "Thelma Ritter was the best. I wrote Birdie Coonan in *All About Eve* for her. A wonderful person and a fine actress. I loved her, bless her. Do you remember that scene in *Letter to Three Wives* when Ritter and Connie Gilcrist are playing cards? I loved that."

"You love people."

He narrows his eyes. "I love *people*."

As Mankiewicz sips lemonade, photographer Richard Harrison moves in for a shot. Mankiewicz stares at him. "Do I know you? I think I know you. You look very familiar." Harrison colors and says, "I'm sure we've never met. I certainly would have remembered." But Mankiewicz shakes his head. "No, I know I've seen you." "Sometimes people say I look like Robert Redford," says Harrison. He does. "Actually," Mankiewicz says without missing a beat, "I was thinking more of Jack Oakie." A rich laugh, a big smile. "Next." Mankiewicz is warming to the interview.

And what of the other stars in *All About Eve*? "Well, you know," Mankiewicz says, "the cast in the picture isn't the one we started out with. Zanuck had read the screenplay and wanted to produce it himself. He loved it. He was looking for Oscars, and a Thalberg for himself. And Zanuck was sure that the knew what the perfect cast was. For Margo he wanted Marlene Dietrich; for Addison, Joe Ferrer; and for Eve, Jeanne Crain. He gives me this cast and I am deeply disappointed, so for the first time I stood up to him. I told him, 'Darryl, you screwed up with *Letter to Three Wives*. I had to overcome the entire opening scene because this Crain girl cannot project anything. She doesn't want to be an actress. She's a very sweet woman who, at the end of the day, hangs her performance on a vaudeville hook and goes home to her husband Paul Brinkman, who happened to be a very nice man. And she was a very nice girl, but she didn't *live* being an actress. There was no way that she could get into the heart . . . if that's the right word . . . of Eve. And so I fought with Zanuck about that. He was tough, but I finally put my foot down and said that I was going to scream and holler. And I won. Marlene was not Margo and I wanted and got Claudette Colbert. How Ferrer lost the role, I don't remember, but he would have been good as Addison. So I got Baxter for Eve, Sanders for Addison, and Claudette. But of course everyone knows the story about how she hurt her back or some such thing, and Davis came in with only two weeks before shooting started. And she was fine. And of course Ritter, bless her. She was my creation and I'm proud of it."

"And Hugh Marlowe?" I ask.

A grunt. "He was a stick." A pause and then, "Remember that line in *Barefoot Contessa*, where Gardner says to Bogart, 'Can you teach me to be an actress?' and he says, 'No one can teach someone to be an actress. If you have talent, I can help you.' That fits here."

"Yes," I say, "but how does one direct a fine actor and, in the same scene, a no-talent one?"

A shake of the head. "It's the same thing. I hesitate to say this, but I've never had anyone complain about the way I've directed him in a scene . . . the great ones and the not-so-great ones. What I always do, I give them a screenplay to read and then I have a one-on-one session with them regarding the character. 'If anything upsets you,' I tell them, 'if anything is phrased badly, tell me, because we're going to correct it now.' I do not rewrite once we start. I did that with Larry Olivier and then, separately, with Michael Caine when we did *Sleuth*. I've done it with any actor or actress I've ever worked with. And it works. That's why I never had a problem about dialogue. Obviously, the better the actor, the better . . . Look, I'm the only human being who could possibly have made four films with Rex Harrison. He could be rough, but he never questioned a line. In his autobiography he makes mention of that and about how much he enjoyed doing *The Honey Pot*." A laugh.

"I could have been Rex Harrison's uncle-in-law. I used to tell him that all the time. Let me explain. It was when I was a kid in Germany. What was I, nineteen? There was this English dance team . . . very much like Fred Astaire and his sister Adele. They were the Kendalls . . . Terry and Pat Kendall . . . and Pat Kendall and I fell madly in love with each other. She was about twenty-two at the time. Anyway, it didn't work out, but Kay Kendall was Terry's daughter, so had I married Pat, I would have been Kay's uncle, and, later, Harrison's uncle-in-law. But . . ." A dismissive wave of the hand.

"What were you doing in Germany?" I ask.

"I was supposed to go the University of Berlin. I had actually registered. I was supposed to study German literature and drama, then, after that, off to Sorbonne to study French Romantic literature. It had all been arranged. And, don't forget all this came after I had graduated from Columbia. And then I hit Berlin at the age of nineteen. There was never such a city in the world as Berlin in 1928! Everything that Paris advertised itself to be, Berlin was. The theater . . . the unbelievable theater. Max Reinhardt. The young Brecht and Weill. It was unbelievable. I became very friendly with Franz Waxman and Fredrich Hollander . . . my God, we ate together three times a week. Waxman was the piano player for The Weintraub Syncopaters. They played at his political cafe, and they were the hottest. They were to Berlin in the twenties what Goodman and Ellington would be to America in the thirties and forties. Hollander was the leader of the group. That's when he wrote the first of all the songs he was to write for Dietrich. Marlene was a chorus girl at that time. Anyway, it was wonderful. Instead of going to graduate school, I ended up working at UFA translating subtitles." A smile. "I ended up getting fired. I think my father was the chief motivator of the plot to get me out of films and back to school. It didn't work. I went from UFA to the Berlin office of the *Chicago Tribune* and worked there. I wanted to get involved in the world, not spend four or more years back in school. What I really wanted to do was to surround myself with theater."

He points at his overflowing bookshelves. "Look at this. All theater. And they're all read, all studied. This is what I've lived with all my life. The theater. (And one hears the voice of Bill Sampson in *All About Eve*, "Listen, junior. And learn. Want to know what the theater is? A flea circus. Also opera . . . The theater's for everybody . . . It may not be your theater, but it's theater for somebody, somewhere . . .")

"And what I thought American film could become is somehow an adjunct to the theater. Just as Griffith brought punctuation to the screen, the screen could bring punctuation to the theater. If you see the moviegoer as a reader, the screen can lead the reader, the viewer, the participant, where the dramatist, the originator, wants them to be. And everything would be much more important, much more understood. Education could happen. But," a shrug, "in order for that to have happened or happen, a lot of people had to feel the same way. It was starting to happen in the forties and fifties with some of us, but now . . ." His sentence trails off and he stares at the bookshelf opposite him.

I break the silence. "But you could have written for the theater. All your characters are so clearly delineated . . ." He chuckles. "Unlike someone like Robert Bolt, you mean? I told him once that all of his characters sound as though they had graduated from Oxford."

"Yes," I say, "you're one of the only writers I know who uses commas." Mankiewicz nods his head. "Oh," he says, "you have to. Look, Karen Richards in *Eve* says, 'Why, I thought, not?' She has to. She went to Radcliffe. Margo would have said 'Why the f—not?' And Eddy O'Brien in *Barefoot Contessa* is a P.R. man. His sentences are long . . . never ending . . . like if he stopped talking someone else might jump in. But I tell you, to write well, you have to have a good ear . . . you have to listen. You also have to remember . . . to have a mental file cabinet and be able to pull out ideas, characters, memories, when you need them. For instance, back to Eddy O'Brien. In one of his speeches in *Contessa* he refers sarcastically to a 'coronet solo on Saturday night.' All right. When I was a kid . . . a little kid . . . my mother took me to the open air movies at St. Nicholas Avenue and 110th Street . . . and there was a coronet solo on Saturday night after the silent film. Used by O'Brien, it becomes a funny topper . . . well, it actually happened. I remember these things. I had a thought once that I filed away and used in *Letter to Three Wives*. Paul Douglas is driving Linda Darnell home in his car . . . you remember, where he is so taken by her that he lights his cigarette and then throws the lighter out of the car? Okey, well, as Linda walks into her house, just at the fade, she closes her front door and the camera stays outside and there's a little thing on the door saying, 'We gave.' Things like that add so much to the scene and to the film as a whole."

The phone rings and I have a chance to look around the room. On a mantle stand four Oscars, two for *A Letter to Three Wives* and two for *All About Eve*; an Edgar, won for *Sleuth*; a D. W. Griffith Special Achievement Award; and, seemingly in a place of honor amid all the other awards, the Sarah Siddons Award for Achievement in the Theater. ("I wouldn't worry too much about your heart. You can always put that award where your heart ought to be.") Mankiewicz sees me staring at it. "That was the prototype. I had others made for the cast members as a wrap gift on *Eve*.

"Tea." Rosemary Mankiewicz stands in the doorway holding a silver tea service. She smiles at her husband. "I thought you'd be ready for some right about now." Mankiewicz holds up his lemonade. "I'll stick with this." As Mrs. Mankiewicz pours for her guests, her husband says, "Here's an interesting story. You were talking about *The Barefoot Contessa* a few minutes ago. I had wanted James Mason to play the nobleman that Ava ends up marrying, but I couldn't get him. Mr. Nicholas M. Schenck, who controlled Loews Incorporated and MGM, was playing games with me. He had been angry with me while we were filming *Julius Caesar* and he waited until the opening at this little theater in New York to let me have it. Well, I wouldn't take it, and I bawled him out in public. That was the most destructive opening of a film. At any rate, I just bawled the sh—out of him in public, and he never forgave me for that. And I end up with Rossano Brazzi, who cannot act, cannot be sensual . . . could hardly speak English, for God's sake, and so we had to hire someone to teach Brazzi his lines phonetically. And in walked this lovely English girl named Rosemary Matthews, who taught Brazzi how to speak the lines, and whom I later married." Rosemary Mankiewicz nods and says to her husband, "How are you doing?" "I am having the time of my life," he tells her, and she excuses herself and quietly leaves the room.

"I'll give you a little trivia here," Mankiewicz says. "Remember *Sleuth*, where we needed all those red herring actors for the credits so you would think there were many characters more than there were? Rosemary's family. Check the names sometime. Mostly her family." He sips his lemonade. "So . . . where were we? We were talking about the little extra things that go into a film, weren't we?"

I tell him that we were and remind him of a scene in *House of Strangers* where Richard Conte and Susan Hayward sit in a bar . . . I never finish. Mankiewicz beams and says, "That's one of my favorite scenes. It's a very honest scene between a man and a woman. They are in trouble with the relationship. There is ice in the air . . . absolutely ice. There is no talking, but there is a lot going on. There is another couple at a table, a young girl and an older man. And she is crying. The older man is making indecent remarks. A waiter takes ashes collected in an ashtray and throws them on the floor. Then he goes back to his chess game. No dialogue. The audience has to become part of the scene, has got to work to fill in the blanks. I do the same thing in *Barefoot Contessa*. Remember the first cafe scene where Ava is performing? You never see her. You see her dance through the eyes of those at the cafe. The men are saying, 'Oh, my, I want her.' A group of whores are sitting there knitting, not paying any attention to someone desired by all the men in the place. An old pervert slips on a glove as he watches Maria dance. And once again, the image of the young girl who is crying, and the older man who had made her cry and is now embarrassed by her carrying on, completes the scene. You can feel the heat in the room though you never see Maria dancing. The audience *thinks* that it has seen her and it never has. It really worked . . . and, frankly, it served another purpose as well. Ava just wasn't that good a dancer. You never would have bought her had you seen her dance . . . but you *had* seen her dance, if you see what I mean, and God was she good!"

"In *Contessa*," I note, "the relationship between Bogart and Gardner is so warm right from the beginning that one would think they would get together."

Mankiewicz nods. "You spoke of dialogue before. Here is an instance where dialogue defined a relationship. The audience has to believe that Bogart would stay with his girlfriend Gerri, a pretty girl, but not an incredible beauty like Gardner. She has to have something to appeal to Bogart's cynical, intelligent Harry Dawes, and that something is a brilliant mind and a quick tongue. Remember Gerri's line to a bitchy star? 'What you got, you used to have.' That wasn't meant to be a wise-ass crack . . . It was meant to show the audience what Gerri had that made Bogart admire her and love her. And not run off with Gardner. Just one line, and it summed up a character and a relationship just like that."

"Speaking of relationship, what about your working relationship with Bette Davis?"

"I wish I could tell you it was a bad one. That would be much more interesting. But in reality, it was quite good." He rubs the bowl of the pipe. "I hadn't thought it was going to be, though. As soon as the word got out that I was going to direct Bette, I get a phone call from Eddie Goulding, who had worked with Davis on *Dark Victory* and *The Old Maid*. 'My dear boy,' he says. 'you're not really going to work with *her*, are you?' I tell him that I am. 'That woman will come onto the set on the first day with a big yellow pad and start changing everything you have written. Look, I know you're a tough guy, but this is a tough broad. I hope you're ready for her.' Well, I knew she had the script and so far I hadn't heard anything from her. First day of shooting, in she comes, letter perfect. Never a bit of trouble. I'm only sorry that I only got to do one picture with her."

"And the feud between Davis and Tallulah Bankhead because of *Eve*?"

Mankiewicz snorts. "All P.R. for Bankhead. Look . . . the first day of shooting on *Eve* was at the Currant Theater in San Francisco. Davis shows up and she has this voice . . . deep, husky. 'Oh my God,' I say to her, 'what happened to you?' It seems she had been out on her lawn the night before yelling at her husband. She's in her nightgown, the fog rolls in and she gets this sore throat. And we're ready to shoot. 'Look,' I say, 'I like the sound of your voice like that, but if we start with it, you're going to have to keep it for the whole picture.' So all through the rest of the film she kept that sore throat. And it sounded like Tallulah. Now remember, Tallulah had a radio show at that time, *The Big Show*. I think they were trying to make it look like radio was still a big deal in the face of television's getting more and more popular. At any rate, Tallulah's press agent, Richard Maney, came up with the Davis/Bankhead feud, with Bankhead mad at Davis for 'imitating' her as Margo. A feud had worked for Fred Allen and Jack Benny, and Maney thought it would work for Bankhead's ratings. I guess it did, too, because people are still talking about it." A pause. "You know, people are always asking me what *All About Eve* would have been like had Claudette played the part. She would have been fine, as would have many other actresses. Claudette would have played it lighter. She would have been a piss elegant drunk. Bette used blunt instruments, where Claudette, or someone like Ina Claire, would have used a rapier. The Davis/Bankhead feud . . ." A chuckle. "Had Colbert played it, you probably would have had *The Big Show* starring Ina Claire. Some P.R. genius would have come up with that."

"Are you getting tired?" I ask.

"I was tired a half hour ago. Next question!"

"The films of today."

Mankiewicz looks uncomfortable. He looks out of the large windows onto his fields. It has started to rain harder. He stares at the rain pelting the windows as he speaks.

"I feel deep sorrow at the condition of film today. It's on its way out. There are no values. Some of the films pretend to be moral. Bull. Maybe the good guys win in the end . . . get to go home to the wives in the last reel . . . have destroyed the villain . . . but there have been ten reels in which the bad guys have had a ball. They've killed people, they've humped people, they get all the money . . . they get all of everything. That's what the young person watching the film is going to remember . . . not the final fade . . . the 'morally' happy ending. They're going to remember what the bad guys did for the majority of the film." He shakes his head. "I wish someone would take the time and spend the money to do a survey on how some of the scenes they film today affect kids. Take that baseball bat killing in *The Untouchables*, for instance. Since then, has the baseball bat become a weapon of choice because of the film? How affected are the young people of today by these films? Whatever happened to love stories? I can't remember the last time I saw a love story. Even that *Pretty Woman*. I liked that film, but it was about a guy falling in love with a prostitute!" Then sadly, "It may have been picking up crumbs, but there was a human relationship there. How few films even bother about human relationships. I wouldn't know how to make a film today. I really wouldn't."

"Let's talk about *Cleopatra*. I think that . . ."

Mankiewicz shakes his head and holds up his hand. "In a minute. I'm still thinking about the brutality in the films of today. And in full color! Do you know that I had only two conditions that I insisted upon when I did *Julius Caesar*? One had to do with the credits, but the other one was about not making the film in color. I insisted on black and white. In color, the assassination scene would have destroyed the movie. You see, the film is not about the blood of Caesar. It's about the eyes of Brutus and the eyes of Caesar and the moment of betrayal. I wanted the audience to get that and they never would have with all that blood splashed around . . . especially in color!" A twinkle. "Okay . . . I'm off my soapbox. But let me tell you it wasn't easy making a film of a play where the audience knows every line when they walk into the theater. There are more cliches in *Julius* . . . try making something fresh of 'Friends, Romans, countrymen.' But there are ways to do it.

"Remember Edmund O'Brien's, 'That's Greek to me'? He just threw it away and it became fresh and new, and the audience loved it. I tell you, I had an epiphany while directing the film. James Mason had done such a great job as Brutus talking to the citizens, the crowd, that when Brando comes in carrying all 200-odd pounds of Louis Calhern playing the dead Caesar, they simply didn't want to hear what Marc Antony had to say. It had become real to the extras and when they saw Caesar they actually started booing him. So there's Marlon carrying Louis and he can't get a word in. I didn't want to cut because the scene was so real, so I starting whispering to Marlon . . . I was out of sight behind a chair or something . . . 'Marlon, get mad. They're not listening to you, so get mad,' and he does and they still are booing, and so in desperation, Marlon, who is a great actor, yells, 'Friends, Romans, countrymen, *lend* me your ears.' You see, he puts the emphasis on 'lend' and right away I realized that is exactly the way Shakespeare had wanted the line to read. They wouldn't listen to Antony if he demanded it, they were too angry, too worked up. But if he pleads with them '*lend* me your ears,' well, maybe they'll quiet down and see what he has to say. He's not demanding it, and they'll listen because of that. He makes them feel important just because of the way he stresses 'lend.' That's the kind of thing that excites me. Just the stress put on a word and the crowd quiets and listens to a man who was loyal to Caesar."

"And speaking of Caesar," I begin, and Mankiewicz knows my direction.

". . . leads us to *Cleopatra*, yes?" I nod. "Well," he says, "so much had been written about that film . . . but I tell you, now that the Taylor/Burton thing has been forgotten, I think the film is being re-evaluated in a more kindly way than it was when it first came out.

Harrison was very proud of his Caesar. He writes about it in his autobiography. As for me . . . ," he sweeps his hand around the room, "it
bought us this house. I think, though, that I corrupted myself by making *Cleopatra*. Not because of the finished product . . . I think I did a
good job . . . but for what I had to give up by making it." He grows
pensive. "Look, I have always been fascinated by time . . ."

"The flashbacks used in your films."

"Exactly. There is no such thing as 'today,' 'now,' being separate from
all previous time. I remember I wrote a little piece for Edmund . . .
Irving Edmund . . . my philosophy teacher at Columbia, about how the
letter 'B' has a certain amount of 'A' in it, as all our todays contain
many yesterdays. And the most wonderful representation of this in literature is Lawrence Durrell's *The Alexandria Quartet* . . . and I bought it
for the screen, and after a year of really hard work, I had a treatment. I
had licked the problem of the time and space continuum. When I was
finished with the treatment I wrote on the frontispiece, 'I'm happy this
treatment cannot be read by anyone who has not read all four volumes
of *The Alexandria Quartet*.' The result of that was that no one at Fox read
the treatment. Actually, one person did read it and understood it . . .
young Zanuck . . . Richard. He read it, he got it, and he thought it was
wonderful. Then I take the treatment to Paris . . . to Durell. I buy him a
bottle of cognac and I say, 'You're going to read this!' And he read right
through it.

"Now remember this was a tough one. Here were four different
screenplays about the same woman, told through the eyes of four different people, all of whom are present at every scene in the thing, because
they had to be. Four different stories about the same woman . . . and all
of them are wrong. None of them were right. When Durrell finishes he
says to me, 'I really never thought anybody could do this.' Here I sat
with his blessings, ten thousand minutes of potential film that I knew I
could squeeze so it would work, six hundred double spaced pages . . .
and I get this phone call from Charlie Feldman. Skouras is in big trouble.
They're making this film of *Cleopatra* and everything is falling apart. He's
already spent $9 million and he hasn't got anything to show for it. We
need you, he tells me. And I had a decision to make. And I must tell you
that I look back on my choice with great sadness . . . not because I chose
to do *Cleopatra*, but because by the time it was finished everything fell

apart at Fox and *The Alexandria Quartet* never made it to the screen. My one great disappointment? That's it."

"And Cukor made *Justine*," I say.

For the first time this afternoon, Mankiewicz seems angry. "Cukor made a film of the first book in the *Quartet*. It made no sense. It made absolutely no sense."

"Wasn't anyone interested in your treatment?"

A sigh. "I wasn't. After all the trouble I had with Zanuck . . . I couldn't work for him again. I was just so sick of it . . . Jeez, I took such a beating." A pause, and then he brightens. "But, if anyone asks me, 'Are you as good as your last film?' I just tell them that I was nominated for the Academy Award for mine (*Sleuth*). In fact, it is the only film in history in which the entire cast was nominated for their performances." A wink. We are friends again.

But Mankiewicz does seem to be tiring. Because of his tremendous energy, his great memory and his no-nonsense mien, one tends to forget that this indefatigable man is in his eighties. But, like a child in a magical toy store, I don't want to leave.

"A few more questions?"

"Boy, you don't give up, do you?"

"You call the shots. Whenever you want to stop, just let me know."

"Some quick ones, then."

"Fine. What if I mention some actors and actresses you worked with and you say as much or as little as you wish."

"Let 'er rip."

"Anne Baxter."

"A good actress. She married a son-of-a-bitch and lived with him in the outback of Australia. The outback, for God's sake. The wind is blowing like mad, she had to wash her curtains. She had to kill pigs. She wrote this book about it. I saw her after the book came out, and I said to her, 'Annie, you were playing a part. You were on location the whole time you were married to that guy, and you never got paid.' She agreed with me. She was some actress."

"What about the rumor that Eve was a lesbian?"

Mankiewicz laughs. "Yes, I've heard that. Look, sex has no emotional impact on Eve. It's nothing more than a bodily function. If she can use it, she'll use it. If it was to her advantage, Eve would hump a cat! Next!"

"Elizabeth Taylor."

"If there was any glory associated with *Suddenly, Last Summer*, it was that as much as I thought I had known what Elizabeth could do, she did so much more. She was wonderful. And I don't think she was ever more beautiful than she was in that picture. Beautiful? Gorgeous. Her hair . . . nothing fancy . . . just parted and that's it. And that simple dress. I went up to Edith Head, who did the costumes for the film, and I said, 'Edith, look. I want this girl to look like she's just stepped out of a bathtub. I want an intelligent young woman. No crap. No things hanging from her ears. Simple and beautiful.' And Head did all that and she won an Academy Award for it. And Elizabeth . . . never more beautiful, and, probably, never better as an actress." He remembers something. "Tennessee Williams hated that film. He wished he could take the play back. I think it had to do with his sister and his incredible guilt."

"Ava Gardner."

"Ava never claimed to be the world's greatest actress, but she really loved her part in *Barefoot Contessa*. Actually, I think it affected the rest of her life. She lived in Spain . . . the bullfighters . . . the whole business."

"Marilyn Monroe."

"I've told this story before, but I think it's an important one because it explains a lot about her. With Marilyn, it was one of those freak things. She actually acquired a talent to go with the physical attributes that she thought were enough. And I think everybody was amazed at that, and that she could actually sing a little, move her body a little. Johnny Hyde was so much in love with her. He was a vice president at William Morris. Johnny was the one who said to me, 'Please, you gotta give her this part in *All About Eve*. See, Marilyn had been in the Fox stock company for years. They would give her Betty Grable's old costumes to wear in the background of one western or another. And there were conventions and Marilyn was there with the rest of the girls to do what she was supposed to do. And I said to Johnny, 'Look, Johnny, I've already had problems with the casting of the movie. I'm not going to tear up my contract unless I'm allowed to use Marilyn in the part. I could use anyone with a B cup to play this part.' But I agreed to use her if Zanuck wouldn't make too much of a stink. Johnny said that as a vice president of Morris he had enough on Zanuck so that he would go along with the casting. And, for one reason or another, he did. And Marilyn was very grateful.

"Now one day I see her reading a book on the set. I asked her what she was reading and it turned out to be *Letters to an Unknown Poet* by Rainer Maria Rilke. I asked her how she came to Rilke and she looked surprised and said, 'Oh, you know him?' I told her that of knew *of* him, but hadn't read any of his poems. She said, 'I'm trying to read a lot, but I don't know what to read. So I go to The Pickwick, which was a Hollywood book store, and I just pick up a book and if it look interesting, I buy it. That's wrong, right?' I said, 'No, it's not wrong. It's right. It's the best way for you to read.' Well, she never did finish it, but she did send me a copy, with thanks."

"That's very revealing."

"The most revealing thing of all is what I wrote about in *More About All About Eve* (Random House, 1972). "Everybody today is saying that Marilyn was a lonely girl. I think she was not lonely, but rather, alone. During the shooting of *Eve* we'd all go out in the evening and have a few drinks. I'd see Marilyn come into the restaurant and we would have to pull her over to join us. She'd have drinks with us and then we'd almost have to force her to have dinner with us. The next night the same thing, and the next. She never assumed that she was part of the crew. She was an outsider. I remember talking about it with Annie Baxter. I think Marilyn lived and died an outsider."

Mankiewicz pushes new tobacco into the bowl of his pipe. He tamps it down. "One more question, and then we call it an interview."

"W. C. Fields."

"Have I got stories about Fields! Most people forget that I wrote his segment of *If I Had a Million*. 'My little chickadee' and all those other Fieldsisms were written by yours truly for that picture. His segment was called 'Rollo and the Roadhogs.' At any rate, Fields loved those little asides I had given him in the film, and one day I'm sitting in my office and in walks Fields. God, I was twenty, twenty-one at the time, and in walks Fields with the bound volumes of Audobon's *The Birds of North and South America* under his arms. He says (and here Mankiewicz breaks into a Fields imitation) 'I want to buy that material.' I ask him what material he is talking about, and he says (again the imitation), 'The material you wrote for me to say in "Rollo and the Roadhogs."' So I said,

'That doesn't belong to me. That belongs to Paramount.' But he insisted, saying, 'No, you wrote it and I like to use new material,' and he puts a $50 bill on my desk. Here I am making $65 a week. I had never even *seen* a $50 bill in my whole life. Anyway, he made me take it. He respected material and the exclusivity of it.

"You know, there are a lot of stories about Fields . . . well . . . let's say he was not loved by many people in Hollywood. But there was one incident that happened for which no one blamed Fields. It was when Fields was in *The Ziegfeld Follies*. Fields used to do a routine with a billiard cue. All of a sudden, he's getting more laughs than he ever got before, and this for only chalking his cue. Well, he figured something was up, and it turns out that while he's chalking the cue, Ed Wynn is hiding under the pool table and starts doing his Ed Wynn faces to break up the audience. That night, up goes the curtain at the Ziegfeld Follies and sure enough, Wynn is doing the same thing again. Fields hears the laughter from the audience, turns the cue around, walks to the end of the table, and when Ed Wynn's head pops out, he smashes the cue on Wynn's head. Wynn had to be taken to the hospital, but he never brought action of any kind against Fields. And none of the papers covered it. As I say, it's one of the few things that Fields did in his act that nobody blamed him for. That's how valuable material was to a vaudevillian. Your act was everything.

"When I came to California in 1929, vaudeville was just dying, and the vaudevillians came out there and settled, like the lost tribes of Israel, in the San Fernando Valley. On any Sunday you could drive out there, and on these little green lawns there they all were rehearsing with their medicine clubs and their costumes." A match flares and he draws on the pipe, "But that, as they say, is another story." His neck is stiff, and he rubs it with his other hand. "It looks," he says, "as though we started in 1928 and have come full circle."

And what a circle it has been, this career of Joseph L. Mankiewicz. A circle made of brilliant words and images. "This bed looks like a dead animal act" intertwines with a long travelling shot up a dark staircase, to a flashback in which Edward G. Robinson sits in a bathtub singing an aria from *Martha*. "It was always Violet and Sebastian, Sebastian and Violet," mixes and roils with a freeze frame of hands reaching to accept an award. "Always make the moon your key light" fades and is replaced by a young Egyptian queen making an entrance into Rome. A painting of a dead sea captain startling a young widow who has come across it for the first time . . . Katherine Hepburn descending in an open elevator . . . three women watching as a telephone they all long to use slips further and further out of their reach. The circle and the world of Joseph L. Mankiewicz, full of fire and music. Or, as Mankiewicz would probably end this piece (after breaking into a rash from all the praise), "Yeah, and there's a coronet solo on Saturday night."

INDEX

The collected interviews with notable modern directors, including

Robert Aldrich • Woody Allen • Pedro Almodóvar • Robert Altman • Theo Angelopolous • Ingmar Bergman • Bernardo Bertolucci • Tim Burton • Jane Campion • Frank Capra • Charlie Chaplin • The Coen Brothers • Francis Ford Coppola • George Cukor • Brian De Palma • Clint Eastwood • Federico Fellini • John Ford • Terry Gilliam • Jean-Luc Godard • Peter Greenaway • Howard Hawks • Alfred Hitchcock • John Huston • Jim Jarmusch • Elia Kazan • Buster Keaton • Stanley Kubrick • Akira Kurosawa • Fritz Lang • Spike Lee • Mike Leigh • George Lucas • Sidney Lumet • Roman Polanski • Michael Powell • Satyajit Ray • Jean Renoir • Martin Ritt • Carlos Saura • John Sayles • Martin Scorsese • Ridley Scott • Steven Soderbergh • Steven Spielberg • George Stevens • Oliver Stone • Quentin Tarantino • Andrei Tarkovsky • Lars von Trier • François Truffaut • Liv Ullmann • Orson Welles • Billy Wilder • John Woo • Zhang Yimou • Fred Zinnemann